M O R — — — — E N

the
Saddest Pleasure

"Never has the South American scene been painted with such heart-breaking fidelity."

NORMAN LEWIS

"You will not get your hands on a finer travel book this year."

Financial Times

"Nothing like this one has happened before, nor will happen again."

MARTHA GELLHORN

"Probably the purest travel book I've read in years."

ANTHONY QUINN *New Statesman*

"A new and unique voice in the literature of travel."

COLIN THUBRON

"...an absorbing and lovely book in haunting prose."

MARY WESLEY

THE SUMACH PRESS · £5.99

GRANTA

THE WOMANIZER

40

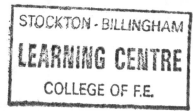

Editor: Bill Buford
Deputy Editor: Tim Adams
Managing Editor: Ursula Doyle
Editorial Assistant: Robert McSweeney
Contributing Editor: Rose Kernochan

Managing Director: Derek Johns
Financial Controller: Geoffrey Gordon
Circulation Manager: Sally Lewis
Subscriptions Assistant: Deanna Holmes

Picture Editor: Alice Rose George
Design: Chris Hyde
Executive Editor: Pete de Bolla
US Associate Publisher: Anne Kinard, Granta, 250 West 57th Street, Suite 1316, New York, NY 10107.

Editorial and Subscription Correspondence: Granta, 2–3 Hanover Yard, Noel Road, Islington, London N1 8BE. Telephone: (071) 704 9776. Fax: (071) 704 0474. Subscriptions: (071) 704 0470.
A one-year subscription (four issues) is £19.95 in Britain, £27.95 for the rest of Europe, and £34.95 for the rest of the world.
All manuscripts are welcome but must be accompanied by a stamped, self-addressed envelope or they cannot be returned.

Granta is printed in the United States of America. The paper used in this publication meets the minimum requirements of American National Standard for Information Sciences—Permanence of Paper for Printed Library Materials, ANSI Z39.48-1984 ∞

Granta is published by Granta Publications Ltd and distributed by Penguin Books Ltd, Harmondsworth, Middlesex, England, Viking Penguin, a division of Penguin Books USA Inc, 375 Hudson Street, New York, NY 10014, USA; Penguin Books Australia Ltd, Ringwood, Victoria, Australia; Penguin Books Canada Ltd, 2801 John Street, Markham, Ontario, Canada L3R 1BR; Penguin Books (NZ) Ltd, 182-190 Wairau Road, Auckland 10, New Zealand. This selection copyright © 1991 by Granta Publications Ltd.

Cover by Senate. Photo: Marc Ribaud (Magnum)

Granta 40, Summer 1992
ISBN 0-14-014051-4

As a young soldier, Manfred fought a war for the British in Italy and North Africa; he married a beautiful Jewish girl who survived Birkenau; they had a son; but in the long shadow of the war, Manfred begins to destroy the things he loves most...

From the award-winning author of RIPLEY BOGLE.

Hardback   UK Publication Date: 5 June 1992

The myth of Marilyn Monroe has foiled countless attempts to uncover the truth about the greatest sex symbol of them all. Rare is the book which dispels the obscuring shadows to reveal the complexities of a flesh and blood woman. QUEEN OF DESIRE succeeds.

Hardback   UK Publication Date: 10 July 1992

In the stillness of a bitterly cold February weekend the phone rings sharply.
The Chilean writer Christian Huneeus, a life-long friend of Tony Gould, has tragically died of a brain tumour.
Thus begins Tony Gould's journey into the heart of a volatile Latin American country to uncover the truth about his exotic Chilean friend.

Hardback   UK Publication Date: 10 July 1992

PICADOR

OUTSTANDING INTERNATIONAL WRITING

CONTENTS

Woody Allen

A biography

ERIC LAX

"A unique insight on Allen's working methods"
Time Out

£7.99
A VINTAGE PAPERBACK V

RICHARD FORD
THE WOMANIZER

Austin turned up the tiny street—rue Sarrazin—at the head of which he hoped he would come to a larger one, one he knew, rue de Vaugirard, possibly, which he could take all the way to Josephine Belliard's apartment by the Luxembourg Gardens. He was going to sit with Josephine's son, Leo, while Josephine went to her lawyers to sign papers divorcing her husband, and then he was going to take Josephine for a romantic dinner. Her husband, Bernard, was a cheap novelist who'd published a scandalous novel with her in it; her name used, her infidelity exposed in every salacious detail. The book had just reached the stores, and everybody she knew was reading it.

'It is not so bad to *write* such a book,' Josephine had said the first night Austin had met her, only the week before, when he had also taken her to dinner. 'It is his choice. I am an editor. OK? But. To publish this? No. I'm sorry. My husband—he is a shit. What can I do? I say goodbye to him.'

Martin Austin was from Chicago. He was married without children and worked for an old, family-owned company that sold expensive, specially-treated paper to foreign textbook publishers. He was forty-four and had worked for the same company, the Lilienthal Company of Winnetka, for fifteen years. He had met Josephine Belliard at a cocktail party at the Intercontinental Hotel, a party thrown by a publisher he called on, for one of its important authors. He'd been invited only as a courtesy since his company's paper hadn't been used for the author's book, a sociological text that calibrated the suburban loneliness of immigrant Arabs using sophisticated differential equations. Austin's French was lacking—he had always been able to speak much more than he could understand—and consequently he had stood by himself at the margins of the party and drunk champagne, looking pleasant and hoping to hear English spoken and to find someone he could talk to instead of someone who might hear him speak French and then start a conversation he couldn't make sense of.

Josephine Belliard was a sub-editor at the publishing house. She was a small, slender, dark-haired French woman in her thirties and of an odd beauty—a mouth slightly too wide and too thin, her chin soft, almost receding, but with a smooth, caramel

Photo: Marc Ribaud/Magnum

11

skin and dark eyes and dark eyebrows that Austin found appealing. He had caught a glimpse earlier in the day when he had visited the publisher's offices in the rue de Lille. She'd been sitting at her desk in a small, shadowy office, rapidly and animatedly speaking English into the telephone. He had peered in at her as he passed by but had forgotten about her until she came up to him at the party and smiled and asked in English how he liked Paris. Later that night they had gone to dinner, and at the end of the evening he'd taken her home in a taxi then returned to his hotel alone and gone to sleep.

The next day, though, he called her. He had nothing special in mind, just an aimless, angling call. Maybe he could sleep with her—not even that he thought that. It was just a possibility, an inevitable option. When he asked her if she would like to see him again, she said she would if he wanted to. She didn't say she'd had a good time the night before. She didn't mention that at all. It was almost, Austin felt, as if that time had never happened. But it was an attitude he found attractive; she was smart. She judged things. It wasn't American at all. In America a woman would have to seem to care, more, probably, than she did or could after one harmless encounter.

That evening they had gone to a small, noisy Italian restaurant near the Gare de l'Est, a place with bright lights and mirrors on the walls and where the food was not very good. They'd ordered light Ligurian wine, gotten a little drunk and engaged in a long and in some ways intimate conversation. Josephine told him she had been born in the suburb of Aubervilliers, north of Paris, and couldn't wait to leave home. She had gone to a university and studied sociology while living with her parents, but now had no relationship with her mother, or with her father, who had moved to America in the late seventies and not been heard from. She said she had been married eight years to a man she once liked, and had had one child with but did not especially love, and that two years ago she had begun an affair with another man, a younger man, which lasted only a short time then ended, as she had expected it might. Afterwards, she had believed she could simply re-enter life more or less as she'd left it, a lifelong bourgeois muddle of continuance.

But her husband had been shocked and incensed by his wife's infidelity and had moved out of their apartment, quit his job at an advertising firm, found a woman to live with and gone to work writing a novel which had as its only subject his wife's supposed indiscretions—some of which, she told Austin, he'd obviously made up, but others of which, amusingly enough, were surprisingly accurate.

'It's not so much I blame him, you know?' Josephine had said and laughed. 'These things come along. They happen. Other people do what they please.' She looked out the restaurant window at the row of small parked cars along the street. 'So?'

'But what's happening now?' Austin said, trying to find a part of the story that would allow him into it. A phrase, a niche that could be said to invite his closer interest—though there wasn't such a phrase.

'Now? I am living with my child. Alone. That is my all of life.' She unexpectedly looked up at Austin and her eyes opened wide, as though to say, 'What else is there?' 'What more else?' she in fact did say.

'I don't know,' Austin said. 'Do you think you'll go back with your husband?' This was a question he was quite happy to ask.

'Yes. I don't know. No. Maybe,' Josephine said, extending her lower lip slightly and raising one shoulder in a gesture of carelessness Austin believed was typical of French women. He didn't mind it in Josephine, but he usually disliked people for affecting that gesture. It was patently false and always came at the service of important matters a person wished to pretend were not important.

Josephine, though, did not seem like a woman to have an affair and then talk about it matter-of-factly to someone she barely knew (she seemed more like an unmarried woman looking for someone to be interested in). Obviously she was more complicated, maybe even smarter than he'd thought, and quite realistic about life, though slightly disillusioned. Probably if he wanted to press the matter of intimacy he could take her back to his room with him—a thing he'd done before on business trips, and even if not so many times, enough times that to do so now wouldn't be extraordinary or meaningful, at least not to him. To share an unexpected intimacy might intensify both their holds on life.

Yet there was a measure of uncertainty surrounding that very thought—a thought he was so used to having he couldn't keep from it. Maybe it was true that even though he liked her, liked the frankness and direct nature of her conduct toward him, intimacy was not what he wanted. She appealed to him in a surprising way, but he was not physically attracted to her. And maybe, he thought, looking at her across the table, an intimacy with him was the last thing on earth *she* was interested in. She was French. He didn't know anything about them. An illusion of potential intimacy was probably what all French women broadcast, and everyone knew it. Possibly she had no interest in him at all and was just passing the time. It made him feel pleased even to entertain such a multi-layered view.

They finished dinner in thoughtful, weighted silence. Austin felt ready to begin a discourse on his own life—his marriage, its length and intensity, his feelings about it and himself. He was willing to talk about the uneasy, unanchored sensation he'd had lately of not knowing exactly how to make the next twenty-five years of life as eventful and important as the previous twenty-five, a sensation buttressed by the hope that he wouldn't fail of courage if courage was required, and by the certainty that everybody had their life entirely in their hands and were required to live with their own terrors and mistakes, etc. Not that he was unhappy with Barbara or that he lacked anything. He was not the conventionally desperate man on the way out of a marriage that had grown tiresome. Barbara, in fact, was the most interesting and beautiful woman he'd ever known, the person he admired most. He wasn't looking for a better life. He wasn't looking for anything. He loved his wife, and he hoped to present to Josephine Belliard a different human perspective from the ones she might be used to.

'No one thinks your thoughts for you when you lay your head on the pillow at night,' was a sobering expression Austin often used addressing himself, as well as when he'd addressed the few women he'd known since being married—including Barbara. He was willing to commence a frank discussion of this sort when Josephine asked him about himself.

But the subject did not come up. She did not ask about his thoughts or about him in any way. Not even that she talked about herself. She talked about her job, about her son, Leo, about her husband and about friends of theirs. He had told her he was married. He had told her his age, that he had gone to college at the University of Illinois and grown up in the small city of Peoria. But to know no more seemed fine to her. She was perfectly nice and seemed to like him, but she was not very responsive, which he felt was unusual. She seemed to have more serious things on her mind and to take life seriously—a quality Austin liked. In fact it made her appealing to him in a way she had not seemed at first, when he was only thinking about how she looked and whether he wanted to sleep with her.

But when they were walking out to her car, down the sidewalk at the end of which were the bright lights of the Gare de l'Est and the Boulevard Strasbourg swarming with taxis at eleven o'clock, Josephine put her arm through his arm and pulled close to him, put her cheek against his shoulder and said, 'It's all confusion to me.'

And Austin wondered: what was all confusion? Not him. He was no confusion. He'd decided he was a good-intentioned escort for her, and that was a fine thing to be under the circumstances. There was already plenty of confusion in her life. An absent husband. A child. Surviving alone. That was enough. Though he took his arm from her grip and reached it around her shoulder and pulled her close to him until they reached her little black Opel and got in, where touching stopped.

When they reached his hotel, a former monastery with a walled-in courtyard garden, two blocks from the great lighted confluence of St Germain and the rue de Rennes, she stopped the car and sat looking straight ahead as if she were waiting for Austin to get out. They had made no mention of another meeting, and he was scheduled to leave in two days.

Austin sat in the dark without speaking. A police station occupied the next corner down the shadowy street. A police van had pulled up with blinking lights, and several uniformed officers in shiny white Sam Browne belts were leading a line of handcuffed men inside, their heads all turned down like penitents. It was April,

15

and the street surface glistened in the damp spring air.

This was the point, of course, to ask her to come inside with him if such a thing was ever to be. But it was clearly the furthest thing from possibility, and each of them knew it. And apart from privately acknowledging that much, Austin had no real thought of it. Although he wanted to do *something* good, something unusual that would please her and make them both know an occurrence slightly out of the ordinary had taken place tonight —an occurrence they could both feel good about when they were alone in bed, even in fact if nothing much had taken place.

His mind was working on what that extra ordinary something might be, the thing you did if you didn't make love to a woman. A gesture. A word. What?

All the prisoners were finally led into the police station, and the officers had gotten back in their van and driven it straight up rue de Mezières where Austin and Josephine Belliard were sitting in the silent darkness. Obviously she was waiting for him to get out, and he was in a quandary about what to do. Though it was a moment he relished. It was the exquisite moment before anything is acted on and when all is potential, before life turns this way or that—towards regret or pleasure or happiness, towards one kind of permanence or another. It was a wonderful, tantalizing, important moment, one worth preserving, and he knew she knew it as well as he did and wanted it to last as long as he wanted it to.

Austin sat with his hands in his lap, feeling large and cumbersome inside the tiny car, listening to himself breathe, conscious he was on the verge of what he hoped would be the right—rightest—gesture to enact. She had not moved. The car was idling, its headlights shining bleakly on the empty street, the dashboard instruments turning the interior air faintly green.

Austin abruptly—or so it felt to him—reached across the space between them, took Josephine's small soft, warm hand off the steering wheel and held it between his two large equally warm ones like a sandwich, though also in a way that would seem protective. He would be protective of her, guard her from some as yet unnamed harm or from her own concealed urges, though most immediately from himself, since he realized it was her reluctance more than his that kept them apart now, kept them from parking the car and going inside and spending the night in each others' arms.

He squeezed her hand tightly then eased up.

'I'd like to make you happy somehow,' he said in a sincere voice, then waited while Josephine said nothing. She did not remove her hand, but neither did she answer. It was as though what he'd said didn't mean anything, or that possibly she wasn't even listening to him. 'It's just human,' Austin said, as though she *had* said something back, had said, 'Why?' or 'Don't try,' or 'You couldn't possibly,' or 'It's too late.'

'What?' She looked at him for the first time since they'd stopped. 'It's what?' She had not understood him.

'It's only human to want to make someone happy,' Austin said, holding her warm, nearly weightless hand. 'I like you very much, you know that.' These were the perfect words, as ordinary as they sounded.

'Yes. Well. For what?' Josephine said in a cold voice. 'You are married. You have a wife. You live far away. In two days, three days, I don't know, you will leave. So. For what do you like me?' Her face seemed impenetrable, as though she were addressing a cab driver who'd just said something inappropriately familiar to her. She left her hand in his hand, but looked away, straight ahead.

Austin wanted to speak again then. He wished to say something—likewise absolutely correct—into this new void she had opened between them, words no one could plan to say or even know in advance, but something that admitted to what she'd said, conceded his acquiescence to it, yet allowed another moment to occur during which the two of them would enter on to new and uncharted ground.

Though the only thing that Austin could say—and he had no idea why these were the only words that came to him, since they seemed asinine and ruinous—were: 'People have paid a dear price for getting involved with me,' which were definitely the wrong words, since to his knowledge they weren't particularly true, and even if they were they were so boastful and melodramatic as to cause Josephine or anyone else to break out laughing.

Still, he could say that and immediately have it all be over

17

between them and forget about it, which might be a relief. Only relief was not what he wanted. He wanted something to go forward between them, something definite and realistic and in keeping with the facts of their lives; to advance into that area where nothing actually seemed possible at the moment.

Austin slowly let go of Josephine's hand. Then he reached both of his hands to her face and turned it towards him, and leaned across the open space and said, just before he kissed her, 'I'm at least going to kiss you. I feel like I'm entitled to do that, and I'm going to.'

Josephine Belliard did not at all resist him, though she did not in any way concur. Her face was soft and compliant. She had a plain, not in the least full, mouth, and when Austin put his lips against her lips she did not move towards him. She let herself be kissed, and Austin was immediately, cruelly aware of it. This is what was taking place: he was forcing himself on this woman, and a feeling came over him as he moved his lips more completely on to hers that he was delusionary and a fool and pathetic—the kind of man he would make fun of if he heard himself described using only these facts as evidence. It was an awful feeling, like being old, and he felt his insides go hollow and his arms become heavy as cudgels. He wanted to disappear from this car seat and never remember any of the idiotic things he had just an instant before been thinking. This had now been the first permanent move, when potentiality ended, and it had been the wrong one, the worst one possible. It was ludicrous.

Though before he could move his lips away, he realized Josephine Belliard was saying something, speaking with her lips against his lips, faintly, and that by not resisting him she was in fact kissing him, her face almost unconsciously giving up to his intention. What she was saying all the while Austin was kissing her thin mouth was—whisperingly, almost dreamily—'Non, non, non, non, non. Please. I can't. I can't. No, no.'

Though she didn't stop. 'No' was not what she meant exactly. She let her lips part slightly in a gesture of recognition. And after a moment, a long suspended moment, Austin inched away from her lips, sat back in his seat and took a deep breath, put his hands back in his lap and let the kiss fill the space between them he had somehow hoped to fill with words. It was the most unexpected and enticing thing that could've come of his wish to do right.

She did not take an audible breath. She merely sat as she'd sat before he'd kissed her, and did not speak or seem to have anything in her mind to say. Things were mostly as they had been before he'd kissed her, only he *had* kissed her—they had kissed —and that had made all the difference in the world.

'I'd like to see you tomorrow,' Austin said very resolutely.

'Yes,' Josephine said almost sorrowfully, as if she couldn't help agreeing. 'OK.'

And he was satisfied then that there was nothing else to say. It was as it should be. Nothing else could go wrong.

'Good night,' Austin said with the same resolution as before. He opened the car door and hauled himself out on to the street.

'OK,' she said. She didn't look out the door, though he leaned back into the opening and looked at her. She had her hands on the steering wheel, staring straight ahead, appearing no different really from when she'd stopped to let him out five minutes before—possibly slightly fatigued.

He wanted to say one more good word that would help balance how she felt at that moment—not that he had the slightest idea how that might've been. She was opaque to him, completely opaque, and it was not even so interesting. And all he could think to say was something as inane as the last thing had been ruinous. 'Two people don't see the same landscape.' These were the terrible words he thought, though he didn't say them. He just smiled in at her, stood up, pushed the door closed firmly and stepped slowly back so Josephine could turn and start down rue de Mezières. He watched her drive away, but could tell that she did not look at him in the rear-view mirror. It was as though in a moment he did not exist at all.

2

What Austin hoped would be the rue de Vaugirard, leading around and up past Josephine's apartment, turned out instead to be the rue St Jacques. He had gone much too far and was near the medical college, where there were only lightless shop windows containing drab medical texts and dusty, passed-over antiques.

He did not know Paris well—only a few hotels he'd stayed in and a few restaurants he didn't want to eat in again. He couldn't keep straight which *arrondissement* was which, or in what direction anything was from anything else, or how to take the Metro or even how to leave town except by airplane. All the large streets looked the same and travelled at confusing angles to each other, and all the famous landmarks seemed to be in unexpected locations when they peeked up into view above the building tops. In the two days he'd been back in Paris now—after leaving home in a fury and taking the plane to Orly—he'd tried to make a point at least to remember in which direction on the Boulevard St Germain the numbers became larger. But he could not keep it straight, and in fact he could not always find the Boulevard St Germain when he wanted to.

At rue St Jacques he looked down towards where he thought would be the river and the Petit Pont bridge, and there they were. It was a warm, spring day, and the sidewalks along the river banks were jammed with tourists, cruising the little picture stalls and gaping at the huge cathedral on the other side.

The view down the rue St Jacques seemed for an instant a familiar view—a pharmacy-front he recognized, a café with a distinctive name. Horloge. He looked back up the street he'd come up and saw that he was only half a block away from the small hotel he'd once stayed in with Barbara. The Hotel de Tour de Notre Dame, which had promised a view of the great cathedral but from which no such view was possible. The hotel was run by Pakistanis and had rooms so small you couldn't both have your suitcase open and also reach the window. He'd brought Barbara with him on business—it was four years ago now—and she had shopped and visited museums and eaten lunch along the Quai de la Tournelle while he made his customer calls. They had stayed out of the room as much as possible until fatigue dumped them in bed in front of the indecipherable French TV, which eventually put them to sleep.

Austin remembered very clearly now, standing on the busy sidewalk on his way to Josephine Belliard's apartment, that he and Barbara had left Paris on the first of April—taking a direct flight back to Chicago. Only, when they'd struggled their heavy luggage out of the room, crammed themselves into the tiny, airless elevator and emerged into the lobby ready to settle their bill and depart—looking like beleaguered refugees—the Pakistani room clerk who spoke crisp British English looked across the reception desk in an agitated way and said, 'Oh, Mr Austin, have you not heard the bad news, I'm sorry?'

'What's that?' Austin had said. 'What bad news?' He looked at Barbara, holding up a garment bag and a hat box, not wanting to hear any bad news now.

'There is a quite terrible strike,' the clerk said and looked very grave. 'The airport's closed down completely. No one can leave Paris today. And, I'm sorry to say, we have already booked your room for another guest. A Japanese. I'm so, so sorry.'

Austin stood amid his suitcases, breathing in the air of defeat and frustration and anger he felt certain it would be useless to express. He stared out the hotel window at the street. The sky was cloudy and the wind slightly chilled. He heard Barbara say behind him as much to herself as to him, 'Oh well. We'll do something. We'll find another place. It's too bad. Maybe it'll be an adventure.'

Austin looked at the clerk, a little brown man with neat black hair and a white cotton jacket, standing behind the marble desk. He was smiling. This was all the same to him, Austin knew; that they had no place to go; that they were tired of Paris; that they had brought too much luggage and bought too much to take home; that they had slept badly every night; that the weather was changing to colder; that they were out of money and sick of the arrogant French. None of this mattered to this man—in some ways, Austin sensed, it may even have made him pleased, pleased enough to smile.

'What's so goddamned funny?' Austin had said to the little subcontinental. 'Why's my bad luck a source of such goddamned amusement to you?' This man would be the focus of his anger now. He couldn't help himself. Anger couldn't make anything worse. 'Doesn't it matter that we're guests of this hotel, and we're in a bit of a bad situation here?' He heard what he knew was a pleading voice.

'April fool!' The clerk said and broke out in squeaking little laughter. 'Ha, ha, ha, ha, ha, ha, ha. It is only a joke, *monsieur*,' the man said, so pleased with himself now, more even than when he'd told Austin the lie. 'The airport is perfectly fine. It is open. You can leave. There is no trouble. It's fine. It was only a joke. *Bon voyage*, Mr Austin. *Bon voyage*.'

3

For the two days after she had left him standing in the street at midnight, after he had kissed her the first time and felt that he had done something exactly right, Austin saw a great deal of Josephine Belliard. He'd had plans to take the TGV to Brussels and then go on to Amsterdam, and from there fly to Chicago and home. But the next morning he sent messages to his customers and to the office complaining of 'medical problems' which had inexplicably 'recurred', although he felt it was 'nothing serious'. He would conclude his business by fax when he was home the next week. He told Barbara he'd decided to stay in Paris a few extra days—just to relax, to do things he'd never taken the time to do. Visit Monet's house maybe, he said. Walk the streets like a tourist. Rent a car. Drive to Fontainebleau.

With Josephine Belliard he decided he would spend every minute he could. He did not for an instant think that he loved her, or that keeping each other's company would lead him or her to anything important. He was married; he had nothing to give her; to get deluded about such a thing was to bring on nothing but trouble—the kind of trouble that when you're younger you glanced away from, but when you're older, you ignored at risk.

Hesitancy in the face of trouble, he felt, was probably a virtue.

But short of that he did all he could. Together they went to a movie. They went to a museum. They visited Notre Dame and the Palais Royal. They walked together in the narrow streets of the Faubourg St Germain. They looked in store windows. They acted like lovers. Touched. She allowed him to hold her hand. They exchanged knowing looks. He knew what made her laugh, listened carefully for her small points of pride. She stayed as she had been—seemingly uninterested, but willing—as if it was all his idea and her duty, only a duty she surprisingly liked. Austin felt this very reluctance in her was compelling, attractive, and caused him to woo her in a way that made him admire his own intensity. He took her to dinner in two expensive places, went with her to her apartment, met her son, met the country woman she paid to care for him during the week, saw where she lived, slept, ate, gazed out her apartment windows to the Jardins du Luxembourg and down to the peaceful streets of her neighborhood. He saw her life, which he found he was curious about and which, when he satisfied that curiosity, made him feel as though he'd accomplished something, something that was not easy or ordinary to do.

She told him not much more about herself and asked nothing about him, as if his life didn't matter to her or simply didn't exist. She told him she had once visited America, had met a musician in California and decided to live with him in his small wooden house by the beach in Santa Cruz. This was in the early seventies. She had been a teenager. Only one day—it was after four months—she woke up one morning on a mattress on the floor, underneath a rug made out of a tanned cow hide, got up, packed her bag and left.

'This was too much,' Josephine said, sitting in the window of her apartment, looking out at the twilight and the streets where children were kicking a soccer ball. The musician had been disturbed and angry, she said, but she had come back to France and her parents' house. 'You cannot live a long time where you don't belong. Is true?' She looked at him and elevated her shoulders. He was sitting in a chair, drinking a glass of red wine, contemplating the rooftops, enjoying how the tawny light burnished the delicate scrollwork cornices of the apartment buildings opposite visible from the one he was in. Jazz was playing softly on the stereo. A sinuous saxophone solo. 'It's true, no?' she said. 'You can't.'

'Exactly right,' Austin said. He had grown up in Peoria, Illinois. He lived on the north-west side of Chicago now. He'd attended a state U. He felt she was exactly right, although he saw nothing wrong in being here at this moment, enjoying the sunlight as it gradually faded then disappeared from the roofs of houses he could see from this woman's rooms. That seemed permissible. It seemed perfect.

She told him about her husband. His picture was on the wall in Leo's room—a bulbous-faced, dark-skinned Jew with a thick black moustache that made him look like an Armenian. Somewhat disappointing, Austin had thought. He'd imagined Bernard as being handsome, a smooth-skinned Louis Jourdan type with the fatal flaw of being boring. The real man looked like what he was—a man who wrote French radio jingles.

Josephine said that her affair had proved to her that she did not love her husband, although perhaps she once had, and that while for some people to live with a person you did not love was possible, it was not possible for her. She looked at Austin again, as if to underscore the point. This was not, of course, how she had first explained her feelings for her husband, when she said she'd felt she could resume their life after her affair, but that her husband had left her flat. It was how she felt now, Austin thought, and the truth certainly lay somewhere in the middle. In any case it didn't matter to him. She said her husband gave her very little money now, saw his son infrequently, had been seen with a new girl-friend who was German, and of course had written a terrible book which everyone she knew was reading, causing her immense pain and embarrassment.

'But,' she said, and shook her head as if shaking the very thoughts out of her mind. 'What I can do, yes? I live my life now, here, with my son. I have twenty-five more years to work, then I'm finished.'

'Maybe something better will come along,' Austin said. He didn't know what it would be, but he disliked her being so pessimistic. It felt like she was somehow blaming him, which he thought was very French. A more hopeful American point of view, he thought, would help.

'What is it? What will be better?' Josephine said, and she looked at him not quite bitterly, but helplessly. 'What is going to happen? Tell me. I want to know.'

Austin set his wine glass carefully on the polished floor, climbed out of his chair and walked to the open window where she sat, below which the street was slowly being cast in grainy darkness. There was the bump of a soccer ball still being kicked over and over aimlessly against a wall, and behind that the sound of a car engine being revved down the block. Austin put his arms around her arms and put his mouth against her cool cheek, and held her to him very tightly.

'Maybe someone will come along who loves you,' Austin said. He was offering encouragement, and he knew she knew that, and would take it in a good spirit. 'You wouldn't be hard to love. Not at all,' he said, and held her more tightly to him. 'In fact,' he said, 'you'd be very easy to love.'

Josephine let herself be pulled, be gathered in. She let her head fall against his shoulder. It was perilous to be where she was, Austin thought, in the window, with a man holding her. He could feel the cool, outside air on the backs of his hands and against his face, half in, half out, himself. It was thrilling, even though Josephine did not put her arms around him, did not reciprocate his touch in any way that made any difference, only let him hold her as if pleasing him was easy and did not matter to her at all.

That night, he took her to dinner at the Closerie des Lilas, a famous place where writers and artists had been frequenters in the twenties—a bright, glassy and noisy place where the two of them drank champagne, held hands, but did not talk much. They seemed to be running out of things to say. The next most natural things would be subjects between them, subjects with some future built in. But Austin was leaving in the morning, and those future subjects didn't seem to interest either of them, though Austin could feel their pull, could imagine below the surface of unyielding facts that there could be a future for them. Certainly under different, better circumstances they would be lovers, would immediately begin to spend more time together, see what there was to see between them. Austin had a strong urge to say all these very things to her as they silently sat over their champagne, just go ahead and put that much on the table from his side, and see what it called forth from hers. But it was too noisy in the restaurant. Once he started to say it, but it sounded like words said too loud. And these were not that kind of words. These were important words and needed to be said respectfully, even solemnly, with their inevitable sense of loss built-in.

The words, though, stayed in his mind as she drove the short distance back to rue de Mezières and the corner where she'd left him the first night. The words seemed to have missed their moment. They needed another context, a more substantial setting. To say them in the dark, in a crummy Opel with the motor running, at the moment of parting, would give them a sentimental weightiness they didn't mean to have, since they were, for all their built-in sorrow, an expression of optimism.

When Josephine stopped the car, the gate into the hotel just a few steps away, she kept her hands on the steering wheel and stared straight ahead, as she had two nights ago. She did not offer him anything, a word, a gesture, even a look. To her, this night, the last one, the night before Austin left for Chicago and home and his wife, never to come back again, never to try to pick up from where they were at that moment—this night was just like the first one, one Josephine would forget about as soon as the door slammed shut, and her headlights swung on to the empty street towards home.

Austin looked out her window at the rustic, wooden hotel gate beyond which was a ferny, footlit courtyard, then the double glass doors, then the lobby, then the stairs up two flights to his small room. What he wanted was to take her there, lock the door, close the curtains and make sorrowful love until morning, until, in fact, he had to call a cab to leave for the airport. But that was the wrong thing to do, having gotten this far without complication, without greater confusion or harm being caused to each of them. Harm *could* be caused by getting involved with him, Austin thought. They both knew it, and it didn't require saying. She wouldn't think of sleeping with him in any case. *No* meant *no* to her. And that was the right way to play this.

Austin sat with his hands in his lap and said nothing. It was the way he knew this moment of leaving would occur. Sombrely on his part. Coldly on hers. He didn't think he should reach across and take her hands again as he had before. That became play-acting the second time you did it, and he had already touched her that way plenty of times—sweetly, innocently, without trying anything more except possibly a brief, soft kiss. He would just let this time—the last time—go exactly according to her wishes, not his.

He waited. He thought Josephine Belliard might say something, something ironic or clever or cold or merely commonplace, something that broke her little rule of silence and that he could then reply to and perhaps have the last good word, one that would leave them both puzzled and tantalized and certain that a small but important moment had not entirely been missed. But she did not speak. She was intent on there being nothing that would make her do anything different from what she did naturally. And Austin knew if he had simply climbed out of the car right then and without a goodbye, she would've driven straight away. Maybe this was why her husband had written a book about her, Austin thought. At least he'd know he'd gotten her attention.

Josephine seemed to be waiting for the seat beside her to become empty. Austin looked across at her in the car-darkness, and she for an instant glanced at him, but did not speak. This was annoying, Austin thought; annoying and stupid and French to be so closed to the world, to be so unwilling to let a sweet and free moment cause you happiness—when happiness was in such short supply. He realized he was on the verge of getting angry, of saying nothing else and simply getting out of the car and walking away.

'You know,' Austin said, more irritably than he wanted to sound. 'We could be lovers. We're interested in each other. This isn't a sidetrack for me. This is real life. I like you. You like me. All I've wanted to do is take advantage of that in some way that

27

makes you glad, that puts a smile on your face. Nothing else. I don't need to sleep with you. That would cause me as much trouble as it would cause you. But that's no reason we can't just like each other.' He looked at her intently inside the dark car, her silhouette softened against the lights above the hotel gate across the street. She said nothing. Though he thought he heard a faint laugh, hardly more than an exhaled breath, intended, he presumed, to express what she'd thought of all he'd just said. 'Sorry. Really, I am,' Austin said angrily, swivelling his knees into the doorway to get out.

But Josephine put her hand on his wrist and held him back, not looking at him, but speaking towards the cold windshield. 'I am not so strong enough,' she whispered and squeezed his wrist.

'For what?' Austin said, also whispering, one foot already on the paving stones, but looking back at her in the darkness.

'I am not so strong enough to have something with you,' she said. 'Not now.' She looked at him, her eyes soft and large, her one hand holding his wrist, the other in her lap, half curled.

'Do you mean you don't feel strongly enough, or you aren't strong enough in yourself?' Austin said, still over-assertive, but feeling good about it.

'I don't know,' Josephine said. 'It is still very confusing for me now. I'm sorry.'

'Well that's better than nothing,' Austin said. 'At least you gave me that much. That makes me glad.' He reached across and squeezed her wrist where she was holding his wrist tightly. Then he stood out of the car into the street. She put her hand on the gear shift and pushed it into gear with a loud rasping.

'If you come back,' she said in a husky voice through the doorway, 'Call me.'

'Sure,' Austin said, 'I'll call you. I don't know what else I'd do in Paris.'

He closed the door again firmly, and she drove away, spinning her tires on the slick stones. Austin walked across the street to the hotel gate without looking back at her tail-lights as they disappeared.

A t one a.m., when it was six p.m. in Chicago, he had called Barbara, and they had come close to having a serious argument. It made Austin angry because when he had dialled the number, his own familiar number, and heard the familiar ring, he'd felt happy—happy to be only hours away from leaving Paris, happy to be coming home, and not to have just a wife to come home to but this wife—Barbara, whom he both loved and revered; happy also to have effected his 'contact' with Josephine Belliard (that was the word he was using; at first it had been *'rapprochement'*, but that had easily given way); happy that there were no consequences to dread—no false promises inspiring false hopes, no tearful partings, no sense of entrapping obligations or feelings of being in over your boot-tops. No damage to control.

Which was not to say nothing had taken place, because plenty had—things he and Josephine Belliard both knew about and that had been expressed when she held his wrist in the car and admitted she wasn't strong enough, or that something was too strong for her.

What does one want in the world, Austin thought, sitting against the headboard of the bed in his room that night, having a glass of warm champagne from the mini-bar? He was in his blue pajama bottoms, on top of the bed covers, barefoot, staring across the room at his own image in the smoky mirror that occupied one entire wall—a man in a bed with a lighted bedlamp beside him, a glass on his belly. What does one want most of all, when one has experienced much, suffered some, persevered, tried to do good when good was within reach? What does that experience teach us that we can profit from? That the memory of pain, Austin thought, mounts up and lays a significant weight upon the present—a sobering weight—and what one has to discover is, given that, what's possible but also valuable and desirable between human beings, on a low level of event.

No easy trick, Austin thought. Certainly not everyone could do it. But he and Josephine Belliard had in an admittedly small way brought it off, found the point of contact whose consequences were only positive for each of them. No damage. No confusion. Yet not insignificant either. He realized, of course, that if he'd had his own way, Josephine would be in bed beside him right now; though in God knows what agitated frame of mind, the late hours ticking by, sex their only hope of satisfaction. It was a distasteful thought. *There* was trouble and nothing would've been gained—only lost. But the two of them had figured out a better path to take, which had eventuated in his being alone in his room and feeling quite good about everything. Even virtuous. He almost raised his glass to himself in the mirror, only it seemed slightly ridiculous.

He waited a while before phoning Barbara because he thought Josephine might call—a drowsy late-night voice from bed, an opportunity for her to say something more to him, something interesting, maybe serious, something she hadn't wanted to say when they were together in the car and could reach each other.

But she didn't call, and Austin found himself staring at the foreign-looking telephone, willing it to ring. He'd had a lengthy conversation between himself and Josephine playing in his mind for several minutes: he wished she was here now—that's what he wanted to say to her, even though he'd already decided that was distasteful. Still, he thought of her lying in bed asleep, alone, and that gave him a hollow almost nauseated feeling. Then, for some reason, he thought of her meeting the younger man she'd had the calamitous affair with, the one that had ended her marriage. He picked up the receiver to see if it was working. Then he put it down. Then he picked up the receiver again and called Barbara.

'What did you do tonight, sweetheart? Did you have some fun?' Barbara was in jolly spirits. She was in the kitchen fixing dinner for herself. He could hear pots and pans rattling. He pictured her in his mind, tall and beautiful, confident about life.

'I took a woman to dinner,' Austin said bluntly. There was no delay on the line—it was as if he were calling from the office. Something, though, was making him feel irritated. The sound of the pans, he thought. The fact that Barbara considered fixing her dinner to be important enough to keep doing it as she was talking to him. His feeling of virtue was fading.

'Well, that's wonderful,' Barbara said. 'Anybody special or just somebody you met on a street corner who looked hungry?'

She wasn't serious.

'A woman who works at Editions Perigord,' Austin said sternly. 'An editor.'

'That's nice,' Barbara said, and what seemed like a small edge rose in her voice. He wondered if there was a signal in *his* voice, something that alerted her no matter how hard he tried to seem natural, something she'd heard before over the years and couldn't be hidden.

'It *was* nice,' Austin said. 'We had a good time. But I'm coming home tomorrow.

'Well, we're waiting for you,' Barbara said brightly.

'Who's we?' Austin said.

'Me. And the house. And the plants and the windows. The cars. Your life. We're all waiting with big smiles on our faces.'

'That's great,' Austin said.

'It *is* great,' Barbara said. Then there was silence on the line—expensive, transoceanic silence. Austin felt the need to reorganize his good mood. He had nothing to be mad about. Or uncomfortable. All was well. Barbara hadn't done anything, but neither had he. 'What time is it there?' she said casually. He heard another pot clatter, then water turn on in the sink. His champagne glass had gotten warm, the champagne flat and sweet.

'After one,' he said. 'I'm sleepy now. I've got a long day tomorrow.'

'So go to sleep,' Barbara said.

'Thanks,' Austin said.

There was more silence. 'Who *is* this woman?' Barbara said somewhat brittly.

'Just a woman I met,' Austin said. 'She's married. She has a baby. It's just *la vie moderne*.'

'*La vie moderne*,' Barbara said. She was tasting something now. Whatever she was cooking she was tasting.

'Right,' Austin said. 'Modern life.'

'I understand,' Barbara said. '*La vie moderne*. Modern life.' She tapped a spoon hard on the rim of a pan.

'Are you glad I'm coming home?' Austin said.

'Of course,' Barbara said and paused again while Austin

31

tried to particularize for himself the look that was on her face now. All the features in her quite beautiful face seemed to get thinner when she got angry. He wondered if they were thin now. 'Do you think,' Barbara said trying to sound merely curious, 'that you might just possibly have taken me for granted tonight?' Silence. She was going on cooking. She was alone in their house, cooking for herself, and he was in a nice hotel in Paris—a former monastery—drinking champagne in his pajamas. There was some discrepancy. He had to admit that. Though it finally wasn't very important since each of them was well fixed. But he felt sorry for her, sorry that she thought he took her for granted when he didn't think he did; when in fact he loved her and was eager to see her. He was sorry she didn't know how he felt right now, how much regard he had for her. If she did, he thought, it would make her happy.

'No,' Austin said finally answering her question, 'I don't think I do. I really don't think so. Do you think I do?'

'No? It's fine then,' Barbara said. He heard a cabinet door close. 'I wouldn't want you to think that you took me for granted, that's all.'

'Why do we have to talk about this now?' Austin said plaintively. 'I'm coming home tomorrow. I'm eager to see you. I'm not mad about anything. Why are you?'

'I'm not,' Barbara said. 'Never mind. It doesn't matter. I just think things and then they go away.' More spoon banging.

'I love you,' Austin said. The rim of his ear had begun to ache from the receiver being pressed into it with his shoulder.

'Good,' Barbara said. 'Go to sleep loving me.'

'I don't want to argue.'

'Then don't argue,' Barbara said. 'Maybe I'm just in a bad mood. I'm sorry.'

'Why are you mad?' Austin said.

'Sometimes,' Barbara said. Then she stopped. 'I don't know. Sometimes you just piss me off.'

'Well, shit,' Austin said.

'Shit is right. Shit,' Barbara said. 'It's nothing. Go to sleep.'

'Fine. I will,' Austin said.

'I'll see you tomorrow, sweetheart,' Barbara said.

'Sure,' Austin said, wanting to sound casual. He started to say something else. To tell her he loved her again in the casual voice. But Barbara had put down the phone.

Austin sat in bed in his pajamas, staring at himself in the smoky mirror. It was a different picture from before. He looked grainy, displeased, the lights beside his bed harsh, intrusive, his champagne glass empty, the night he'd just spent unsuccessful, unpromising, vaguely humiliating. He looked like he was on drugs. That was the true picture, he thought. Later he knew he would think differently, would see events in a kinder, more flattering light. His spirits would rise as they always did and he would feel very, very encouraged by something, anything. But now was the time to take a true reading, he thought, when the tide was out and everything was exposed—yourself—as it really, truly was. *There* was the real life, and he wasn't deluded about it. It was this picture you had to act on.

He sat in bed and felt gloomy, drank the rest of his warm champagne and thought about Barbara in the house alone, probably doing something to prepare for his arrival the next afternoon—arranging some fresh flowers or preparing to cook something he especially liked—maybe that's what she was doing when they were talking, in which case he was certainly wrong to have been annoyed. After thinking along these lines for a while, he reached over and dialled Josephine's number. It was two a.m. He would wake her up, but that was all right. She'd be glad he had. He would tell her the truth—that he couldn't keep from calling her, that she was on his mind, that he wished she was here with him, that he already missed her, that there was more to this than it seemed. But when he dialled her number the line was busy. And it was busy in five minutes. And in fifteen. And in thirty. And then he turned out the harsh lamplight beside the bed, put his head on the crisp pillow and passed quickly into sleep.

4

Near the Odéon, striding briskly up the narrow street that ended at the Palais du Luxembourg, Austin realized he was arriving at Josephine's apartment with nothing in his hands—a clear mistake. Possibly some bright flowers would be a good idea, or a toy, a present of some minor kind which would encourage Leo, whom he was keeping for an hour while Josephine visited her lawyer, to like him. Leo was four and ill-tempered and spoiled. He was pale and had limp, wispy-thin dark hair, and dark, penetrating eyes, and when he cried—which was often—he cried loudly and had the habit of opening his mouth and leaving it open for as much of the sound to come out as possible, a habit which accentuated the simian quality of his face, which on occasion he seemed to share with Josephine. Austin had seen documentaries on TV that showed apes doing virtually the same thing while sitting in trees—always it seemed just as the daylight was vanishing and the advent of another long, imponderable night was at hand. Possibly that was what Leo's life was like. 'It is because of my divorce from his father,' Josephine had said matter-of-factly the one time he had been in her apartment, the time they had listened to jazz and he had sat and admired the golden sunlight on the building cornices. 'It is too hard on him. He is a child. But . . . ' She'd shrugged her shoulders and begun to think about something else.

Austin had seen no store selling flowers, so he crossed over to a chic little shop that had wooden toys in its window: bright wood trucks of ingenious meticulous design, bright wood animals—ducks and rabbits and pigs in preposterous detail. Even a French farmer wearing a red neck kerchief and a black beret. An entire wooden farm house was painstakingly constructed with roof tiles, little dormer windows and Dutch doors, and cost a fortune—more than he intended to pay. Kids were fine, but he'd never wanted any for himself, and neither had Barbara. It had been their first significant point of agreement when they were in college in the sixties, and he was a Lambda Chi and she was the Lambda Chi Beauty Queen—the first reason they'd found to make them think they might be made for each other. Years ago now, Austin thought—twenty-two—all of it slid past, out of reach.

The little shop, though, seemed to have plenty of nice things inside that Austin *could* afford—a wooden clock whose hands you moved yourself, a wooden replica of the Eiffel Tower, likewise one of the Arc de Triomphe. There was a little wood pickaninny holding a tiny red and green wood water-melon and smiling out through bright painted-white teeth. The little pickaninny reminded Austin of Leo—minus the smile—and he thought about buying it as a piece of Americana and taking it home to Barbara.

Inside, the saleslady seemed to think he would naturally want that and started to take it out of the case. But there was a little wicker basket full of painted eggs on the counter top, all for twenty francs, and Austin picked up one of those, a bright green enamel and gold paisley one made of perfectly turned balsa that felt hollow. They were left over from Easter, Austin thought, and had probably been more expensive. There was no reason Leo should like a green, wooden egg, but *he* liked it, and Josephine would like it too. Once the child set it aside in favor of whatever he liked better, Josephine could claim it and put it on her night table or on her desk at work and think about him.

Austin paid the clerk for the nubbly-sided little egg and started for the door—he was going to be late on account of being lost. But just as he reached the glass door Josephine's husband came in, accompanied by a tall, beautiful, vivacious blonde woman with a deep tan and thin, shining legs. The woman was wearing a short silver-colored dress that encased her hips in some kind of elastic fabric, and she looked, Austin thought, standing by in complete surprise, rich. Josephine's husband—short and bulgy with his thick, dark Armenian-looking moustache and soft, swart skin—was at least a head shorter than the woman, but was dressed in an expensively-shapeless black suit. They were talking in a language which sounded like German, and Bernard—the husband who had written the salacious novel about Josephine, and who provided her little money and his son precious little attention, and whom Josephine was that very afternoon going off to secure a divorce from—was seemingly intent on buying a present in the store.

Bernard glanced at Austin disapprovingly. His small, almost black eyes flickered with some vague recognition. Though there couldn't be any recognition. Bernard knew nothing about him, and there was, in fact, nothing to know. Bernard had certainly never laid eyes on Austin. It was just the way he had of looking at people, as though he had your number and didn't much like you. Why, Austin wondered, would that be an attractive quality in a man? Suspicion. Disdain. A bullying nature. Why marry an asshole like that?

Austin paused inside the shop door, looking down into the display window from behind. He studied the little wooden Eiffel Tower and Arc de Triomphe, saw that they were parts of a whole little Paris made of wood, a kit a child could play with and arrange any way he saw fit. A wooden Notre Dame, a wooden Louvre, an Obelisque, a Musée Pompidou, even a little wooden Odéon like the one a few steps down the street. The whole set of buildings was expensive as hell—nearly 3,000 francs—but you could also buy the pieces separately. Austin thought about buying something to accompany the enamel egg—give the egg to Josephine and the building miniature to Leo. He stood staring down at the little city in wood, beyond which out the window the real city of metal and stone went on unmindful.

Bernard and his blonde friend were laughing at the little pickaninny holding his red and green water-melon. The clerk had it out of the case, and Bernard was holding it up and laughing derisively at it. Once or twice Bernard said, 'a leetle neegger,' then said 'voilà, voilà,' then the woman said something in German and both of them burst out laughing all over again. Even the shopkeeper laughed behind the counter.

Austin fingered the green egg in his pants pocket, a lump against his leg. He considered just going up and buying the whole goddamned wooden Paris and saying to Bernard in English, 'I'm buying this for *your* son, you son of a bitch,' and threatening him with his fist. But that was a bad idea, and he didn't have the stomach for a row. It was even remotely possible that the man might not be Bernard at all, that he only looked like the picture in Leo's room, and he would be a complete idiot to threaten him.

He slipped his hand in his pocket, felt the enamel paint of the egg, and wondered if this was an adequate present, or would it be ludicrous? The German woman turned and looked at him, the smile of derisive laughter still half on her lips. She looked at Austin's face, then at his pocket where his hand was gripping the little egg. She leaned and said something to Bernard, something in French, and Bernard turned and looked at Austin across the shop, narrowed his eyes in a kind of disdainful warning. Then he raised his chin slightly and turned back. They both said something else, then they both chuckled. The proprietress looked at Austin and smiled in a friendly way. Then Austin changed his mind about buying the wooden city and opened the glass door and stepped out on to the sidewalk where the air was cool and he could see up the short hill to the park.

5

In the small suburban community of Oak Grove, Illinois, Austin meant to take straight aim on his regular existence —driving to and from his suburban office in nearby Orchard Park; helping coach a little league team sponsored by a friend's Oak Grove linoleum company; spending evenings at home with Barbara, who was a broker for a big firm that sold commercial real estate and who was herself having an excellent post-recession selling season.

Austin could sense that something was wrong with himself, which bewildered him. But Barbara had decided to continue everyday life as if that were not true, or as if whatever was bothering him was simply outside her control, and that since she loved him eventually his problem would either be solved privately or be carried away by the normal flow of ordinary happy life. Barbara's was a systematically optimistic view: that with the right attitude everything works out for the best. She said it was because her family had all been Scottish Presbyterians. And it was a view Austin admired, though it was not always the way he saw things. He thought ordinary life had the potential to grind you into dust—his parents' life in Peoria for instance, a life he couldn't have stood—and sometimes unusual measures were called for. Barbara said this point of view was typically shanty Irish.

On the day Austin returned—into a hot, springy airport sunshine, jet-lagged and forcibly good-spirited—Barbara had cooked venison haunch in a rich secret fig sauce, something she'd had to sleuth the ingredients for in a Hungarian neighborhood in West Diversey, plus brabant potatoes and roasted garlics (Austin's favorite), plus a very good Merlot that Austin had drunk too much of while earnestly, painstakingly lying about all he'd done in Paris. Barbara had bought a new spring dress, had her hair restreaked and generally gone to a lot of trouble to orchestrate a happy homecoming and to forget about their unpleasant late-night phone conversation. Though Austin felt it should be his responsibility to erase that uncomfortable moment from memory and see to it his married life of long standing was once again the source of seamless, good-willed happiness.

Late that night, a Tuesday, he and Barbara made brief, boozy love in the dark of their thickly curtained bedroom, to the sound of a neighbor's springer spaniel barking unceasingly one street over. Theirs was practiced, undramatic love-making, a set of protocols and assumptions lovingly followed like a liturgy which points to but really has little connection with the mysteries and chaos which had once made it a breathless necessity. Austin noticed by the digital clock on the chest of drawers that it all took nine minutes, start to finish. He wondered bleakly if that was of normal or less than normal duration for Americans his and Barbara's age. Less, he supposed, though no doubt the fault was his.

Lying in the silent dark afterwards, side by side, facing the white plaster ceiling (the neighbor's dog had shut up as if on cue from an unseen observer to their act), he and Barbara tried to find something to say. Each knew the other's mind was seeking it; an up-beat, forward-sounding subject that conjured away the past couple or maybe it was three years, which hadn't been so wonderful between the two of them—a time of wandering for Austin, and patience from Barbara. They wished for something unprovoking that would allow them go to sleep thinking of themselves the way they presumed they were.

'Are you tired? You must be pretty exhausted,' she said, matter-of-factly into the darkness. 'You poor old thing.' She reached and patted him on his chest. 'Go to sleep. You'll feel better tomorrow.'

'I feel fine now. I'm not tired,' Austin said alertly. 'Do I seem tired?'

'No. I guess not.'

They were silent again and Austin felt himself relaxing to the sound of her words. He was, in fact, corrosively tired. But he wanted to put a good end to the night, which he felt had been a nice night, and to the homecoming, and to the time he'd been gone and ridiculously infatuated by Josephine Belliard. That encounter—there *was* no encounter, of course—but those pronouncements and preoccupations could be put to rest. They could be disciplined away. They were not real life—at least not the bedrock, real-*est* life, the one everything depended on—no matter how he'd felt and protested for an instant. He wasn't a fool. He wasn't stupid enough to lose his sense of proportion. He was a survivor, he thought, and survivors always knew in which direction the ground was.

'I just want to see what's possible now,' Austin said unexpectedly. He was half-asleep and had been having two conversations at once—one with Barbara, his wife, and one with himself about Josephine Belliard—and they were getting mixed up. Barbara hadn't asked him anything to which what he'd just mumbled was even a remotely logical answer. She hadn't, that he remembered, asked him anything at all. He was just babbling, talking in his near sleep; and a cold, stiffening fear gripped him—that he'd said something, half-asleep and half-drunk, that he'd be sorry for, something that would incriminate him with the truth about Josephine. Though in his current state of mind, he wasn't at all sure what that truth might be.

'That shouldn't be hard, should it?' Barbara said out of the dark.

'No,' Austin said, wondering if he was awake. 'I guess not.'

'We're together. And we love each other. Whatever we want to make possible we ought to be able to do.' She touched his leg through his pajamas.

'Yes,' Austin said. 'That's right.' He wished Barbara would go to sleep now. He didn't want to say anything else. Talking seemed like a minefield since he wasn't sure what he would say.

Barbara was silent while his insides contracted briefly then slowly began to relax. He resolved to say nothing else and didn't. After a couple of minutes Barbara turned and faced the curtains. The street light showed palely between the fabric closings, and Austin wondered if he had somehow made her cry without realizing it.

'Oh well,' Barbara said. 'You'll feel better tomorrow I hope. Good night.'

'Good night,' Austin said. And he settled himself helplessly into sleep, feeling that he had not pleased Barbara very much, and that he was a man who probably pleased no one very much now, and that, in fact, even in his own life—of the things that should and always had made him happy—very little pleased him much at all.

In the next days Austin went to work as he usually did. He made make-up calls to his accounts in Brussels and Amsterdam. He told a man he'd known for ten years and deeply respected that doctors had discovered a rather 'mysterious inflammation' high-up in the upper quadrant of his stomach but that there was reasonable hope surgery could be averted with the aid of drugs. He tried to think of the name of the drug he was 'taking' but couldn't. Afterwards he felt gloomy about having told such a pointless falsehood and worried that the man might mention something to his boss.

He wondered, staring at the elegantly framed azimuth map which Barbara had given him when he'd been awarded the prestigious European accounts and that he'd hung behind his desk with tiny red pennants attached denoting where he'd increased the company's market share—Brussels, Amsterdam, Düsseldorf, Paris—wondered if his life, his normal carrying-on, was slipping out of control, only gradually so as not to be noticed. But he decided that it wasn't, and as proof he offered the fact that he was entertaining this idea in his office, on an ordinary business day, with everything in his life arrayed in place and going forward, rather than entertaining it in some Parisian street café in the blear aftermath of a calamity; a man with soiled lapels, in need of a shave and short of cash, scribbling his miserable thoughts into a tiny spiral notebook like all the other morons he'd seen who'd thrown their lives away. This feeling now, this sensation of heaviness and of life's coming unmoored, was actually a feeling of vigilance, the weight of responsibility accepted, and the proof that carrying life to a successful end was never an easy matter.

On Thursday, the moment he arrived in the office he put in a call to Josephine at work. She'd been on his mind almost every minute, her little oddly-matched but inflaming features, her boyish way of walking with her toes pointed out like a country bumpkin. But also her soft, shadowy complexion and soft arms, and her whispered voice in his memory: 'No, no, no, no, no.'

'Hi, it's me,' Austin said. There was a bulky delay in his connection this time, and he could hear his voice echo on the line. He didn't sound like he wanted to sound. His voice was higher pitched, like a kid's voice.

'OK. Hi,' was all she said. She was rustling papers, a habit that annoyed him.

'I was just thinking about you,' Austin said. A long pause occurred after this announcement, and he endured it uncomfortably.

'Yes,' she said, then another pause. 'Me, too. How are you?'

'I'm fine,' Austin said, though he didn't want to stress that. He wanted to stress that he missed her. 'I miss you,' he said and felt feeble hearing his voice inside the echo.

'Yeah,' she said finally though flatly. 'Me, too.'

Austin wasn't sure if she'd actually heard what he'd said. Possibly she was actually talking to someone else, someone in the office. He felt disoriented and considered just hanging up. But he knew how he'd feel if that happened. Wretched beyond imagining. In fact, he needed to persevere now or he'd end up feeling wretched anyway.

'I'd like to see you very much,' Austin said, his ear pressed to the receiver.

'Yeah,' Josephine said. 'Come and take me to dinner tonight.' She laughed a harsh, ironic laugh. He wondered if she was saying this for someone else's benefit, someone in her office who knew all about him and thought he was stupid. He heard more papers rustle. He felt things spinning.

'I mean it,' he said. 'I would.'

'When are you coming back to Paris?' she said.

'I don't know. But very soon I hope.' He didn't know why he'd said that since it wasn't true, or at least wasn't in any plans he currently had. Only in that instant it seemed possible. Anything was possible. And indeed this seemed imminently possible, though he had no idea how. France wasn't Wisconsin. You couldn't decide to go for a weekend.

'So. Call me, I guess,' Josephine said. 'I would see you.'

'I will,' Austin said, his heart already beginning to thump. 'When I come I'll call you.'

He wanted to ask her something. He didn't know what, though. He didn't know anything to ask. 'How's Leo?' he said, using the English pronunciation.

Josephine laughed, but not ironically. 'How is Leo?' she said, using the same pronunciation. Leo is OK. He is at home. Soon I'm going there. That's all.'

'Good,' Austin said. 'That's great.' He swivelled quickly and stared at Paris on the map. As usual, he was surprised at how much nearer the top of France it was instead of perfectly in the middle the way he always thought of it. He wanted to ask her then why she hadn't called him the last night he'd seen her, to tell her that he'd hoped she'd call, but then he remembered her line had been busy, and he wanted to know who she'd been talking to. But he couldn't ask that. It wasn't his business.

'Fine,' he said. And he knew that in five seconds the phone call would be over and Paris would instantly be as far from Chicago as it ever was. He almost said, 'I love you,' into the receiver. But that would be a mistake, and he didn't say it, though part of him furiously wanted to. Then he nearly said it in French, thinking possibly it might mean less than it meant in English. But again he refrained. 'I want to see you very much,' he said as a last, weak, compromise thing to say.

'So. See me. I kiss you,' Josephine Belliard said, but in a strange voice, a voice he'd never heard before, almost an emotional voice. Then she quietly hung up the phone.

Austin sat at his desk staring at the map, wondering what that voice had been, what it meant, how he was supposed to interpret it. Was it the voice of love or some strange trick of the phone line? Or just some trick of his ear to confect something he wanted to hear and so allow him not to feel as wretched as he figured he'd feel but in fact didn't feel. He felt wonderful now. Ebullient. The best he'd felt since the last time he'd seen her. Alive. And there was nothing wrong with that, was there? If something makes you feel good for a moment and no one is crushed by it, what's the use of denying yourself? Other people denied. And for what? The guys he'd gone to college with, who'd never left the track once they were on it, never had a moment of ebullience, and maybe never knew the difference. But he *did* know the difference, and it was worth it, no matter the difficulties you endured living with the consequences. You had one life, Austin thought. Use it up. He'd heard what he'd heard.

That evening he picked Barbara up at the realty offices and drove them to a bar. It was a thing they often did. Barbara frequently worked late, and they both liked a semi-swanky Polynesian restaurant in Skokie called Hai-Nun, a dark, teak-and-bamboo place where the drinks were all doubles and eventually when you were too drunk to negotiate your way to a table you could order a platter of fried specialties and sober up eating dinner at the bar.

For a while an acquaintance of Austin's, a commodities trader named Ned Coles, had stood beside them at the bar (their friends routinely circulated through the place) and made chit-chat about how the salad days at the Board of Trade were a thing of the past, and then about the big opportunities in Europe after 1992 and how the US was probably going to miss the boat, then about how the Fighting Illini were sizing up the skilled positions during the spring drills, and finally about his ex-wife, Suzie, who was moving to Phoenix in the next week so she could participate more in athletics. She was interested in competing in iron woman

43

competitions.

'Can't she be an iron woman in Chicago?' Barbara said. She barely knew Ned Coles and was bored by him. Ned's wife was 'kidnapping' their two kids to Arizona, which had Ned down in the dumps, but not wanting to make a fuss.

'Of course,' Ned said. Ned was a heavy, beet-faced man who looked older than forty-six. He had gone to Harvard then come home to work for his old man's company and quickly become a drunk and a bore. Austin had met him in M.B.A. night school fifteen years ago. They didn't see each other socially. 'But that's not the big problem.'

'What's the big problem?' Austin said, muddling an ice-cube in his gin.

'*Moi-même*,' Ned said. 'Me.' Ned looked grim about it. 'She contends I'm a force field of negativism that radiates into all the north suburbs. So I have to move to Indiana for her to stay. And that's way too big a sacrifice.' Ned laughed humorlessly. Ned knew a lot of Indiana jokes which Austin had already heard. Indiana, to Ned Coles, was the place where you caught sight of the flagship of the Polish navy and visited the Argentine war heroes memorial. He was old Chicago, and he was, Austin thought, an idiot. He wished Ned's wife a good journey to Arizona.

When Ned wandered away into the restaurant, leaving Austin and Barbara alone at the lacquered teak bar, Barbara grew quiet. Both of them were drinking gin, and in silence they let the bartender pour them another two on the rocks. Austin knew he was a little drunk now, and that Barbara was probably more drunk than he was. He sensed there could be a problem lurking—about what he wasn't sure. He longed for the feeling he'd had when he put the phone down with Josephine Belliard that morning. Ebullience. To be fiercely alive. It had been a temporary feeling, he understood perfectly well. But he longed for it now all the more achingly on account of its illusory quality, its innocent smallness. Even realists, he thought, needed a break now and then.

'Do you remember the other night?' Barbara began as if she were choosing her words with extreme precision. 'You were in

Paris, and I was back here at home. And I asked you if you thought you might be taking me for granted?' Barbara focused on the rim of her glass, but quickly her eyes cast up and found his. There was one other couple in the bar, and the bartender had seated himself on a stool at the end and was silently reading a newspaper. This was the dinner hour, and many people were in the restaurant. Someone had ordered a dish that required fire be brought from the kitchen to their table, and Austin could see the yellow flame lick up at the ceiling, hear the loud *sssss* sound and the delighted diners say, 'Oooo.'

'I didn't think that was true,' Austin said quietly in answer to her question.

'I know you didn't,' Barbara said and nodded her head slowly. 'And maybe that's exactly right. Maybe I was wrong.' She stared at her glass of gin again. 'What *is* true, though, Martin, and what's worse—about you—is that you take *yourself* for granted.' Barbara kept nodding her head without looking at him, as if she'd discovered an interesting but worrisome paradox in philosophy. When Barbara got mad at him, particularly if she was a little drunk, she nodded her head and spoke in this overly meticulous way, as if she'd already done a considerable amount of thinking on the subject at hand and wished to illuminate her conclusions as a contribution to common sense. Austin called this habit, 'reading the ingredients off the Molotov cocktail,' and he disliked it and wished Barbara wouldn't do it, though there was never a good moment to bring the subject up.

'I'm sorry but I don't think I know what you mean by that,' he said in the most normal voice he could call upon.

Barbara looked at him curiously, her perfect Lambda-Chi beauty-queen features grown as precise and angular as her words. 'What I mean is that you think—about yourself—that you can't be changed. On your insides, I mean. You think of yourself as a given, that what you go off to some foreign country and do won't have any effect on you, won't leave you different. But that isn't true, Martin, because you *are* different. In fact, you're unreachable, and you've been becoming that way for a long time. For two or three years. I've just tried to get along with you and make you happy, because making you happy has always made me happy. But now it doesn't, because you've changed and I don't feel like I can reach you or that you're even aware of what you've become, and frankly I don't even care. All this just occurred to me while I was ordering a title search this afternoon. I'm sorry it's such a shock.'

Barbara sniffed and looked at him and seemed to smile. She wasn't about to cry. She was cold-eyed and factual now, as if she were reporting the death of a distant relative neither of them much cared about.

'I'm sorry to hear that,' Austin said slowly, wanting to remain as calm she was, though not as cold. He didn't exactly know what this meant or what could've brought it about, since he didn't think he'd been doing anything wrong. Nothing had happened two or three years ago that he could remember. Josephine Belliard had had a small effect on him, but it would pass the way anything passed. Life had seemed to be going on. He thought, in fact, that he'd been acting about as normal as he could hope to act.

But did this mean that she had taken all she intended to and was through with him? That would be a shock, he thought, and something he didn't want to happen. Or did she only mean to say he needed to shape up and become more reachable, go back to some nice way he'd been that she approved of—some way he would've said he still was. Or maybe she was just saying she intended to change herself dramatically now, be less forgiving, less interested in him, less loving, take more interest in herself; that their marriage was going to start down a new, more equitable road—something else he didn't like the sound of.

He sat in the silence she was affording him now for just this purpose. He certainly needed to offer a response. He needed intelligently and forthrightly to answer her charges and demonstrate sympathy for her embattled point of view, but also he needed to stand up for himself, while offering a practical way out of this apparent impasse. Much, in other words, was being asked of him. He was, in essence, expected to solve everything; take both points of view—hers and his—and somehow join them so that everything was either put back to a way it had been, or else made better so that both of them were happier and could feel that if life was a series of dangerous escarpments you scaled with difficulty, at least you eventually succeeded, whereupon the plenteous rewards of happiness made all the nightmares worthwhile.

It was an admirable view of life, Austin thought. It was a sound, traditional view, absolutely in the American grain, and one that sent everybody to the altar starry-eyed and certain. It was a view Barbara had always maintained and he'd always envied. Barbara was in the American grain. It was one of the big reasons he'd been knocked out by her years ago, and why he knew she would be the best person he or anyone else could ever love. Only he didn't see at that moment what he could do to make her wishes come true, if he in fact knew anything about what her wishes were. So that what he said, after admitting he was sorry to hear what she'd already said, was: 'Only I don't think there's anything I can do about it. I wish there was. I'm really sorry.'

'Then you're just an asshole,' Barbara said and nodded again very confidently, very conclusively. 'And you're also a womanizer and you're a creep. And I don't want to be married to any of those things any more. So.' She took a big emptying swig out of her glass of gin and set the thick tumbler down hard on its damp little napkin coaster. 'So,' she said again as if admiring her own voice, 'Fuck you. And goodbye.' With that, she got up and walked very steadily and straight out of the Hai-Nun (so much so that Austin didn't wonder about whether she was in any condition to drive) and disappeared around the bamboo corner just as another fat lick of yellow flame swarmed into the dark dining-room air and another hot, loud sizzling sound went up, and another 'ooo' was exhaled from the dazzled diners, a couple of whom even clapped.

This was certainly an over-response on Barbara's part, Austin felt. In the first place she knew nothing about Josephine Belliard because there was nothing to know. No incriminating facts. She was only guessing, and unfairly. In all probability she was just feeling bad about herself and hoping to make him responsible for it. In the second place, it wasn't easy to tell the truth about how you felt when it wasn't what someone you loved wanted to be the truth. He'd done his best by saying he wasn't sure what he could do to make her happy. That was a place to start. He'd thought her opening certitude had just been a positioning strategy and that possibly a big fight was brewing, but it would be one which they could settle over the course of the evening, ending with apologies, after which they'd both could feel better, liberated. It had gone like that in the past when he'd gotten temporarily distracted by some woman he met far from home. Ordinary goings-on, he thought.

Women were sometimes a kind of problem—he enjoyed their company, enjoyed hearing their voices, knowing about their semi-intimate lives and daily dramas. But his attempts at knowing them often left him feeling peculiar, as if he had secrets he didn't want to keep, and on the other hand, left in him an odd residue of life—his life with Barbara, especially—not fully appreciated, gone somewhat to waste.

But Barbara had gone out of all bounds with this leaving. Now they were both alone in separate little cocoons of bitterness and self-explanation, and that was when matters did not get better but worse. Everyone knew that. She had brought this situation into existence, not him, and she would have to live with the outcome, no matter how small or how large. Drinking had something to do with all this, Austin thought. His and hers. There was a lot of tension in the air at the moment, and drinking was a natural response. He didn't think either of them had a drinking problem *per se*—particularly himself. But he resolved, sitting at the teak bar in front of a glass of Beefeater's, that he would quit drinking as soon as he could.

When Austin walked outside into the dark parking lot, Barbara was nowhere in sight. A half hour had gone by. He thought he might find her in the car mad or sleeping. It was eight-thirty. The air was cool, and Old Orchard Road was astream with automobiles.

When he drove home, all the lights were off and Barbara's car, which she had left at her office when he had picked her up, was not in the garage. Austin walked in through the house turning on lights until he got to their bedroom. He opened the door gingerly, so as not to wake Barbara if she were there asleep flung across the top-covers. But she wasn't there. The room was dark except for the digital clock. He was alone in the house, and he did not know where his wife was, only that she conceivably was leaving him. Certainly she'd been angry. The last thing she had said was, 'fuck you.' And she'd walked out—something she hadn't done before. Someone, he understood, might conclude she was leaving him.

Austin poured himself a glass of milk in the brightly-lit kitchen and considered testifying to these very moments and facts as well as to the unpleasant episode in the Hai-Nun and to the final words of his wife, in a court of law. A divorce court. He featured himself sitting at a table with his lawyer, and Barbara at a table with her lawyer, both of them, eyes straight ahead, facing a judge's bench. In her present state of mind Barbara wouldn't be persuaded by his side of the story. She wouldn't have a change of heart or decide just to forget the whole thing in the middle of a court room once he'd looked her square in the eye and told only the truth. Though divorce was certainly not a good solution, he thought.

Austin walked up to the sliding glass door that gave on to the back yard and to the fenceless yards of his neighbors, all now bathed in darkness—their soft house-lights and the reflection of his kitchen cabinets and of himself holding his glass of milk and of the breakfast table and chairs all combined and cast in perfect half-lit diorama.

On the other hand, he thought (the first being a messy divorce attempt followed by sullen reconciliation once they realized they lacked the nerve for divorce) *he was out.*

He hadn't left. *She* had. *He* hadn't made any threats or complaints or bitter, half-drunk, name-calling declarations or soap-operaish exits into the night. *She* had. *He* hadn't wanted to be alone. *She* had wanted to be alone. And as a result he was free. Free to do anything he wanted, no questions asked or answered, no suspicions or recriminations. No explanatory half-truths.

In the past, when he and Barbara had had a row and he had felt like just getting in the car and driving to Montana or Alaska to work for the Forest Service—never writing, never calling, though not actually going to the trouble of concealing his identity or whereabouts—he'd found he could never face the moment of actual leaving. His feet simply wouldn't move. And about himself he'd said and felt proud of the fact that he was no good at departures. There was in leaving, he believed, the feel of betrayal—of betraying Barbara. Of betraying himself. You didn't marry somebody so you could leave, he'd said to her. He could never in fact even seriously think about leaving. About the Forest Service he could only plot as far as the end of the first day —when he was tired and bruised from hard work but his mind emptied of worries. After that he was confused about what would be happening next—another toilsome day like the one before. And he'd decide that meant he didn't want to leave; that his life, his love for Barbara were simply too strong. Leaving was what weak people did. Again his college classmates were called upon to be the bad examples, the cowardly leavers. All of them had been divorced, strewn kids of all ages all over the map, routinely and grimly posted big checks off to Dallas and Seattle and Atlanta, fed on regret. They had left and now they were plenty sorry. His love for Barbara, though, was simply worth more. Some life force was in him too strongly, too fully, to leave—which meant something, something lasting and important. It was, he felt, what all the great novels ever written were about.

It had occurred to him, of course, that what he might be was just a cringing, lying coward who didn't have the nerve to face a life alone; couldn't fend for himself in a complex world full of his own acts' consequences. Though that was merely a conventional way of understanding life, another soap-opera view—about which he knew better. He was a stayer. He was a man who did not have to do the obvious thing. He would be there to preside over the messy consequences of life's turmoils. It was, he thought, his one innate strength of character.

Only now, oddly, he was in limbo. The 'there' where he'd promised to stay seemed to have suddenly separated into pieces and receded. And it was invigorating. He felt, in fact, that although Barbara had seemed to bring it about, he may have caused this himself, though it was probably inevitable, too—destined to happen between the two of them no matter what the cause or outcome.

He went to the bar cart in the den, poured some scotch into

his milk and came back and sat in a kitchen chair in front of the sliding glass door. Two dogs trotted across the grass in the rectangle of light that fell from the window. Shortly after, another two dogs—one, the springer spaniel he often heard yapping at night—came through. And then a small scruffy lone dog, sniffing the ground behind the other four. This dog stopped and peered in at Austin, blinked, then trotted out of the light and disappeared.

Austin had been imagining Barbara checked in to an expensive hotel downtown, drinking champagne, ordering a Cobb salad from room service, and thinking the same things he'd been thinking. But what he was actually beginning to feel now, and grimly, was that when push came to shove, the aftermath of almost anything he'd done in a very long time really *hadn't* given him any pleasure. Despite good intentions, and despite loving Barbara as he felt few people ever loved anybody, and feeling that he was to blame for everything that had gone on tonight, he considered it unmistakable that he could do his wife no good now. He was bad for her. And as if his own puny inability to satisfy her candidly expressed and possibly partly legitimate grievances was not adequate proof of his failure, then her own judgement certainly was: 'You're an asshole,' she'd said. And he concluded that she was right. He *was* an asshole and he was the other things, too, and he hated to think so. Life didn't veer, you discovered it *had* veered—later. Now. And he was as sorry about it as anything he could imagine ever being sorry about. But he simply couldn't help it. He didn't like what he didn't like, and he couldn't do what he couldn't do.

What he *could* do, though, was leave. Go back to Paris. Immediately. Tonight if possible, before Barbara came home certainly, and before he and she became swamped all over again and he had to wade back into the problems of his being an asshole, and their life. He felt as if a fine, high-tension wire strung between his toes and the back of his neck had been forcefully plucked by an invisible finger, causing him to feel a chilled vibration, a bright tingling that radiated into his stomach and out to the ends of his fingers.

He sat up straight in his chair. He was leaving. Later he

would feel awful and bereft and be broke, maybe homeless, on welfare and sick to death from a disease born of dejection. But now he felt scintillated, primed, jittery with excitement. And it wouldn't last for ever, he thought, probably not even very long. The mere sound of a taxi door closing out in the street would detonate the whole fragile business, and sacrifice his chance to act.

He stood and quickly walked to the kitchen and called a taxi, then left the receiver dangling off the hook. He walked back through the house, checking all the doors and windows to be certain they were locked. He walked into his and Barbara's bedroom, turned on the light, hauled his two-suiter from under the bed, opened it and began putting exactly that in one side, two suits, and in the other side underwear, shirts, another pair of shoes, a belt, three striped ties, plus his still-full dopp kit. In response to an unseen questioner, he said out loud, standing in the bedroom: 'I really didn't bring much. I just put some things in a suitcase.'

He closed his bag and brought it into the living-room. His passport was in the secretary. He put that in his pants pocket, got a coat out of the closet by the front door—a long rubbery rain jacket bought from a catalog—and put it on. He picked up his wallet and keys, then turned and looked into the house.

He was leaving. In less than twenty seconds he'd be gone. Likely as not he would never stand in this doorway again, surveying these rooms, feeling this way. Some of it might be the same, OK, but not all. And it was so easy; one minute you're completely in a life, and the next you're completely out. Just a few items to round up.

A note. He felt he should leave a note and walked quickly back to the kitchen, dug a Day-Glo green grocery list pad out of a drawer, and on the back scribbled: 'Dear B,' and then wasn't sure what exactly to continue with. Something meaningful would take sheets and sheets of paper and then would be both absurd and irrelevant. Something brief would be ironic or sentimental, and demonstrate in a completely new way what an asshole he was—a conclusion he wanted this note to make the case against incontrovertibly. He turned the sheet over. A sample grocery list was printed there with blank spaces provided for pencil checks.

Pain	___
Lait	___
Cereal	___
Oeufs	___
Veggies	___
Hamburger	___
Lard	___
Fromage	___
Les Autres	

He could check '*Les Autres*', he thought, and write 'Paris' beside it. Paris was certainly '*autres*'. Though *only* an asshole would do that. He turned it over again to the 'Dear B' side. Nothing he could think of was right. Everything seemed to want to stand for their life but couldn't stand for their life. Their life was their life and couldn't be represented by anything but their life, not something scratched on the back of a grocery list. His taxi honked outside. For some reason he reached up and put the phone receiver back on the hook, and almost instantly it started ringing—loud, brassy, shrill, unnerving rings that filled the yellow kitchen as if the walls were metal. He could hear the other phones ringing in other rooms. It suddenly was intolerably chaotic inside the house. Below 'Dear B' he furiously scribbled, 'I'll call you. Love M,' and stuck the note under the jangling phone. Then he hurried to the front door, grabbed his suitcase, and exited his empty home into the soft spring suburban nightfall.

6

During the first few dispiriting days back in Paris Austin did not call Josephine Belliard. There were more pressing matters; to arrange, over terrible phone connections, to be granted a leave of absence from his job selling paper. 'Personal problems,' he said squeamishly to his boss, and felt certain as he said it his boss was concluding he'd had a nervous breakdown. 'How's Barbara?'

Fred Carruthers said cheerfully, which annoyed him.

'Barbara's great,' he'd said, 'She's just fine. Call her up yourself. She'd like to hear from you.' Then he'd hung up thinking he'd never see Fred Carruthers again and didn't give a shit if he didn't, only that his own voice had sounded desperate, the one way he didn't want it to sound.

He arranged for his Chicago bank to send him money—enough, he thought, for six months. Ten thousand dollars. He called up one of the two people he knew in Paris, a former Lambda Chi brother who was a homosexual and a would-be novelist living someplace in Neuilly. Dave, his old frat bro, asked him if he was a homosexual himself now, then laughed like hell. Finally, though, he remembered he had a friend who had a friend—and eventually after two unsettled nights in his old Hôtel de la Monastère, during which he'd worried about money, he'd been given the key to a luxurious, metal-and-velvet faggot's seraglio with enormous mirrors on the bedroom ceiling, just down the rue Bonaparte from the Deux Magots, where Sartre was supposed to have liked to sit in the sun and think.

Much of these first days—bright, soft mid-April days—Austin was immensely jet-lagged and exhausted and looked sick and haunted in the bathroom mirror. He didn't want to see Josephine in this condition. He had been back home only three days, then in the space of one frenzied evening had had a big fight with his wife, driven to the airport, waited all night for a flight and taken a middle row stand-by between two French children to Orly. It was crazy. A large part of this was definitely crazy. Probably he *was* having a nervous breakdown and was too out of his head even to have a hint about it and eventually Barbara and a psychiatrist would have to come bring him home heavily sedated and in a strait-jacket. But that would be later.

'Where are you?' Barbara said coldly, when he reached her finally at home.

'In Europe,' he said. 'I'm staying a while.'

'How nice for you,' she said. He could tell she didn't know what to think about any of this. It pleased him to baffle her, though he also knew it was childish.

'Carruthers might call you,' he said.

'I already talked to him,' Barbara said.

'I'm sure he thinks I'm nuts.'

'No. He doesn't think that,' she said, without offering what he did think.

Outside the apartment the traffic on the rue Bonaparte was noisy, so that he moved away from the window. The walls in the apartment were dark red and green suede with glistening tubular steel abstract wall-hangings and thick black velvet carpet and furniture. He had no idea who the owner was, though he realized just at that moment that in all probability the owner was dead.

'Are you planning to file for divorce?' Austin said. It was the first time the word had ever been used, but it was inescapable, he thought, and he was remotely satisfied to be the first one to put it into play.

'Actually I don't know what I'm going to do,' Barbara said. 'I don't have a husband now, apparently.'

He almost blurted out that it was she who'd walked out, not him, she who'd actually caused this. But that wasn't entirely true, and in any case saying anything about it would start a conversation he didn't want to have, and that no one *could* have at such long distance. It would just be bickering and complaining and anger. He realized all at once that he had nothing else to say and felt jittery. He'd only wished to announce that he was alive and not dead, and was now ready to hang up. 'You're in France, aren't you?'

'Yes,' Austin said. 'That's right. Why?'

'I supposed so,' Barbara said as though the thought of it disgusted her. 'Why not, I guess? Right?'

'Right,' Austin said.

'So. Come home when you're tired of whatever it is, whatever her name is.' She said this very mildly.

'Maybe I will,' Austin said.

'Maybe I'll be waiting, too,' Barbara said. 'Miracles still happen. I've had my eyes opened now, though.'

'Great,' he said, and he started to say something else, but he thought he heard her hang up. 'Hello?' he said, 'Hello? Barbara, are you there?'

'Oh, go to hell,' Barbara said, and then she did hang up.

T011395

For two days Austin took long, exhausting walks in completely arbitrary directions, surprising himself each time by where he turned up, then taking a cab back to his apartment. His instincts still seemed all wrong, which frustrated him. He thought the Place de la Concorde was farther away from his apartment than it was, and in the opposite direction. He couldn't always remember which way the river ran. And unhappily he kept passing the same streets and movie theater playing *Cinema Paradiso*, and the same news kiosk over and over as if he continually walked in a circle.

He called his other friend, a man named Hank Bullard who'd once worked for Lilienthal, but had decided to start an air-conditioning business of his own in Vitry. He was married to a French woman and lived in a suburb. They made plans for a lunch, then Hank cancelled for business reasons—an emergency trip out of town. Hank said they should arrange another date, but didn't talk about it specifically. Austin ended up having lunch alone in an expensive brasserie on the rue Montparnasse —seated behind a glass window, trying to read *Le Monde* but growing discouraged as the words he didn't understand piled up. He could read the *Herald Tribune*, he thought, to keep up with the world and let his French build gradually.

There were even more tourists than a week ago when he'd been here. The tourist season was beginning, and the whole place, he thought, would probably change and become unbearable. The French and the Americans, he decided, looked exactly like each other, only their language and some qualities you couldn't see distinguished them. Sitting behind his tiny, round boulevard table removed from the swarming passers-by, Austin thought this street was full of people walking along dreaming of doing what he was actually doing, of picking up and leaving everything behind, coming here, sitting in cafés, walking the streets, possibly deciding to write a novel, or to paint watercolors or just to start an air-conditioning business like Hank Bullard. But there was a price to pay for that. And the price was that it didn't feel the least romantic to be doing it. It felt purposeless, as if he himself had no purpose, and there was no sense of a future now—as he had always experienced the future—as a palpable thing you looked forward to confidently even if what it held might be sad or tragic or unwantable. It was still there, of course. But he didn't know how to imagine it. He didn't know, for instance, exactly what he was in Paris for, though he could recount perfectly everything that had gotten him here, to this table, to his plate of *moules meunières*, to this feeling of great fatigue, observing tourists all of whom might dream whatever he dreamed, but in fact knew precisely where they were going and precisely why they were here. It was possible they were the wise ones, he thought, with their warmly lighted, tightly constructed lives on far-away landscapes. Maybe he had reached a point, or even gone far by a point now, when he no longer cared what happened to himself—the linkages of a good life, he knew, being small and subtle and in most ways just lucky things you hardly even noticed. But you could fuck them up and never know quite how you'd done it. Only everything just started to go wrong and unravel. Your life could be on a track to ruin, to your being on the street, to your disappearing from view entirely, and you, in spite of your best efforts, your best hope that it go differently, could only stand by and watch it happen.

For the next two days he did not call Josephine Belliard, although he thought about calling her all the time. He thought he might possibly bump into her as she walked to work. His garish little roué's apartment was only four blocks from the publishing house where she worked on rue de Lille, and where, in a vastly different life, he had made a perfectly respectable business call a little more than a week before.

He walked down the nearby streets as often as he could—to buy a newspaper or to buy food in the little market stalls on the rue de Seine, or just to pass the shop windows and begin to find his way along narrow brick alleys. He disliked thinking that he was only in Paris because of Josephine Belliard, because of a woman, and one he really barely knew, but whom he nevertheless thought about all the time and made persistent efforts to see 'accidentally'. He felt he was here for another reason, a subtle and insistent, albeit a less specific one he could not exactly express to himself, but which he felt would be expressed only and finally by his being here and feeling the way he felt.

Not once, though, did he see Josephine Belliard on the rue de Lille, or walking along the Boulevard St Germain on her way to work, or walking past the Café Flore or the Brasserie Lipp, where he'd had lunch with her only the week before and where the sole had been full of grit but he had not mentioned it.

Much of the time, on his walks along strange streets, he thought about Barbara; not with a feeling of guilt, or even of loss, but involuntarily, habitually. He found himself shopping for her; noticing a blouse or a scarf or an antique pendant or a pair of emerald ear-rings he could buy and bring home. He found himself storing away things to tell her—that France, for instance, was seventy per cent nuclear, a headline he deciphered off the front page of *L'Express* and that coursed around his mind like an electron with no polarity other than Barbara who, as it happened, was a supporter of nuclear power. She occupied, he recognized, the place of final consequence in his life—the destination for practically everything he cared about or noticed or imagined. And you did not get two of those in life. Only now, or at least for the present time, that situation was undergoing a change. Such things as being in Paris and waiting his chance to see Josephine had no destinations now, or else they all started and stopped in himself. And that was how he wanted them. That was the fuzzy explanation he had not exactly articulated in the last few days. He wanted things, whatever things there were, to be for him and only him.

On the third day, at four in the afternoon, he called Josephine Belliard. He called her at home instead of her office, thinking she wouldn't be at home and that he could leave a brief, possibly inscrutable recorded message, and then not call her for a few more days, as though he was too busy to be held accountable to specific times. But when her phone rang twice she answered.

'Hi,' Austin said, stunned at the suddenness of Josephine actually being on the line and only a short distance from where he was standing, and sounding unquestionably like herself. It made him feel vaguely faint. 'It's Martin Austin,' he managed to say feebly.

He heard a child scream in the background before Josephine could say more than hello. 'Nooooooo!' the child, certainly Leo, screamed again.

'Where are you?' she said in a hectic voice. He heard something fall loudly in the room where she was. 'Are you in Chicago now?'

'No, I'm in Paris,' Austin said, grappling his composure and speaking very softly.

'What are you doing *here*?' Josephine said. She was surprised. 'Are you on business again now?'

Somehow this was an unsettling question. 'No,' he said, still very faintly. 'I'm not on business. I'm just here. I have an apartment.'

'*Tu as un appartement!*' Josephine said in even greater surprise. 'What for?' she said. 'Why? Is your wife with you?'

'No,' Austin said. 'I'm here alone. I'm planning on staying for a while.'

'*Oooo-la-laaa,*' Josephine said. 'Do you have a big fight at home? Is that the matter?'

'No,' Austin lied. 'We didn't have a big fight at home. I decided to take some time away. That's not so unusual is it?'

Leo screamed again savagely. '*Ma-man!*' Josephine spoke to him patiently in French. 'Please be quiet, sweetheart' she said, 'I'm coming to listen to you in one minute.' One minute didn't seem like very much time, but Austin didn't want to stay on the phone long. Josephine seemed much more French than he remembered. In his mind she had been almost an American, only with a French accent. 'OK. So,' she said, a little out of breath. 'You are here now. In Paris.'

'I want to see you,' Austin said. It was the moment he'd been waiting for—more so even than the moment when he would finally see her—the moment when he would declare himself to be present. Unencumbered. Available. Willing. That mattered a great deal. He actually slipped his wedding ring off his finger then and laid it on the table beside the phone.

'Yes?' Josephine said. 'What . . . ' she paused then resumed. 'What do you like to do with me? When do you like? What?' She was impatient.

'Anything. Any time,' Austin said. In that instant he felt the best he'd felt in days. 'Tonight,' he said. 'Or today. In twenty minutes.'

'In twenty minutes! Come on. No!' she said and laughed, but in an interested way, a pleased way—he could tell. 'No, no, no,' she said. 'I have to go to my lawyer in one hour. I have to find my neighbor now to stay with Leo. It is impossible now. I'm divorcing. You know this already. It's very upsetting. Anyway.'

'I'll stay with Leo,' Austin said rashly.

'*You'll* stay with him!' Josephine said and laughed again. 'You don't have children, do you? You said this.'

'I'm not going to adopt him,' Austin said. 'But I'll stay with him for an hour. Then you can have your neighbor come, and I'll take you to dinner. How's that?' He felt confident. This would all turn out perfectly.

'He doesn't like you,' Josephine said. 'He likes only his father best. He doesn't even like me.'

'I'll teach him English,' Austin said. 'I'll teach him to say "Chicago Cubs".' He could feel his enthusiasm leaching off immediately. 'We'll be great friends.'

'What is Chicago Cubs?' Josephine said.

'It's a baseball team.' And he felt, just for a sudden instant, bleak. Not because he wished he was home, or wished Barbara was here, or wished really that anything was different. Everything was how he'd hoped it would be. He simply wished he hadn't mentioned the Cubs. It was over-confident, he thought. It was the wrong thing to say. A mistake.

'So. Well,' Josephine said, sounding business-like. 'You come here, then? I go to my lawyers to sign my papers. Then maybe we have a dinner together, yes?'

'Absolutely,' Austin said, all bleakness vanished. 'I'll come right away. I'll start in five minutes.' On the dark suede wall, under a little metal track-light positioned to illuminate it, was a big oil painting of two men naked and locked in a strenuous kiss and embrace. Neither man's face was visible, and their bodies were weight-lifters' muscular bodies with genitals hidden by their embroiled pose. They were seated on a rock which was very crudely painted in. It was like Laocoön, Austin thought, only corrupted. He'd wondered if one of the men had been the one who owned the apartment, or possibly the owner was the painter or the painter's lover. He wondered if either one of them was alive this afternoon. He hated the painting and had decided to haul it down before he brought Josephine here. And that was what he meant to do—bring her here, tonight if possible, and keep her with him until morning when they could walk up and sit in the cool sun at the Deux Magots and drink coffee. Like Sartre.

'Martin?' Josephine said. He was just about to put the phone down and go move the smarmy Laocoön painting. He almost forgot he was talking to her.

'What? I'm here, sweetheart,' Austin said. Though it might be fun to leave it up. It could be an ice-breaker, to give them something to gas about, like the mirrors on the ceiling, before things got more serious.

'Martin, what are you doing here?' Josephine said oddly. 'Are you OK?'

'I'm here to see you, darling,' Austin said. 'Why do you think? I said I'd see you soon and I meant it. I guess I'm just a man of my word.'

'You are a very silly man, though,' Josephine said and laughed, not quite so pleased as before. 'But,' she said. 'What I can do?'

'You can't do anything,' Austin said. 'Just see me tonight. After that you never have to see me again.'

'Yeah. OK,' Josephine said. 'That's a good deal. Now. You come to here. *Ciao.*'

'*Ciao,*' Austin said oddly, not really being entirely sure what *ciao* meant.

7

Josephine's apartment block was an unexceptional one on a street of similar older buildings with white modernistic fronts overlooking the Jardins du Luxembourg. In the tiny, shadowy lobby, there was an elegant old beaux-arts grille-work elevator that worked. But since Josephine lived only on the third level,

Austin walked up, taking the steps two at a time, the little green paisley egg lumping against his leg with each exaggerated stride.

When he knocked, Josephine immediately threw open the door and flung her arms around his neck. She hugged him then held her hands on his cheeks and kissed him hard on the mouth. Little Leo, who'd just been running from one room to another waving a wooden drumstick, stopped stock-still in the middle of the floor and stared, shocked by his mother kissing a man he didn't remember seeing before.

'Now I must hurry,' Josephine said, releasing his face and hurrying back to the open window which overlooked the side-street to the park. She was putting on her eye-shadow using a tiny compact mirror and the light from outside.

Josephine was dressed in a simple white blouse and a pair of odd, loose-fitting trousers that had pictures of circus animals all over them helter-skelter and in loud colors. They were odd, unbecoming pants, Austin thought, and they fit so that her small stomach made a noticeable round bulge below the waist band. Josephine looked slightly fat and a little sloppy. She turned and smiled at him as she fixed her face. 'How do you feel?' she said.

'I feel great,' Austin said. He smiled down at little Leo, who had not stopped staring at him, holding up his drumstick like a little cigar-store Indian. The child had on short trousers and a white T-shirt that had the words BIG-TIME AMERICAN LUXURY printed across the front above a huge red Cadillac convertible which seemed to be driving out from his chest.

Leo uttered something very fast and in French, then looked at his mother and back at Austin, who hadn't gotten far into the room since being hugged and kissed.

'*Non, non, Leo,*' Josephine said and laughed with an odd delight. She said something back in French. 'He asks if you are my new husband. He thinks I need a husband now. He is very mixed up.' She went on darkening her eyes. She looked pretty in the window light, and Austin wanted to go over right then and give her a much more significant kiss. But the child kept staring at him, holding his drumsticks up and making Austin feel awkward and reluctant, which wasn't how he thought he'd feel. He thought he'd feel free and completely at ease and on top of the world about everything.

He reached in his pocket, palmed the wooden egg and knelt in front of the little boy showing two closed fists.

'*J'ai un cadeau pour toi,*' he said. He'd practiced these words and wondered how close he'd come. 'I have a nice present for you,' he said in English to satisfy himself. '*Choissez le main.*' Austin tried to smile. He jiggled the correct hand, his right one, trying to capture the child's attention. '*Choissez le main,* Leo,' he said again and smiled a little grimly. Austin looked at Josephine for encouragement, but she was still appraising herself in her little mirror. She said something very briskly, though, to Leo, who beetled his dark little brow at the two presented fists. Slowly he pointed his drumstick at Austin's right fist, the one he'd been jiggling. Very slowly—as though he were opening a chest filled with gold—Austin opened his fingers to reveal the bright little green egg with gold paisleys and red snowflakes. Some flecks of the green paint had come off on his palm, which surprised him. '*Voilà,*' Austin said dramatically. '*C'est une jolie oeuf!*'

Little Leo stared intently at the clammy egg in Austin's soft palm. He looked up at Austin with a look of practiced inquisitiveness, his little thin lips growing pursed as though something worried him. Very timidly he extended his wood drumstick and touched the egg, then nudged it with the shaped tip, the end intended to strike a drum. Austin noticed that Leo had two or three big gravelly warts on his tiny fingers, and a cold wretchedness from his own childhood opened in him, making Leo for an instant seem frail and sympathetic. But with startling swiftness the child raised the drumstick and struck the egg—still in Austin's proffered palm—a fierce blow, hoping apparently to smash it and splatter its contents and give Austin's fingers a painful slashing for good measure.

But the egg, though the blow chipped its glossy green enamel and Austin felt the impact like a shock, did not break. And little Leo's pallid face assumed a look of controlled fury. He instantly took two more vengeful back-and-forth swipes at it, the second of which struck Austin's thumb a stinging then numbing blow, then he turned and fled out of the room and down the hall and through a door which he slammed behind him.

Austin looked up at Josephine, who was just finishing at the window.

'I tell you before,' she said and shook her head.

'That didn't work out too well,' he said and squeezed his thumb so as not to have to mention it.

'It's not important,' she said, going straight to the couch and putting her compact into her purse. 'He is angry all the time. Sometimes he hits *me*. Don't feel bad. You're sweet to bring something for him.'

What Austin felt though was that he wanted to kiss Josephine—now that they were alone—kiss her in a way that said he was here, and it wasn't just a coincidence, that he'd had her on his mind this whole time, and wanted her to have him on her mind, and that this whole thing that had started last week in discretion and good-willed restraint was rising to a new level, a level to be taken more seriously. She could love him now. He could conceivably even love her. Much was possible that only days ago was not even dreamed of.

He moved towards where she was, re-pocketing the egg, his injured thumb throbbing. She was leaned over the couch in her idiotic animal pants, and he rather roughly grasped her hips—covering the faces of a yellow giraffe and a gray rhino with his hands—and pulled, tried to turn her towards him so he could give her the kiss he wanted to give her, the authoritative one that signalled his important arrival on to the scene. But she jumped, as though he'd startled her, and she shouted, 'Stop, what is it!' as he was negotiating her face around in front of his. She had a lipstick tube in her hand, and she seemed irritated to be so close to him, though she smelled sweet, surprisingly sweet. Like a flower, he thought.

'There's something important between us, I think,' Austin said directly into Josephine's irritated face. 'Important enough to bring me back across an ocean and to leave my wife and to face the chance that I'll be alone here.'

'What?' she said. She contorted her mouth and without exactly pushing, exerted a force to gain a few inches from him. He still had her by her hips, cluttered with animal faces. A dark crust of eye shadow clung where she had doctored her eyelids.

'You shouldn't feel under any pressure,' he said and looked at her gravely. 'I just want to see you. That's all. Maybe have some time alone with you. Who knows where it'll go?'

'You are very fatigued, I think.' She struggled to get backwards. 'Maybe you can have a sleep while I am going.'

'I'm not tired,' Austin said. 'I feel great. I've got a clean slate. Nothing's bothering me.'

'That's good,' she said and smiled and pushed firmly away from him just as Austin was moving in to give her the important kiss. Josephine quickly kissed him first, though, the same, hard unpassionate kiss she'd greeted him with five minutes before and that had left him dissatisfied.

'I want to kiss you the right way, not that way,' Austin said. He pulled her firmly to him again, taking hold of her soft waist and pushing his mouth towards hers again. He kissed her as tenderly as he could with her back stiff and resistant, and her mouth not shaped to receive a kiss but ready to speak when the kiss ended. Austin held the kiss for a long moment, his eyes closed, his breath going out his nose, trying to feel his own wish for tenderness igniting an answering tenderness in her. But if there was any tenderness it was of an unintended type—more like forbearance. And when he had pressed her lips for as many as six or eight seconds, until he had breathed her breath and she had relaxed her resistance, he stood back and looked at her—a woman he felt he might love—and took her chin between his thumb and index finger and said, 'That's really all I wanted. That wasn't all that bad, was it?'

She shook her head in a perfunctory way and very softly almost compliantly said, 'No.' Her eyes were cast down, though not in a way he felt confident of, more as if she were waiting on something. He felt he should let her go now; that was the thing to do. He'd forced her to kiss him. She'd relented. Now she could be free to do anything she wanted.

Josephine hurriedly turned back towards her purse on the couch, and Austin walked to the window and surveyed the vast trees of the Jardins du Luxembourg. The air was cool and soft and the light seemed creamy and rich in the late afternoon. He heard music, guitar music from somewhere, and the faint sound of a voice singing. He saw a jogger running through the park gate and out into the street below, and he wondered what anyone would think who saw him standing in this window—someone glancing up a moment out of the magnificent garden and seeing an American man in a French woman's apartment. Would it be clear he was an American? Or would he possibly seem French? Would he seem rich? Would his look of satisfaction be visible? He thought almost certainly it would be visible.

'I have to go to the lawyer now,' Josephine said behind him.

'Fine. Go,' Austin said. 'Hurry back. I'll look after little Gene Krupa. Then we'll have a nice evening.'

Josephine had a thick sheaf of documents she was forcing into a plastic briefcase. 'Maybe,' she said in a distracted voice.

Austin was picturing himself talking to Hank Bullard about the air-conditioning business. They were in a café on a sunny side-street. Hank's news was good, full of promise about a partnership.

Josephine hurried into the hall, her flat shoes scraping the boards. She opened the door to Leo's room and said something quick and very soft to him, something that did not have Austin's name in it. Then she closed the door and entered the W.C. and used the toilet without bothering to shut herself in. Austin couldn't see down the hall from where he stood in the living-room, but he could hear her pissing, the small trickle of water hitting more water. It was a sound he'd heard a thousand times—Barbara always closed the door, and he did, too—but it was a sound he didn't particularly like and usually tried to avoid hearing. Not that he was squeamish, but the sound seemed so inert to him, so factual, that hearing it threatened to take away a layer of his good feeling. He was sorry to have to hear it just now, sorry Josephine didn't bother to close the door.

In an instant, however, she was out and down the hallway. She picked up her briefcase while water sighed in the pipes. She gave Austin a peculiar, fugitive look across the room as if she was surprised he was there and wasn't sure why he was. It was, he felt, the look you gave an unimportant employee who had said something inexplicable.

'So. I am going now,' she said.

'I'll be here,' Austin said, looking at her and feeling suddenly helpless. 'Hurry back, OK?'

'Yeah, sure. OK,' she said. 'I hurry. I see you.'

'Great,' Austin said. She went out the door and hurried down the echoing steps towards the street.

For a while Austin walked around the apartment looking at things—things Josephine Belliard liked or cherished or had kept when her husband cleared out. There was an entire wall of books across one side of the little sleeping alcove she'd constructed for her privacy using fake Chinese rice paper dividers. The books were the sleek French soft-covers, mostly on sociological subjects, though other books seemed to be in German. Her modest bed was covered with a clean, billowy white counterpane and big fluffy white pillows—no headboard—just the frame, but very neat, Austin thought. A copy of her soon-to-be-ex-husband's scummy novel lay on the bed table with several pages roughly bent down. Folding a page up, he read a sentence in which a character named Solange was performing an uninspired act of fellatio on someone named Albert. He recognized the charged words: *Fellation. Lugubre.* Albert was talking about having his car repaired the whole time it was happening to him. *Un Amour Secret* was the book's uninspired title and Bernard's scowling, condescending visage was nowhere apparent.

He wondered what Bernard knew that he didn't know. Plenty, he supposed, if the book was even half true. But the unknown was interesting. You had to face it one way or another. Though it might as well be your own unknown rather than somebody else's. The idea of fellatio with Josephine, though—nothing up to this moment he'd even thought about—inflamed him, and he began to think there was something distinctly sexual about roaming around examining private belongings and her bedroom, a room and a bed he could easily imagine occupying in the near future. Before he moved away he laid the green paisley egg on her bed table beside the copy of her husband's smutty book. It would create a contrast, he thought, possibly a reminder that she had choices in the world.

He looked out the bedroom window on to the park. It was the same view as the living-room—the easeful formal garden with great leafy horse-chestnut trees and tonsured green lawns with topiaries and yew shrubs and pale gravel paths criss-crossing, and the old École Superieure des Mines looming along the far side and the Luxembourg Palace to the left. Some hippies were sitting in a tight little circle on one of the grass swards with their legs crossed, sharing a joint around. No one else was in view, though the light was cool and smooth and inviting and birds soared through it. A clock chimed somewhere nearby. The guitar music had ceased.

It would be pleasant to walk there, Austin thought—with Josephine—to breathe the sweet air of chestnut trees and to stare off. Life was very different here. This apartment was very different from his house in Oak Grove. *He* felt different here. Life, in fact, seemed to have improved remarkably in a short period of time. All it took, he thought, was the courage to take control of things and to live with the consequences.

He assumed little Leo to be asleep down the hall and that he could simply leave well enough alone there. But when he'd sat leafing through the French *Vogue* for perhaps twenty minutes he heard the hall door open and seconds later the child appeared at the corner, looking confused and drugged and still in his BIG TIME AMERICAN LUXURY shirt with the big red Cadillac barging off the front. He still had his little shoes on.

Leo rubbed his eyes and looked pitiful. Josephine no doubt had given him something to knock him out—the sort of thing that wouldn't happen in the States. But in France, he thought, adults treated children differently. More intelligently.

'*Bon soir,*' Austin said in a slightly ironic voice and smiled, setting the *Vogue* down.

Leo eyed him sullenly, suspicious about hearing French spoken by this person who wasn't the least bit French. He scanned the room quickly for his mother's presence. Austin considered a plan of reintroducing the slightly discredited paisley egg but decided against it. He glanced at the clock on the book case: forty-five minutes would somehow need to be consumed before Josephine returned. But how? How would the time be passed in a way to make Leo happy and possibly impress his mother? The Cubs idea wouldn't work—Leo was too young. He didn't know any games or tricks. He knew nothing about children, and he was, in fact, now sorry the boy was awake. Sorry he was here at all.

But he thought of the park—the Jardins du Luxembourg—available just outside the window. A nice walk in the park could set them on the right course, he thought. He wasn't able to talk to the child, but he could watch him while he enjoyed himself.

'*Voulez-vous aller au parc?*' Austin said and smiled a big, sincere smile. '*Maintenant? Peut-être? Le parc? Oui?*' He pointed at the open window and the cool, still evening air where swallows soared and flittered.

Leo frowned at him and then the window, still dazed. He fastened a firm grip on the front of his shorts—a signal Austin recognized—and did not answer.

'Whatta ya say? Let's go to the park,' Austin said enthusiastically, loudly. He almost jumped up. Leo could understand it well enough. *Parc*. Park.

'*Parc?*' little Leo said and more cravenly squeezed his little weenie. '*Maman?*' he said and looked almost demented.

'*Maman est dans le parc,*' Austin said, thinking that from inside the park they would certainly see Josephine on her way back from the lawyer's, and that it wouldn't turn out to be a complete lie—or if it did, Josephine would eventually come back and take control of things before there was a problem. It was possible, he thought, that he'd never even see this kid after that, that Josephine might come back and never want to see *him* again. Though a darker thought entered his mind: of Josephine *never* coming back, deciding simply to disappear, somewhere on the way from the lawyers. It happened. Babies were abandoned in Chicago all the time and no one knew what happened to their parents or where they went. He knew no one she knew. He knew no one to contact. It was a nightmarish thought.

Inside of five minutes he had Leo into the bathroom and out again. Happily Leo attended to his own privacy while Austin stood outside the door and stared at the picture of Bernard's stuffed, bulbous face on the wall of the boy's room. He was surprised Josephine would even let it stay up. He'd had to suppress an urge to tell her to stick it to Bernard, to get him in the shorts if she could, though later he'd felt a queasiness for conspiring against a man he didn't even know.

As they were leaving the apartment, Austin realized he had no key, neither to the downstairs nor to the apartment itself, and that once the door closed he and Leo were on their own: a man, an American speaking little French, alone with a five-year-old French child he didn't know, in a country, in a city, in a park where he was an absolute stranger. No one would think this was a good idea. Josephine hadn't asked him to take Leo to the park—it was his own doing, and it was a risk. But then everything felt like a risk at the moment and all he needed to do was be careful.

They walked out on to rue Ferou and around the corner, then down a few paces and across a wide street to a corner gate into the garden. Leo said nothing, but insisted on holding Austin's hand and leading the way as if he—Leo—were taking Austin to the park because he didn't know what else to do with him.

Once through the gold-topped gate, though, and on to the pale gravel paths that ran in mazes through the shrubberies and trees and planted beds where daffodils were already blooming, Leo went running straight in the direction of a wide concrete pond where ducks and swans were swimming and a group of older boys was sailing miniature sailboats. Austin looked back to see which building was Josephine's, from which window he'd stood looking down at this very park. But he couldn't distinguish the window, wasn't even sure if from Josephine's window he could see this part of the park. For one thing, there hadn't been a pond, and here there were plenty of people walking in the cool, sustained evening light—lovers and married people both, by the looks of them, taking a nice stroll before going home for dinner. It was probably part of the park's plan, he thought, that new parts always seemed familiar, and vice versa.

Austin strolled down to the concrete border of the pond and sat on a bench a few yards away from Leo who stood raptly watching the older boys tend their boats with long thin sticks.

There was no wind and only the boys' soft studious voices to listen to in the air where swallows were still darting. The little boats floated stilly in the shallows with peanut shells and popcorn tufts, and a number of ducks and swans glided just out of reach, eyeing the boats, waiting for the boys to leave.

Austin could hear tennis balls being hit nearby, but couldn't see where. A clay court, he felt certain. He wished he could sit and watch people playing tennis instead of boys tending boats. Female voices were laughing and speaking in French and laughing again, then a tennis ball was struck once more. A dense wall of what looked like rhododendrons stood beyond a sward of grass, and behind that, he thought, must be the courts.

Across the pond seated on the opposite concrete wall, a man in a tan suit was having his photograph taken by another man. An expensive camera was being employed, and the second man kept moving around, finding new positions from which to see through his viewfinder. 'Su-perb,' Austin heard the photographer say. '*Trés, trés, trés bon.* Don't move now. Don't move.' A celebrity, Austin thought; an actor or a famous writer— somebody on top of the world. The man seemed unaffected, not even to acknowledge that his picture was being taken.

Leo unexpectedly turned and looked at Austin, as if he—Leo —was about to say something, something extremely significant and exciting about the little boats. His face was vivid with importance. Though when he saw Austin seated legs-crossed on the bench, the calculation of who Austin was clouded his pale little features and he looked suddenly devilled and chastened and secretive, and he turned quickly back, inching closer to the water's edge as if he intended to wade in.

He was just a kid, Austin thought calmly, a kid with divorced parents; not a little ogre or a tyrant. He could be won over with time and patience. He thought of his own father, a tall, patient, good-hearted man who worked in a sporting goods store in Peoria. He and Austin's mother had celebrated their fiftieth anniversary two years before, a big to-do under a tent in the city park, with Austin's brother Ted in from Phoenix, and all the older cousins and friends from far-away states and decades past. A week later his father had had a stroke watching the news on

TV and died in his chair.

He'd always had patience with his sons, Austin realized soberly. There'd been no divorces or sudden midnight departures in *his* life, but his father had always tried to understand the goings-on of the later generation. So, what would he think of all this, Austin wondered? France. A strange woman with a son. An empty house back home. Abandonment. Lies. Chaos. He'd have made an attempt to understand everything, tried to find the good in it. Though ultimately his judgement would've been harsh and he'd have sided with Barbara whose success in real estate he'd admired. He thought to imagine his father's very words, his judgement, delivered from his big lounger in front of the TV—the very spot where he'd breathed his last frantic breaths. Only he couldn't. He couldn't for some reason recreate his father's voice, its cadences, the exact tenor of it. It was peculiar not to remember his father's voice, a voice he'd heard all his life. Possibly it had not had that much effect.

He was staring at the man in the tan suit across the lagoon, the man having his photograph taken. The man was up on the concrete ledge now with the shallow pond behind him, his legs wide apart, his hands on his hips, his tan jacket in the crook of his elbow. He looked ridiculous, unconvincing about whatever he was supposed to seem convincing. Austin wondered if he would be visible in the background, a blurry, distant figure staring from across the stale lagoon. Maybe he would see it someplace, in *Le Monde* or *Figaro*, the newspapers he couldn't read. It would be a souvenir he could laugh about at a later date, when he was where? With who?

Not, in all probability, Josephine Belliard. Something about her had bothered him this afternoon. Not her reluctance to kiss him. This was an attitude he could overcome given time. He was good at overcoming reluctances in others. He was a persuasive man, with the heart of a salesman, and he knew it. From time to time it even bothered him, since given the right circumstances he felt he could persuade anybody of anything—no matter what. He had no clear idea what this quality was, but Barbara had occasionally remarked on it, often with an unflattering implication that he did not believe in very much, or at least not in enough. And it always made him uneasy that this might be true or at least thought to be true.

He had believed that he and Josephine could have a different kind of relationship. Sexual, but not sexual at its heart. Rather, a new thing. Founded on realities—the facts of his character and the facts of hers. Whereas with Barbara he was just playing out the end of an old thing. Less real, somehow. Less mature. He could never really love Josephine; that would have to give way, since in his deepest heart he loved only Barbara, for whatever that was worth. Yet he'd for a moment felt compelled by Josephine, found her appealing, considered even the possibility of living with her for months or years. Anything was possible.

Though seeing her in her apartment today, looking just as he knew she would, being exactly the woman he expected her to be, had made him feel bleak in a way he supposed he would never completely quit feeling if he set sail with her for the rest of life. And he was savvy enough to know that if he felt bleak now, at the very beginning, he would feel only bleaker later, and that life would either slowly or quickly become a version of hell for which he would bear all responsibility.

These issues had competed unspecified in his thinking over the last days. But now that he was here, they would work themselves out one way or another. All he had to do was do no harm, cause no unneeded chaos to anyone, and things would become clear.

His thumb still vaguely ached. The women were laughing again on the tennis-courts beyond the flowering rhododendrons. Austin could actually see a pair of woman's calves and tennis shoes, jumping from side to side as though striking a ball, first forehand then back, the little white feet dancing over the red surface. '*Arrête!* Stop!' a woman yelled, and sighed a loud sigh.

French women, Austin thought, all talked like children; in high-pitched, rapid-paced, unpleasingly-insistent voices, which most of the time said, '*Non, non, non, non, non,*' to something someone wanted, some likely-as-not innocent wish. He could hear Josephine saying it, standing in the living-room of her little apartment the only other time he had visited there—a week ago—speaking on the phone to someone, spooling the white phone cord around her finger saying into the receiver, '*Non, non, non, non, non, non. C'est incroyable. C'est in-croy-a-ble!*' It was terrifically annoying, though it amused him at this moment to think of it—at a distance.

Barbara had absolutely no use for French women and made no bones about it. 'Typical Froggie,' she'd remark after evenings with his French clients and their wives, and then act disgusted. It was probably that which bothered him about Josephine: that she seemed such a typical bourgeois little French woman, the kind Barbara would've disliked in a minute—intractable, preoccupied, entirely stuck in her French life, no sense of the wider world, possibly even ungenerous if you knew her very long—as her husband found out. Josephine's problem, Austin thought, looking around for little Leo, was that she took everything inside her life too seriously. Her motherhood. Her husband's ludicrous book. Her boy-friend. Her bad luck. She looked at everything under a microscope, as if she were always waiting to see a mistake she could magnify big enough that she'd have no choice but to go on taking life too seriously. As if that's all adulthood was—seriousness, discipline. No fun. Life, Austin thought, had to be more light-hearted. That's why he'd come here, why he'd cut himself loose—to enjoy life a little more. He admired himself for it. And because of that he didn't think he could be the savior in Josephine's life. That would be a lifelong struggle, and a lifelong struggle wasn't what he wanted most in the world.

When he looked around again for Leo, the little boy was not where he'd been, standing dreamily to the side of the older boys, watching their miniature cutters and galleons glide over the still pond surface. The older boys were there, their long tending sticks in their hands, whispering among themselves and smiling. But not Leo. It had become cooler. Light had faded from the crenellated roofs of the École Superieure, and soon it would be dark. The man having his picture taken was walking away with the photographer. Austin had been engrossed in thought and had lost sight of little Leo, who was somewhere, he was certain, nearby.

He looked at his watch. It was six twenty-five, and Josephine could now be home. He looked up at the row of apartment blocks, hoping to see her window, thinking he might see her there watching him, waving at him happily, possibly with Leo at her side. But he couldn't tell which building was which. One window he could see was open and dark inside. But he couldn't be sure. In any case Josephine wasn't framed in it.

Austin looked all around hoping to see the white flash of Leo's T-shirt, the careening red Cadillac. But he saw only a few couples walking along the chalky paths; two of the older boys carrying their sailboats home to their parents' apartments. He still heard tennis balls being hit—pock, pock, pock. And he felt cold and calm, which he knew to be the feeling of fear beginning, a feeling which could rapidly change to other feelings, and last a long, long time.

Leo was gone, and he wasn't sure where. He called out, 'Leo,' in the American way, then 'Lay-oo,' in the way his mother said. *'Ou êtes-vous?'* Passers-by looked at him sternly, hearing two languages at once. The remaining sailboat-boys glanced around at him and smiled. 'Lay-oo!' he called out again, and he knew his voice did not sound ordinary, that it might sound frightened. Everyone around him, everyone who could hear him was French, and he couldn't precisely explain to any of them all that was the matter here; that this was not his son; that the boy's mother was not here now but was probably close by; that he had let his attention stray a moment.

'Lay-oo,' he called out again. *'Ou êtes-vous?'* He saw nothing of the boy, not a fleck of shirt or a patch of his dark hair disappearing behind a bush. He felt cold all over again, a sudden new wave, and he shuddered because he knew he was alone. Leo, some tiny assurance opened in him to say—Leo, wherever he was, would be fine, was probably fine right now. He would be found and be happy. He would see his mother and immediately forget all about Martin Austin. Nothing bad would befall him. But he, Martin Austin, was alone. He could not find this child, and for him only bad would come of it.

Across an expanse of grassy lawn he saw a park guardian in a dark blue uniform emerge from the trees beyond which were the tennis-courts, and Austin began running towards him. It surprised him that he was running, and half-way there he quit and only half-ran towards the man, who had stopped to permit himself to be approached.

'Do you speak English?' Austin said before he'd arrived. He knew his face had taken on some exaggerated appearance because the guardian looked at him strangely, turned his head slightly, as though he preferred to see him at a different angle, or as if he were hearing an odd tune and wanted to hear it better. At the corners of his mouth he seemed to smile.

'I'm sorry,' Austin said, and took a breath. 'You speak English, don't you?'

'A little bit, why not,' the guardian said, and then he did smile. He was middle-aged and pleasant-looking with a soft sun-tanned face and a small Hitler moustache. He wore a French policeman's uniform with shoulder braid and a white lanyard connected to his pistol and a blue and gold képi. He was a man who liked parks.

'I've lost a little boy here someplace,' Austin said very calmly, even though he remained out of breath. He put the palm of his right hand to his cheek as if his cheek were wet, and felt his skin cold. He suddenly turned and looked again at the concrete border to the pond, at the grass crossed by gravel paths, and then at a dense revetment of yew bushes farther on. He expected to see Leo precisely in the middle of this miniature landscape. Once he'd been frightened and time had gone by, and he'd sought help and strangers had regarded him with suspicion and wonder— once all these had taken place—Leo would appear and all would be returned to calm.

But there was no one. The open sward was empty, and it was nearly dark. He could see weak interior lights from the apartment blocks beyond the park fence, see yellow automobile lights on rue Vaugirard. He remembered once hunting with his father in Illinois. He was a boy, and their dog had run away. And they knew the advent of dark meant he would never see the dog again. They were far from home. The dog wouldn't find its way back. And that is what had happened.

The park guardian stood in front of Austin, smiling, staring at his face very oddly, searchingly, as if he meant to adduce something—if Austin was crazy or on drugs or possibly if he were playing a joke. The man, Austin realized, hadn't understood anything, and was simply waiting for something he would understand to occur.

But he had ruined everything now. Leo was gone. Kidnapped. Assaulted. Merely lost in a hopelessly big city, and all his own newly-won freedom, his clean slate, were in one moment squandered. He would go to jail, and he *should* go to jail. He was an awful man. A careless man. He brought mayhem and suffering to the lives of innocent, unsuspecting people who trusted him. No punishment could be too severe.

Austin looked again at the yew bushes, a long, green clump, several yards thick, the interior lost in tangled shadows. That was where Leo was, he thought with complete certainty. And he felt relief, barely controllable relief.

'I'm sorry to bother you,' he said to the guardian. '*Je regrette.* I made a mistake.' And he turned and ran back towards the clump of yew bushes, across the open grass, the gravel promenade paths and careful beds in bright yellow bloom, the excellent park. He plunged in under the low scrubby branches, where the ground was bare and raked and damp and attended to. With his head ducked he moved forward swiftly. He called Leo's name but did not see him, though he saw a movement, an indistinct fluttering of blue and gray, heard what might've been footfalls on the soft ground, and then he did hear running, like a large creature hurrying in front of him among the tangled branches. He heard laughter from beyond the edge of the yew bushes, where another open grassy terrace opened—the sound of a man laughing and talking in French, out of breath and running all at once. Laughing, then more talking, and laughing again.

Austin moved towards where he'd seen the flutter of blue and gray—someone's clothing glimpsed in flight, he thought. There was a strong old smell of piss and human waste among the thick roots and shrubby trunks of the yew bushes. Paper and trash were strewn around in the foulness. From outside it had seemed cool and inviting, a place to have a nap or to make love.

Leo was there. Exactly where Austin had seen the glimpse of clothing flicker out of the undergrowth. He was naked, sitting on the damp dirt, his clothes strewn around him, turned inside out where they had been jerked off and thrown aside. He looked up at Austin, his eyes small and perceptive and dark, his small feet straight out before him, his legs smudged and scratched, his chest and arms scratched. Dirt was on his cheeks. His hands were between his legs, not covering or protecting him but just limply, as if they had no purpose. He was very white and very quiet. His hair was still combed neatly. Though when he saw Austin, and that it was Austin and not someone else coming, bent at the waist, furious, breathing stertorously, stumbling, crashing arms-out through the yew branches and trunks and roots of that small place, he gave out a shrill, hopeless cry, as though he could see what was next, and who it would be, and it terrified him. And his cry was all he could do to let the world know that he feared his fate.

8

In the days that followed there was to be a great deal of controversy. The police conducted a thorough and publicized search for the person or persons who had assaulted little Leo. There were no signs to conclude he had been molested, only that he'd been lured into the bushes by someone and roughed up there and frightened badly. A small story appeared in the back pages of *Le Monde*, and Austin noticed from the beginning that all the police used the word '*moleste*' when referring to the event as though it were accurate.

The group of hippies he had seen from Josephine's window was generally thought to contain the offender. It was said that they lived in the park and slept in the clumps and groves and yews and ornamental boxwoods and that some were Americans who had been in France for twenty years. But none of them, when the police brought them in to be identified, seemed to be the man who had scared Leo.

For a few hours following the incident there was suspicion among the police that Austin himself had molested Leo, and had found the guardian only as a diversion after he'd finished with the little boy—trusting that the child would never accuse him.

Austin had intelligently and patiently explained that he had not molested Leo and would never do such a thing, but understood plainly that he had to be considered until he could be exonerated —which was not before midnight, when Josephine entered the police station and stated that Leo had told her Austin was not the man who had scared him and taken his clothes off—that it had been someone else, a man who spoke French, a man in blue and possibly gray clothing with long hair and a beard.

When she had told this story and Austin had been allowed to leave the stale, windowless police room where he'd been asked to remain until matters could be determined with certainty, he'd walked beside Josephine out into the narrow street, lit yellow through the tall wire mesh windows of the *gendarmerie*. The street was guarded by a number of young policemen in flak jackets and carrying short machine pistols on shoulder slings, and they calmly watched Austin and Josephine as they stopped at the curb to say good-bye.

'I'm completely to blame for this,' Austin said. 'I can't tell you how sorry I am. There aren't any words good enough, I guess.'

'You are to blame,' Josephine said and looked at him in the face, intently. After a moment she said, 'It is not a game. You know? Maybe to you it is a game.'

'No, it's really not,' Austin said abjectly, standing in the cool night air in sight of all the young policemen. 'I guess I had a lot of plans.'

'Plans for what?' Josephine said. She had on the black crêpe skirt she'd had on the day he'd met her, a week ago. She looked appealing again. 'Not for me! You don't have plans for me. I don't want you. I don't want any man any more.' She shook her head and crossed her arms tightly and looked away, her dark eyes shining in the night. She was very very angry. Possibly, he thought, she was angry at herself. 'You are a fool,' she said, and she spat accidentally when she said it. 'I hate you. You don't know anything. You don't know who you are.' She looked at him bitterly. 'Who are you?' she said. 'Who do you think you are? You're nothing.'

'I understand,' Austin said. 'I'm sorry. I'm sorry about all of this. I'll make sure you don't have to see me again.'

Josephine smiled at him, a cruel, competent smile. 'I don't care,' she said and raised her shoulder in the way Austin didn't like, the way French women did when they wanted to certify as true something that might not be. 'I don't care what happens to you. You are dead. I don't see you.'

She turned and began walking away down the sidewalk along the side of the *gendarmerie* and in front of the young policemen who looked at her indifferently. They looked back at Austin, standing in the light by himself where he felt he should stay until she had gone out of sight. One of the policemen said something to his colleague beside him, and that man whistled a single, long note into the night. Then they turned and faced the other way.

A ustin had a fear in the days to come, almost a defeating fear that deprived him of sleep in his small, risqué apartment above the rue Bonaparte, a fear that Barbara would die soon, a fear that was followed the next day by a feeling that she *had* died, and then that something important in his life he could recognize no other way but by her dying had been lost, exterminated, and by his own doing but also by fate. What *was* that something, he wondered, awake in the middle of the night? It wasn't Barbara herself. She was alive and on the earth to be reunited with if he wanted to try and if she did. But he *had* lost something, and whatever it was, she represented it, and if he could specify it, he felt possibly he could begin to pull things together, see more clearly, could even speak to her again. In a sense, repatriate himself.

Not to know what that something was, though, meant that he was out of control and maybe even something worse about him. And he began to think of his life, in those succeeding days, entirely in terms of what was wrong with him, of his problem, his failure—in particular his failure as a husband; his unhappiness, his ruin which he wanted to undo. He recognized even more plainly now that his entire orientation, everything he'd ever done or presumed or thought had been balanced on Barbara, and that everything he now hoped to do was balanced on the thought that he would go back to Barbara eventually. Everything was in those brackets, impossible to break.

Behind Josephine, of course, was nothing—no fabric or mystery, no secrets, nothing he had curiosity for now. She had seemed to be a compelling woman; not a great object of sexuality, not a source of wit—but a force he had briefly loved with the expectation that she could love him. He remembered kissing her in the car, her soft face and the great swelling moment of wondrous feeling, the great thrill. And her voice saying, 'No, no, no, no, no, no,' softly. That was what Bernard could never get over losing and that had driven him to hate her enough to humiliate her.

For his part he admired her and mostly for the way she'd dealt with him. Proportionately. Intelligently. She had felt a greater sense of responsibility than he had; a greater apprehension of life's importance, of its weight and permanence. To him, it all *did* seem less important, less permanent, and he could never even aspire to her sense of life—a European sense. He *did* feel himself to be a given, a fixed thing. And he knew himself—not at all the way Josephine had said. Josephine was herself a fixed thing, though they were very, very different and could not have been very happy together.

He wondered again in his dreamy moments after the fear of Barbara's dying had risen off and before he went to sleep, wondered what was possible between human beings? What was possible of real value? How could you regulate life, do little harm and still be attached to others? He wondered if as Barbara had said when he had seen her the last time and she had been so angry at him, if he had changed in some way, if he had altered some important linkages that had guaranteed his happiness and become detached, unreachable. Could you become that way? And was it something you controlled yourself, a matter of your character, or a change to which you were only a victim? It was a subject he felt he would have to sleep on many, many nights.

FRONT ROW *Views*

Not in Front of the Audience
Homosexuality On Stage
Nicholas de Jongh, Drama Critic,
The *London Evening Standard*

A pioneering study of the theatre's treatment of homosexuals and homosexuality from the 1920's to the present day. Only in the sixties did theatres confront heterosexual prejudice and in the wake of AIDS, the issue is once again highly charged.

March 1992: 216x138: 232pp:
illus. 6 b+w photographs
Hb: £35.00: Pb: £9.99

Vested Interests
Cross-Dressing and Cultural Anxiety
Marjorie Garber, Harvard University

'There can be no culture without the transvestite' Garber boldly claims, exploring cross-dressing and the West's recurring fascination with it, from Shakespeare to Peter Pan, Elvis and transsexual surgery.

May 1992: 246x189: 500pp: illus. 150 colour and b+w photographs
Hb: £25.00

The Adoring Audience
Fan Culture and Popular Media
Edited by **Lisa A. Lewis,** University of Arizona

With the stories of hysterical teenagers and obsessive fans killing for their heroes, fans and fandom get a bad press. This collection takes a deeper look into the phenomena especially in the way it relates to identity and sexuality.

May 1992: 234x156: 256pp: Hb: £35.00: Pb: £10.99

The Creatures Time Forgot
Photography and Disability Imagery
David Hevey

Traditional imagery of the disabled which typically shows 'tragic but brave' people is attacked by Hevey who shows how disabled subjects have been constructed as 'creatures'.

March 1992: 210x198:
240pp: illus. 30 colour and
30 b+w photographs
Pb: £14.99

Available through booksellers.
For more information please contact:
James Powell, Routledge,
11 New Fetter Lane, London
EC4P 4EE Tel: 071-583 9855.

ROUTLEDGE

PAUL THEROUX
LADY MAX

Yd**Y**ou didn't become a Londoner simply by living there. After seven years I was still an alien. I wanted to write about the city from the inside. I felt it was happening—I was at last becoming a Londoner—the winter I discovered Gaston's.

Only the professionals knew Gaston's. The poet Ian Musprat (*The Dogflud Chronicles*) had shown me the place. It was a small used book dealer in an alley off Chancery Lane. A square of cardboard stuck in the window bore the words NO RICKSHAW PARKING in Chinese characters and in English—an obscure joke. There was no other sign, but there were stacks of books.

Gaston was fussy about the books he bought and sold—they had to be new, unmarked and in demand by libraries. London book reviewers were Gaston's suppliers, and if you lingered by the plain wooden counter where the books were piled you would meet the great names, the savage reviewers, the literary hacks, the strugglers. They entered and left like punters at a pawn shop, trying to put a jaunty face on their shame. All of them were doing something they faintly despised, selling copies of the books they had reviewed, at half-price, cash.

Friday was a popular day, because it was a deadline: copy day for both the Sundays and the weeklies. After lunch I typed my review and made my way from Clapham to Fleet Street, to sell my books. Then I turned in my review at the *New Statesman* nearby. I did round-ups, three or four books, sometimes as many as six: 'The Week's Fiction'. Sometimes it was travel books. The crime reviewer did many more in half the space. The *Statesman* was just on the other side of Lincoln's Inn (barristers looking silly and self-important in wigs and black gowns). After I handed in my review I had money in my pocket, a cheque in the mail and the weekend ahead. Saturday was for shopping, Sunday for outings with Anne and the boys. I never wrote a word those days. On Monday it was back to my novel, and reading the new batch of review copies in the evenings. On Friday I did my review, and then it was time for Gaston's again.

I liked being rid of the books, and I loved the routine. Londoners' routines were as specific as rituals. And the London monotony was helpful to the writing of a long novel.

Photo: Ian Berry/Magnum

'How's your book?' Anne asked on those weekends, when she saw me looking thoughtful.

I always said my book was going fine, and it was, but I would have preferred a bit more: a bit more money; a bit more space in the *Statesman*; a lead review instead of a round-up; one book instead of four; my name on the cover of the magazine. Yet I didn't complain. I was reassured by the routine. Cosy predictable London was at its best, its blackest in the winter, in cold, dead and dreary January, with spring seeming a long way off. Londoners hated January and February, and often muttered as much to strangers on buses.

I was not a Londoner in the way I loved those months, those fogs, those thick white skies. When it rained the city was blackened, and I liked that too. The short days and long nights kept people indoors. I worked in a small pool of lamplight in an upper room, overlooking slate roofs and chimney-pots and the leafless trees in back gardens. Everyone else was inside. In the London winter I never had the feeling I was missing anything.

I often met Ian Musprat in Gaston's. Having done my review a day early, I saw him that dark Thursday in January when I came in with my stack of books. He was negotiating nervously with Gaston—dickering over a book. When they were done he stepped aside, looking fussed. As I sold my four ('God, the price of books,' Gaston said, handing me seven pounds), Musprat covertly slipped a book into his briefcase.

'Gaston made me wait, because Angus Wilson came in to sell that Christmas junk he reviewed in the *Observer*.'

'I wish I had seen him,' I said.

'He looks like the head of Girton.'

'That's a women's college, isn't it?'

'You Americans are so literal,' Musprat said, and we threaded our way through the wet footpaths of Lincoln's Inn, the short cut to the *Statesman*.

I said, 'Did Gaston refuse to buy one of your books?'

Musprat shook his head and said, 'I bought one off him.'

'I've never noticed anyone buying a book there,' I said. 'I thought they sold them by the pound to libraries.'

Musprat inhaled but said nothing, only sighed. He went very quiet. He was just my age but seemed much older. He was balding and had bad teeth, and was cranky in the way only Englishmen in their thirties could be—assertively seedy. He cultivated a look of failure, he boasted of his bad reviews. He smoked heavily, and gnawed his stained fingers. He could have passed for fifty.

I had never seen Musprat without a necktie and jacket, and yet I rarely saw him in a place where he needed them. He wore a tie at home, in his flat in Notting Hill Gate. He told me that he put a tie on before he answered the door—a school habit, he said. So much in English life originated not at home with the family, as it did in Europe, or in the street, as it did in America, but at school: the table manners, the slang, the rules, the habits, the dress code, even the food. What was oddest of all in this school-obsessed country was that people claimed they hated school —Musprat's school poems were angry and sad. He had been thrashed by his sadistic housemaster, mocked for being a loner, disliked for not being a rugger hearty, and yet he still wrote poems about the school he had left twenty years ago. His writing was his way of getting even.

'So what book did you buy?' I asked him.

His briefcase was a battered satchel, like something else from school. He whacked it against his leg as he walked.

'Jesus, you and your bloody questions,' he said. He was genuinely irritated, but he fumbled open the flap of the satchel and took out the book, *The Dogflud Chronicles.*

'You bought your own book?'

'Rescued it,' he said. 'Some bastard sold it to Gaston. I couldn't bear seeing it on the shelf. Half-price, shop-worn, flogged to a library. It's only been out a month.'

'I think I'd do the same if I saw one of my books there.'

'No one sells your books to Gaston,' Musprat said, and he smiled. 'That's the highest compliment a reviewer can pay.'

Waiting outside the literary editor's office at the *New Statesman*, Musprat said, 'This is like a tutorial, isn't it? Clutching our ridiculous essays, waiting for our tutor to summon us.'

Musprat was smoking. He puffed out his cheeks and blew smoke.

'Hoping he'll give us an alpha,' he said crossly. 'Are you going to that Hodders party?'

I said that I didn't know anything about it.

'It's for that boring woman who writes picture books about Nash terraces. Every twit in London will be there.'

'So are you going?'

'It's a drink,' Musprat said, meaning yes. He looked pale and rumpled, leaning clumsily against a torpedo-sized fire extinguisher.

'Are you feeling all right?'

'Of course,' he said. He was offended by the question. 'You're always asking me that.'

There had only been one other time. I had run into him one morning in the Strand. I had said he looked ill, as though he had just thrown up. He said he had been drinking the night before, but that anyway he was sick every morning. 'Don't you throw up every morning?' he asked me.

'Come in Ian!' the literary editor shouted through the closed door.

'Just like my tutor,' Musprat muttered, and shuffled in. He was out in minutes, sighing and rifling the book locker, and then it was my turn. The editor, Graham Heavage, immediately lapsed into his irritating habit.

'*Bonjour M'sieur Theroux, ça va? Il souffle un vent glacial aujourd'hui. Avez-vous des engelures?*'

Heavage often spoke to me in French—because of my name, because he spoke French very well and because he could patronize me that way. I regarded it as an unfriendly gesture. I spoke French badly. So I always replied to him in English. This didn't bother him, but neither did it encourage him to speak to me in English. He had the sort of reddish eyes you see in most geese and some East Europeans.

'I'm fine. No chilblains.'

Wasn't that what *engelures* meant?

Heavage was a highly intelligent but fretful man of fifty or so who had never been friendly with me. He was another tie-wearer. He was said to be an authority on Aleister Crowley. It was hard to reconcile this fastidious editor with the lecherous satanist, but the English sometimes had surprising interests.

Goose-eyes twitching, he went through my copy quickly and frowned in approval, making swift printer's marks in ball-point as he read, and then he said, 'I can't remember when anyone has used the word "crappy" in these pages before.'

'Do you want to change it to "egregious"?'

'No. Crappy will do,' he said. But he didn't smile. It was hard to tell whether he was mocking me. Still he was scrutinizing the review—not reading it, but considering it. 'And you're a trifle severe with Mr Updike.'

'I hate allegories.'

'I would have said pastiche, but never mind.'

Musprat was right: it was a tutorial. No praise, only nit-picking and rather wintry irony.

Shoving the pages into a wire tray on his desk, Heavage said, 'We'll run this next week. On your way out have a trawl through the book locker—see if there's anything you want to do.'

I decided to be blunt. 'I'd like to do one big book instead of four small ones, for a change.'

'I'll keep that in mind,' Heavage said. 'As you say in America, I'll think it over mentally.'

I wanted to hit him. I was sure that he had never had any experience of physical violence, so my slapping his face would be a great shock. In this silence he had levelled his reddish eyes at me, as though he had guessed at my hostility.

'Not many big books in January,' he said, flexing his fingers. 'Very quiet at the moment, though there will be the usual log-jam in the spring. Find yourself a clutch of novels, there's a good chap.'

He was saying no to my doing a lead review. So it was another week as a hack. Then he smiled and broke into French, which was my signal that the meeting was at an end.

I found Musprat on his knees, rooting around in the book locker.

'Look at this,' he said. It was a picture book, *Tennyson at Freshwater: The Record of a Friendship*. 'I bags it.'

'I didn't know you were interested in Tennyson.'

'I'm not,' Musprat said. 'But look at the price. Ten quid. I'll just mention it in my round-up and Gaston will give me a fiver for it.'

It was a beautiful drawing-room in a Nash terrace on the Outer Circle of Regents Park, and everyone there seemed out of place—reviewers, writers, editors, publicists, all drinking wine and watching for the trays of hors d'oeuvres that were carried by waiters and waitresses better dressed than most of the guests. I had the impression of people who had just come in off the street, drifted out of the park, where they had been lurking; they looked damp and grateful and somewhat anxious. I mentioned this to Musprat.

'They're drunk, that's all,' he said, and lunged at a waitress carrying a tray of drinks.

While I was searching for someone I knew, a woman materialized next to me. She was almost my height, and white-faced, with an elegant neck—a pearl and velvet collar encircling it—and full red lips.

'I know who you are,' she said. 'But I thought you were much older.'

People sometimes said this, perhaps because of all my opinionated reviews; but it was only a posture I had adopted. There were comic possibilities in being full of opinions and cracks. I wanted to be the joker who never smiled, and I was surprised when I was taken seriously.

'You're very busy, aren't you? I see your pieces everywhere.'

'But mainly on the back pages.'

'I loathe self-deprecation,' she said. 'Don't be insincere. I thought *A Little Latitude* was brilliant. It was quite the best book I've read in ages. I gave copies to all my friends for Christmas.'

When someone spoke this way I always assumed they were making it up. I simply smiled at the woman and asked no further questions. I thought it might embarrass her if I did. In any case she was still talking.

'Your best review was from a man I saw walking along the platform at Paddington Station. He had a copy of it in his hand.

A man passing by said, "Is that book any good?" and the first man said, "Fucking marvellous, Fred.'"

'I like that.'

'I thought you might,' she said. 'And what are you working on at the moment?'

'A novel.'

She smiled. I loved the fullness of her lips against her thin face.

'About a man,' I said.

Her eyes were dark and deeply set.

'He leaves home and becomes a sort of castaway.'

Still she said nothing. There was a pinkish bloom on her cheeks.

'He dies in the end.'

How was it possible for someone to hear all this and still say nothing? Her silence made me nervous.

But I loved this woman's looks, her lips, her madonna's face, her skin very close against her skull, her high forehead and her black gleaming hair tightly drawn back. Her paleness, her pinkness had no blemish, and I found her slightly protruding teeth another aspect of her beauty. She was wearing a dark dress trimmed with velvet and lace, and although she was thin—with a slender neck and fragile-looking arms and wrists—she had a full deep bosom that her good posture and height elevated and presented. I was accustomed to regarding lovely women as not very intelligent, but she seemed both beautiful and brainy—her silences alone seemed intelligently timed—and this combination I found madly attractive.

My tongue was gummy as I said, 'It's called *The Last Man.*' I looked down and saw that she was wearing stiletto heels—wicked shoes on bony white feet.

'That title has an excellent pedigree. *The Last Man*—it was Mary Shelley's original title for *Frankenstein*,' she said. 'And I'm sure you know that Orwell's first title for *1984* was *The Last Man in Europe.*'

I was sure she realized from my expression that I did not know this at all.

'You could ask Sonia,' the woman said. 'Sonia Orwell. She's

over there by the window—do you want to meet her?'

I said no, not at the moment, because I could not imagine that George Orwell's widow would want to meet me.

'I really do admire your writing,' the woman said. 'In fact, I think you might have that rare combination of qualities that makes a writer of genius.'

'What qualities?' I asked.

'Total megalomania and a nose for what the public likes to read. It's unbeatable. Dickens had it—so did Shaw. Henry James didn't have it, but Maugham did.'

'I've just been reading Hugh Walpole. He was a friend of Henry James. James was always sending him hugs. *The Man With Red Hair.*'

The woman had stiffened each time I uttered a sentence.

'A macabre novel,' I said. 'Set in Cornwall.'

The woman said, 'You're much better than Hugh Walpole.'

It was the first time in my life anyone had ever said that I was better than a dead writer. I had never imagined that I was better than anyone who had written in the past. It had never occurred to me that I might even be compared to another writer, dead or alive. The point about writing was that you were yourself—comparisons were meaningless. Nevertheless, I took this woman's assertion as praise.

She went on praising me—and I felt flustered, embarrassed and confused, like a puppy being squirted with a hose. I also found myself delighting in glancing down at her cleavage. Do women know how this warm smile-like slot excites a man's interest?

Distracted, I asked, 'And who are you?'

But she was looking across the room.

'Will you excuse me?' she said. She gave me a lovely smile, and then she was away, sooner than I wished.

Had I said the wrong thing?

Then Musprat was at my elbow, holding a cigarette and a smeared glass, with flecks of vol-au-vent pastry on his tie and his fingers. His eyes were bloodshot, his suit wrinkled, the knot on his tie yanked small. He was slightly hunched, and looked more fragile and elderly than ever.

'Who is that?' I asked him.

She was standing by the fireplace talking animatedly to a man in a chalk-striped suit.

'Lady Max,' Musprat said. 'She's married to a tick called Alabaster. He's something in the city. They have a house in the Boltons.'

'She seems nice.' I was thinking of her praise.

'That's the one thing she's not.'

'She's attractive,' I said.

'Sort of a bruised peach,' Musprat said.

'I like the way she's dressed.'

'She's always wearing those "fuck me" shoes,' Musprat said.

'Don't you think she's pretty?'

'I hate that word,' he said, in a disgusted way. 'I don't want to hear it. At this point in the evening everyone looks leathery to me.'

He stalked off, chasing the woman with the drinks tray.

I lingered at the party hoping to speak to Lady Max again. She did not return to my end of the room. She was surrounded and I was too shy to approach her.

I loitered, growing sober, and with this heightening sobriety felt strangely superior—not intellectually, but simply stronger and in control. The drunker guests brought out a kind of priggishness in me. Drunk people, loud people, obvious and angry people, people stammering and stumbling, spilling drinks and wolfing small burnt sausages and cheese cubes on toothpicks: they had surrendered all power and direction, they were yelling and gasping. They strengthened me.

I did not want to be that way. I grew calmer, observing them. They seemed, as Musprat often seemed to me, self-destructive and weak. I didn't see how people like that could write anything. That was my yardstick: I measured people by their ability to write. How could these people write well if they could not see straight?

Lady Max flashed past and I made after her, but lost her in the crowd.

It was important in London to leave a party or start home before the pubs closed, for just after eleven o'clock the streets became thronged with drunks—all men, their faces wolfish and ill, yelling at passing cars, staggering and scrapping. Some of them loitered, looking ravenous, eating chips with greasy fingers out of pouches of old newspapers. All over London these men, turned out of the pubs, were pissing in doorways.

That night I was delayed on the underground and by the time I reached Victoria the eruption had occurred—drunks everywhere. The station was over-bright, which made it seem dirtier than it would have seemed in dim light, and it was cold—the wind blowing up the tracks and through the barriers, rustling the newspapers and rattling the plastic cups, moving them through the station the way a flood tide moves flotsam. The news-stand was shut but the *Evening Standard* poster was still stuck to the wall, announcing TV COMEDY STAR IN SUICIDE BID —PICTURE.

That feeling I had had at the party came back to me on the train, as I watched the drunks eating chips and hamburgers, slumped in their seats or swaying feebly, looking weak and tired. It was not merely that I was sober; I was also a stranger, an American, an alien. I saw theirs as a peculiarly English despair. They suffered from London fatigue, London futility. It was their fate, and I wanted to write about it, because no one else had noticed it. I was not any of them.

Three stops, thinking these thoughts, and then I walked through the disorder of my own station, littered and dirty, its posters torn, its black iron gleaming with the sweat of condensed fog. I liked hearing my footsteps in the stillness, and seeing the shadows and the mist falling through the light of the street lamps, as empty double-decker buses moved importantly down the empty high street.

Anne had gone to bed. Before I joined her I crept upstairs in the dark and stood in the boys' room, listening to the rise and fall of their breathing, Louis's an adenoidal snorting, Marcel's a just-audible flutter. They were both still, like buoyant things floating high and peacefully on a sea of sleep. Without waking them I kissed each boy's cheek. Their faces were warm in the cold room, and their breath had made feathers of frost on the window pane.

I undressed in the dark and crept into bed with Anne. She slid against me and sighed—the bedclothes were a nest of warmth. In order to ease myself into sleep I went through the chapters of my unfinished novel, murmuring the number of the chapter and the secret title I had assigned it. There were eleven so far, but I was asleep by the time I got to eight.

London nights were still and clammy and cold in the submarine darkness, and when I woke from a dream of strangulation it was as though I were suspended in this dark vitreous silence. I had the sense of us all in the house swimming through these London nights, of night as a sea swell, and of our sinuously gliding through it as though drifting deep in the face of a wave. I loved sleep, and winter mornings disoriented me— something to do with the darkness, and the clink of milk bottles in crates shifting on the milk float, the only sound in the street, but a deranged one.

'You came home so late last night,' Anne said. 'What time was it?'

'Eleven or so,' I said, wondering why I was lying. She would not have minded me telling her it had been after midnight.

Yet she was silent. She seemed preoccupied. I sensed her disapproval.

'It wasn't much,' I said, being defensive. 'Pretty boring. I got some money at Gaston's, then Ian and I went to a book launch.' Anne said nothing. I said, 'That woman who writes about Nash terraces.'

She had not heard. She said, 'The boys were up until all hours doing homework. Why do they give them so much prep? I'm going to complain.'

'Don't say anything, Mum,' Marcel said.

Louis said, 'You'll get us into trouble.'

'Jeremy's mum complained and Townsend announced it in class and everyone laughed at him.'

They were seated awkwardly at the table wolfing their cereal, their hair sticking up, their rumpled blazers making them look harassed. They ate quickly, nervously, without any pleasure, simply stoking their faces, and then they jumped up and said they had to go or they would be late.

'I'll walk you to the bus-stop,' I said.

Anne said, 'I'll be gone by the time you get back, so I'll say goodbye now.'

She kissed me while the boys tightened the buckles on their satchels.

Mornings were clamorous, and I needed silence, needed the house to myself. I wanted to see them all on their way. I could not sit down until the house was empty.

At the bus-stop Louis said, 'Are you a socialist?'

'I don't vote—Americans can't in Britain,' I said. 'I'm just a spectator.'

'Mum's a Labour supporter,' Marcel said. 'I am too.'

'That's what he told Mr Fitch,' Louis said.

'That's none of your business,' Marcel said.

'You don't have to be dogmatic,' I said.

'What does dogmatic mean?' Louis asked.

Marcel was listening, too, as though he had been too proud to ask.

'Something like inflexible.'

'Mr Beale is inflexible.'

Mr Beale was the hated headmaster.

They were looking up the road for the bus. I hovered and yet held back, wanting to protect them and wanting them to be strong. And they had the same ambivalence, liking my company and resenting the thought that they might need it. They were thin and pale, with a hint of anxiety in their soft brown eyes.

It was a cold, overcast morning, and the dampness gave a greasy look to the black road and the broken pavement. The bus loomed and slowed, and they leaped aboard, catching hold of the rail. I saw them standing, small figures jammed in the aisle among all the heavy coats.

The house was empty when I returned. I went to my study and opened my notebook and read: *Shafts of sunlight filled with brilliant flakes falling through the green leaves to the jungle floor*—which was where I had left off yesterday to write my book review and go to Gaston's.

Shafts of sunlight filled with brilliant flakes.

I looked up and through the window of my study. Outside, London in midwinter was dark, and the brick and stone of the old house backs looked crusty with neglect. The trees were brittle and black too, and the damp night air had left a slimy sheen on the slate roofs. Some windows were lit—you could see the pale bulbs—but the overall impression was of stillness and darkness, of daylight sleepily emerging and seeping out of the low sky.

The darkness was a comfort. I was learning to live here. The stillness, and even that tomb-like quality in the shapes of houses, the sense of being buried alive here, penetrated me: it kept me indoors and calmed me and helped me think. A blue sky would have turned my head and tempted me away, but this grey morning and the backs of these old houses with their brown bricks kept my reverie intact, because I was not dealing with them, or anything like them. There was no distraction here. I was writing about the jungle.

I had sketched the way ahead—I knew what was coming in the next three or four chapters. After that, I had only the vaguest sense of what I was in for. Mocking myself, I said out loud, 'Now what?'

Just as I picked up my pen, the mailman's feet sounded on the stone front steps, and I held my breath, and then letters began plopping through the letter slot. Only one required a reply, an overdue bill, and I did it immediately. Another, from a reader—a woman who said she liked my books—I crumpled and threw away. I lifted my pen again, but when nothing came—no word, no thought—I retrieved the woman's letter from the waste-basket and smoothed it. It was from Stony Plain, Alberta. I pulled out my big atlas and found the place—near Edmonton —and I was so touched by a message from this distance I replied on a postcard, thanking her for her letter.

It was then ten-thirty. I tried again, trying to move on. *The shafts of sunlight.* I struggled to move the sentence, to make a paragraph, but I could not advance it.

The woman's letter from Stony Plain, Alberta, had mentioned a particular story I had written years ago. I found that collection on the bookshelf and read the story. It was good. It held me. Could I still write as well as that? Putting the book away I glanced up and saw a guidebook to Canada. Stony Plain wasn't listed, but Edmonton was. The capital. Oldest city in the province. On the Saskatchewan River. And this: 'Ukrainians played a large role in the settlement of Edmonton and are still the dominant ethnic group.'

I shut the guidebook and dragged my notebook over and tried again, struggling to begin. It was now eleven-twenty. I reread everything I had written in that chapter so far, and as I read I noticed that my finger-nails needed cutting. I immediately attended to this, and as I was doing so the telephone rang. It was Ian Musprat. Did I want to meet for lunch?

Clipping my nails I said, 'I'm writing.'

I believed the lie would commit me to action.

Musprat said, 'I've been thrashing around all morning. I can't do a thing. It's hopeless. How about playing snooker at the Lambourne later on?'

'I'm busy tonight.' Another lie: I must write something, I thought. 'What about tomorrow?'

'Fine. I'll see you at the Lambourne at seven. If we eat early the table will be free. I'll let you get on with your writing. I don't know how you do it.'

But after I hung up I did not write. I finished clipping my nails and then I filed them. It was almost noon.

At last, very carefully, I began to copy what I had written on the previous page in the notebook on to a fresh page, as though to give myself momentum. I improved it, but when I got to the end nothing more came. It was ten minutes to one. I tugged. I saw something.

I wrote, *Just then they looked up and saw a brown face staring at them through the leaves, and after they saw the first one they saw more—three, seven, a dozen human faces suspended like masks.*

A breakthrough at last. But I stopped writing. It was one o'clock: time for lunch.

Fish fingers—I loved the improbable name, like *shoe-trees* —three of them in a sandwich, a cup of coffee, two chocolate cookies, and while I ate this I listened to *The World at One*, and I read *The Times*, and I sat. The radio, the food, the newspaper—it all left me calm, and when the programme ended I hurried upstairs and almost without thinking I wrote another sentence: *They looked again and the faces were gone.*

This was all I needed, because in that thought—the sight of the faces in the jungle—I saw the whole situation: my own characters, the Indians spying on them, the hint of an ambush, the jungle, the narrow paths, the hidden village. And so I spent the rest of the afternoon bringing my characters nearer and nearer—and intermittently they saw the faces—to the point where their path ran out, they arrived at the village and were mobbed. End of chapter.

I had written thirty-five words in the morning and in the afternoon something like fifteen hundred. But what gave me the greatest pleasure was a sentence containing the image *limp green leaves like old dollar bills.*

I made notes for the next chapter, to prepare for tomorrow: *the village, smoke, trampled earth, frightened children, barking dogs, a conversation, 'We cannot help you,' 'Ice is life,' the hidden strangers.*

The act of writing produced ideas and events. It was late afternoon and I was growing excited at the thought that I had moved on. I guessed that I was half done with the book. I wanted so much to be done before the summer. Ten chapters more, ten weeks, would take me into March. I might be through by my birthday in April. Looking over what I had written I became hopeful. The book was strange, true, comic and unexpected—that was what mattered most. I wanted people to believe it and like it, and to find something of themselves expressed in it.

With these thoughts—my pen twitching words on to the bright paper in the pool of light on my desk, and darkness all around—night had fallen.

The door to my room opened. It was Louis.

'Marcel's downstairs making tea,' he said.

He looked exhausted. His face was smudged, his hair spiky, and his hand-me-down school blazer had shrunk on him. Instead of making him look bigger, it only made him look skinnier, with a thin neck and knobby shoulders.

'Hi Dad.'

He kissed me. His hair smelled of cigarette smoke. When I mentioned this, he said, 'I had to sit on the top deck of the bus.'

He slumped into the armchair opposite my desk. He said, 'What page are you on?'

I looked down. 'Two hundred and eighty-seven.'

'Are you almost done?'

'Half done, I think. I don't know for sure.'

'I did an essay for Wilkins today. Two sides. *Macbeth.*'

'The hen-pecked hero.'

Louis nodded. 'It's true. I should have said that.'

'You look tired, Lou.'

'We had rugby. And an English essay. And in chemistry we did an experiment with sulphuric acid and Ragget burnt a hole in his blazer. In the morning there was a rehearsal for the school play. Lunch was stew. It was gristle and fat. I didn't eat it. Jam sponge for afters. Beale told me I needed a haircut. And some of the boys hid my satchel and when I found it they made fun of me. The sole of my shoe is coming off. Wesley told me he hates me.'

School.

I said, 'Why don't you watch television?'

'I have tons of homework. Latin prep, chemistry and history.'

'What would you like for dinner?'

'Dunno, do I? Maybe spaghetti. The vegetarian kind.'

'I'll make the sauce,' I said. 'We'll have salad. I think there's ice cream for dessert.'

He yawned like a cat. 'I'll have a bath first. The showers weren't working, so we ran straight from rugby to chemistry. We were all dirty.'

That explained the mud streaks on his face and the dirt under his finger-nails. My sons knew I loved them, but they had no idea how much I admired them.

Marcel yelled to Louis to say the toast and tea were ready, and while they sat at the table, saying little, I made the spaghetti sauce. I chopped the onion and garlic and green pepper, and sautéed them with some mushrooms, then scalded and peeled the tomatoes, and tossed it all into a pot with a large bunch of fresh basil and a stock cube and a pinch of crushed red pepper and a dollop of tomato paste. While the sauce reddened and simmered the boys went upstairs to their rooms to do their homework, and I went out. I bought the *Evening Standard* and took it to the Fishmonger's Arms to read over a pint of Guinness. There was a mention in 'Londoner's Diary' of Anthony Burgess staying at Claridge's, and I thought how Londoners knew nothing of London hotel rooms.

Later, waiting for Anne to come home, I watched a television game show with Marcel, who had finished his homework, and when the host of the show quipped 'You're like the Irishman who thought an innuendo was a suppository,' Marcel laughed out loud, and I thought, *I am happy*. There was nothing so joyous on earth as this: the darkness, the harmless game show, the thought that I had written something today, the knowledge that I was home, the anticipation that Anne would be home soon, the spaghetti sauce simmering, a pint of Guinness inside me, and—most of all—the explosive sound of my child's laughter, generous and full-throated. I felt blessed.

Anne was home at seven, a bit later than usual. She too was tired, but she helped Louis with his Latin while I boiled the water for the spaghetti and made salad. We ate together. The boys cleared the table. Anne did the dishes, because I had cooked, and after the boys went upstairs I read her the chapter I had just finished.

'It's good,' she said.

'Say something more.'

'Isn't that enough?'

'Just a little more.'

'I like the image about the leaves like dollar bills. And it's menacing at the end. I would want to read on. How's that?'

'OK.'

We watched the *Nine O'Clock News*, and the beginning of a programme about fruit-bats, and then Anne yawned and said, 'I'm tired.'

So we went to bed. Then the house was in darkness. I was happy. What had happened today to make me so? I could not say why I was reassured. Perhaps because my novel had gone better than I expected—I had finished a chapter—but more likely it was that we were together, a complete family, a whole healthy organism, fully alive.

This ordinariness was what I liked and needed. It had been a perfect day.

L ondon lies in a bowl-shaped valley sloping into the Thames, downhill from Clapham to the river and uphill again from the Embankment to the West End. London pedestrians and cyclists can feel the earth's contours beneath all these bricks. I sensed this on my last half-mile up the steepness of St James's Street on my way to the Lambourne Club, and I was imagining, not that I was meeting Musprat, but that I was a member, going here each evening in the London darkness and finding it a refuge, reading *Punch* and *The Times* in an armchair in the reading room, sitting in front of the big fireplace in the lounge, standing by the bar with old men in rumpled suits.

The Lambourne Club was a bright place with tall windows and high ceilings, and it smelled of pipe tobacco and brass polish and the hot ashes in the fire baskets. It seemed to me the essence of London—a carpet-quiet place, slightly too warm, a blend of old folk's home and school, the safest place in the world, if you were an older white male.

Joining the club was a lazy ambition, I knew that, and it didn't suit my impatient temperament—and what did I have in common with the members? But these difficulties interested and provoked me.

On the stairs, when I saw some men in pin-striped suits, I mentioned to Musprat that I felt out of place in the Lambourne because I was an American.

'This club is full of Americans,' Musprat said. 'Lawyers and bankers mostly. The club wants their money. Them, for example.'

He indicated the men in the pin-striped suits. Was that the sort of person I wanted to turn into? American Anglophiles, predictable in their Burberrys and kidding themselves rigid, and going hee-haw in the club lounge with schooners of sherry?

My main objections were the strict dress code and the

absence of women. How could anyone relax while wearing a suit and tie? How could any man find pleasure in a place that was so sternly masculine?

'Doesn't it bother you that there are no women here?'

We were at the bar, among the old men who looked like morticians, and the toothy young men shouting at each other, and the over-dressed Americans.

Musprat looked around. He shrugged and made a sound in his nose. He said, 'How many women are there in your local—what's it called?'

'The Fish,' I said. 'Fishmonger's Arms. Not many.'

'Exactly,' he said. 'Irish, isn't it? All bog-trotters.'

We had gone there for a pint once when he had come over to borrow a book, and he had looked around and said *I hate places like this.*

'I suppose the Lambourne's a bit like school in that way,' he said, and glanced around. 'Everything in London is a bit like school.'

I had already worked that out for myself.

Making a face he said, 'The food here at the Lambourne is school food. But that's not as bad as some places. Wilton's Restaurant? Posh old buffers eat there. It costs a fortune. Because of the food.'

'Nouvelle cuisine?'

He had a particularly aggressive laugh—the harsh triumphant laughter of a deeply insecure person.

'Nursery food,' he shrieked, showing his stained teeth.

We went into the Lambourne dining-room. The idea in this club was that rather than eat alone the members ate at a long refectory table in the centre of the room. In this way a shipping magnate might find himself seated next to a journalist, a diplomat next to a novelist, but the chances were that you would find yourself next to a barrister or a solicitor—so Musprat said—because there were so many of them in the Lambourne. Once it had been mainly writers, the likes of H. G. Wells and Arnold Bennett, Saki and Shaw, and its reputation had been literary and raffish. But now it was old grey men in old grey suits.

Musprat winced at the menu, pinching it distastefully in his chewed fingers. The menu was a small single sheet of paper inserted in a leather holder.

'See what I mean?' he said. 'School food.'

'They didn't have smoked buckling at my school. What is it anyway?'

'Fish,' Musprat said, and smiled sourly at me in a one-upping way. It struck me again that the English often made a conscious effort to be bad company, made a virtue of being peevish. Musprat certainly did. You could see them up and down the long table, frowning at their food—their school food—loading their forks as though they were baiting hooks.

We ordered our food, and I began to hate being here.

Not only did Musprat seem older than me, he also seemed fixed and certain in his life. I had no idea what was going to happen to me. Musprat said that he knew what his whole life would be like. Already he had been married and divorced. It was an unhappy and bitter marriage but an amicable divorce, and now he was quite friendly with his ex-wife, so he said. He disliked children.

Like many insecure people he was deeply and cynically opinionated, perhaps in an effort to give the impression that he was very sure of himself. But his talk made me uneasy. The more certain he sounded the more I feared for him. He said he knew exactly what he wanted: the very narrow and predictable life that the English seemed to assume was the ideal, a life without change or upheaval or, apparently, without passion. He could be tetchy and a scold—he was truthful and blunt in the way of an unhappy person who takes a little satisfaction in the hurt he inflicts on others. I sometimes reflected with sadness that I had no other friends.

He used soon-to-be-obsolete and fogeyish words like 'pantechnicon' for removal van and 'beaker' for mug. In the country, he said, he wore gaiters. *Gaiters?* He called the radio 'the wireless'. To annoy him one day I said, 'Do you call airplanes "flying machines"?' and he replied, 'No, I call them aeroplanes, which is what they are.'

We talked at dinner about his radio plays. He was writing

one at the moment, about a gypsy who moved an entire caravan piece by piece into his one-room apartment in Islington.

'I want to go on writing plays for the wireless,' Musprat said.

And as though to ensure the failure of the effort at the outset, the plays were often written in blank verse, and sometimes they rhymed.

'What about poetry?'

'Poetry-writing is shovelling shit. Radio plays reach a huge audience,' he said. 'I'm going to do that for the rest of my life. And I want to go on being in this club. I don't want to travel. I don't want to turn into a book reviewer. And I never want to go to America again. It's hideous there.'

'Sometimes I miss Boston,' I said. It was a timid confession. I missed it every day—its space and its familiar streets and smells. I missed its food, I missed the laughter, I missed the feel of American money, which was like the feel of flesh. Reality for me was the past, and it was elsewhere. London was like a role I had been assigned to play, and I was as yet still unsure of my lines.

Musprat said, 'I was in Boston for that colour mag story two years ago. Boston isn't a city. Not a real city. It's about ten small towns clustered around that poxy harbour. And you find'— Musprat was cutting a very small muscle of meat, his mouth set rather severely as he sawed the grey sinew—'that in fact, Boston does not exist except as a rather spurious urban concept. I hated the food, the traffic's appalling, and you can't drive ten feet without propelling your car straight into a pot-hole. The police carry these bloody great revolvers and they're always reaching for them.'

'I lived in Boston for twenty-two years,' I said, hoping to shut him up. He knew so little of the city it was futile to argue the merits of it. I had to be gentle. He was at his most vulnerable when he was generalizing like this, and his feelings were easily wounded even though he could be brutal with others.

'I preferred New York City,' he said.

'New York is never dark and never quiet,' I said. 'I can't sleep there.'

'London's worse in some ways,' he said. 'The air's foul from everyone breathing, shop assistants are rude and the food's filthy.'

He was still eating, chewing quickly with his stained and protruding teeth, like a rodent.

'I suppose that's why I like London,' he said. He was not a Londoner, though I would never have known.

'Money's not important here. Class matters. And class has nothing to do with money.'

I kept noticing in the English their love of being right or of setting you straight, the schoolteacher sternness—perhaps because they had once been cringing students. In Musprat's case it was slightly worse, because he was from the provinces, somewhere in the Midlands, possibly Lichfield—he often made references to Doctor Johnson. He needed to prove himself and yet he loathed himself for having to do it. He had a keen awareness of class and with this a hatred of the class system. This caused him conflict and sometimes pain.

'People are always imitating their charlady. "The lie-dee wot does for me, comes on a weekly bie-sis, innit?"'

And when I laughed—his imitation was a success—he was torn, having succeeded at the very thing he hated.

'Money's such a big thing in America. But no one has money here.'

He was signing the chit on the pad the waiter had brought. The waiter looked Malay but when I asked the old man next to me he said they were all Filipinos.

The old man had a white moustache that was stained with nicotine, and he spoke in a roaring voice.

'They're absolutely indestructible! They work for a pittance. They can live on rice and fish heads. Their only fault is they believe in an afterlife.' He shifted his gaze around the table, as though seeking more listeners. 'Very superstitious. You wouldn't want to put your life in their hands, because they don't mind dying. You want an atheist as your batman, see. But they get on willy-nilly. This isn't America. You don't need to take an examination to be admitted to Britain.'

The old man opposite, straining to hear, said, 'Quite. My nephew is taking his examinations. I have no idea what it's all about. When I was in school my father simply rang his old tutor and said I was ready. I went up to Trinity.'

'Maybe your nephew is in one of those comprehensive schools,' the other man said.

'Yes, I believe he is. Are they very expensive?'

As these old men continued to talk, the Filipino waiter went around the room, no one taking any notice of him. It seemed to me that he could go anywhere and see anything. He was invisible.

As I watched the silent waiter, Musprat said, 'You see? That's why I like this club. Those old men.'

We were on our way to the coffee room.

There were more old men in the coffee room, among the aquatints of Indian ruins.

One was saying, 'She is a very handsome woman. She absolutely has her pick of men. They send her roses. Her husband knows about it, of course. Turns a blind eye. Very keen cricketer, you know.'

Another said, 'It was well-known that the prince was having a little fling with her. Her husband was in the picture then. But you know, people are always rather proud when their wives or daughters have a thing with a member of the royal family. In fact, people look up to them. It is rather an accomplishment.'

'No such luck for me,' Musprat said, and he began talking to the old man, as though he were one of them.

I had two thoughts. One was that this was like every overseas club I had ever been in—male, old-fangled, English, fussy and foolish—only cleaner. And the other was more in the nature of a fear, that this life of the club and London and this talk was a sort of permanent condition. You joined and this was how your life went on, changelessly, passing from the dining-room to the bar to the library, with a stop at the Gents, among these men, predictably, without surprises, until you died.

Musprat looked irritable and slightly drunk. He took a deep breath, looked briefly youthful, smiled at me, then began to cough and, coughing, became elderly once more.

'I really am glad you suggested this,' I said. Was I saying this because of my guilty feeling, which was the opposite of what I said? 'I remember the first time I came here, about a year ago.

That winter night, when the snow—'

'Jesus, are you actually reminiscing?'

He was angry, disgusted, embarrassed. He drank some wine and made an ugly chewing face as he swallowed.

'Let's bag the snooker table before someone else does,' he said.

From the way he behaved, in this abrupt and sneering way, usually bristling, I guessed that he had been bullied at school. He was small and pale. He wore thick glasses. He chewed his fingers. He wrote poems.

In the snooker room a long bar of light hung over the table, brightening the green felt and putting the rest of the room in shadow.

Musprat chalked our names on the slate that hung above the scoreboard of beads on wires, like an abacus. He had lovely handwriting, regular and upright. School had made him, and then unmade him.

'You know who those old buffers are talking about?'

'That woman?'

'Yes. Your friend, Lady Max.'

'I don't even know her.'

And I thought: I have no friends, except you. I spend all my time writing. I have a wife and two children and they are the whole of my life, my society in London. I could not tell Musprat the truth, that he was my only friend, that this outing to the Lambourne twice a month was my only outing.

'I met her at that party,' I said. 'That's all.'

But I saw her clearly: her white forehead, her drawn-back hair, her bright eyes, her pretty mouth and thin fingers.

He had set the triangle of balls on the table. We were taking our shots with the cue balls to see who would break. Musprat strained and stroked and his cue ball came to rest an inch from the cushion.

So he went first. He pondered his break, and took his shot, a purist's poke. He nicked the edge of the cluster of balls, hardly disturbing the triangular arrangement.

'Your shot,' he said.

At this rate we would be playing for a week. There was a

slow tactical you-can't-see-me game of snooker that I hated, although it was said to be the real thing. And there was a speedier version, nearer the American game of pool that I was more used to, with bolder strokes and more obvious moves, played more on the open table and less in the shadow of other balls.

I lined up the cue ball and hit the clustered balls hard, blasting them apart.

'How rash,' Musprat said. The balls were still caroming, and none was potted. 'How convenient.'

And he began potting balls. When he finally kissed one, snookering me, and I went to take my answering shot, I nudged the cue ball with the tip of the cue.

'It moved. You touched it. That's your shot.'

'It was an accident, Ian.'

'That's your shot,' he said firmly, in the stern prissy voice he had learned at school. He chalked his cue. 'No exceptions. If we start making exceptions where will we be?'

He was ponderous as only a drunken man can be. He fought for every point, and when I realized how badly he wanted to win I became bored by the whole business—the desperate fussing of his insistent competitiveness—and wished I were home with my little family.

'Get in there,' he said, speaking to the brown ball. 'I've potted the pink but it's got to go back on the table.'

The idea was that as long as the player went on potting, his opponent flunkeyed for him, replacing the balls that were hit out of sequence. Flunkeying was another school role, for the younger, newer, duller boys.

We were about evenly matched, yet he won more often than I did, partly because I always let him have the disputed point and also because he was the more consistent player—not aggressive, but tenacious. No one held on like the English, and when they wanted something they knew no embarrassment. They were never more obvious or disregarding or single-minded than in this tenacity. No surrender was Musprat's way, but winning gave him very little pleasure; it simply made him chattier.

'And it seems,' he said, continuing the line of talk that he had broken off earlier, 'that she's an admirer of yours. The Lady Max. She told Heavage. He told me.'

This was news—that she knew Heavage, who had a reputation as an obnoxious and persistent womanizer. *Poor Gillian*, people always said of his wife. He was niggardly, a trait I associated with most lechers. And I hated him for speaking French to me and treating me like a hack.

'What do you think of her?'

'A bruised peach,' Musprat said. It was his only summing-up.

'I thought she was witty.'

'That's the one thing she's not,' he said.

'So you don't like her?'

'What does "like" mean? I don't care one way or the other.' Musprat was still sinking balls. 'She always gets what she wants though.'

'What's wrong with that?'

'She wants everything.'

He could not pot the green. He lined up his shot and sent the cue ball gently into it, and it came to rest between the pink and the blue.

'Snookered,' he muttered with satisfaction.

'Oh, I say,' an old man cried out from the shadows, and soon afterwards I conceded the game.

Musprat was uncharacteristically jaunty afterwards, and friendliness gave him an air of confidentiality. He wanted another drink, and then he wanted to sit by the fire, and then he wanted to talk.

He began to behave like an uncle. He said, 'How would you like me to put you up for membership? The drill is that I simply put you in the book and the other members scribble remarks next to your name.'

I did not know how to say no without offending him, so I equivocated, knowing that he would drop the idea when he was sober.

'You look like a wet weekend,' he said. 'Don't worry. I'll let you have a rematch.'

He did not know how sad I was. It was worse than he knew,

and it depressed me. He had been my only friend. I had nowhere else to go.

'Doesn't she know you're married?' Anne asked me, the night of Lady Max's dinner party.

'I'm sure I told her,' I said, hedging. But had I? 'I only met her once.'

'I don't understand why she didn't invite me.'

The flames were gone from the grate, and there was heat from the mass of coals, but little light. It was almost eight o'clock. I had sat with Anne while she had eaten—cold chicken and salad—and now she was drinking her customary cup of tea, sipping it neatly and looking comfortable in her big warm chair. She would read or watch television for an hour or so and then, growing sleepy, would crawl into bed.

Reflecting on this, I began to wish that I hadn't agreed to this late dinner with Lady Max. I was tired after a day of writing and I needed to rest, nestling against my wife in bed. These days I slept nine hours like that and in the morning, thinking of my novel, saw light breaking through the tree-tops of the jungle clearings.

I said, 'Would you have come with me if you'd been invited?'

'And sit in some stuffy house in the Boltons,' she said, suddenly defiant, 'listening to a lot of old bores droning on about poetry? No, thank you very much. I'd rather watch *Dallas*.'

Before I left the house I put my head into the boys' bedroom. The room was cool but the children seemed to radiate warmth, and this warmth from each small bed I associated with their good hearts. They still smelled soapily of their baths, and I kissed their warm cheeks and whispered good night. What is it in darkness that makes us whisper?

They were in that mild twilight of fatigue that was like sinking in warm water. Their breathing became shallower as they slipped softly from wakefulness into the depths of sleep.

'Why are you all dressed up, Dad?' Marcel asked.

'I'm going to see a lady. Lady Max.'

'See a fine lady on a white horse,' Louis said, calling softly from his bed. 'Is she rich?'

'Probably. I don't know. Money's not important here. Class is the thing,' I said, and was annoyed with myself when I realized I was quoting Musprat. 'You know, middle class. Upper class.'

'What class are we?'

'None. We don't care about that.' I wanted to say *I'm a spectator*, but I only half believed it. I wanted more.

The way the boys kissed me said that all was well between Anne and me.

When I left the room, I heard Marcel whispering across the room to Louis, 'I think we're middle class.'

Going out alone into the winter night took an effort of will, like crossing a frontier, because I was re-entering London after a full day in the fastness of my tall house.

It was such a quiet and gentle city at night, with shadows on its face; it was a city that slept, a city with a bed-time. And in this part of the city the skyline was old-fashioned chimney-pots, slate roofs and church spires. On these winter nights I had the illusion of being a part of it, an alien being swallowed by the city's shadows, and transformed.

I loved night-time London's sulphurous skies. At Chelsea Reach the light shimmering in the river had the watery dreamy quality of one of Whistler's *Nocturnes*. I was intensely conscious of where I was, and I thought of another trait that Londoners possessed: they could find their way around in the dark.

All this from the upper deck of the bus, sitting at the front window, with the sense of piloting a very old, low-flying plane.

Lady Max's house, a short walk from the bus-stop, was one of those newly painted cream-coloured Victorian façades, almost phosphorescent in the light of the street lamps, with tall bay windows and pale pillars at the top of an intimidating flight of stairs, in an empty corner of the square.

A small woman, with a pretty face and a nimble, simian way of walking, greeted me in a sing-song accent and took my coat. Another Filipino.

Imposing from the outside, the house was moribund within, like a walk-in sarcophagus. It was the foyer's marble floor, it was the dust, it was the brittle flowers and dry plants and gloomy pictures in ornate frames, it was most of all the temperature and the smell of decaying carpets. There was a chilly sullen lifelessness, as though no one had eaten or slept here for a long time. Just as I thought of my own warm house on the other side of the river I heard my name being called from a room beyond this foyer.

'Paul,' Lady Max cried out.

She remained in her chair in a queenly way. But she was so friendly and familiar I was encouraged, and she quickly introduced me to the people present, who were arrayed around the room. Graham Heavage smiled and showed no sign that he had rebuffed my willingness to write a lead review. There was an elderly novelist named Dunton Marwood, and a couple called Lasch from South Africa whose name I associated with anti-apartheid protests. There was a woman named Pippa who blinked repeatedly when she spoke, and the American poet, Walter Van Bellamy.

'My wife couldn't make it,' Bellamy explained to me, twirling his forefinger in a shock of his hair.

He was famously crazy and very tall, and when he drew me over to the fire—too close to the flames, he was crowding me—he smiled his wild staring smile and said, 'You're from Boston too.'

The fire burned but gave less heat than mine, which only smouldered. This one simply gasped in the chimney.

'I'm from Medford, actually.'

But Bellamy had a crazy man's deafness and distractedness, and the glazed eyes of someone on medication.

'We Bostonians have to stick together,' he said.

I was flattered until he squeezed my arm—too hard; it hurt, and conveyed more desperation than friendliness. He then lost all interest in me and staggered towards the bookshelves, where he pulled out a volume of his own poems.

'Max was just telling us about you, so you arrived on cue, as it were.'

This was Marwood, the novelist. I knew his name from the *New Statesman* fiction cupboard, and there were always stacks of his books at Gaston's. He was married to a rich woman whom no one knew and his reputation—although all my information was from Ian Musprat—was that of an envious and conceited bore.

'Are you working on a novel at the moment?' I asked.

'Good for you! I usually have to tell people that I'm a novelist. "You won't have heard of me," I say. "I write what's called quality fiction."'

'Not popular fiction?' Heavage said.

'God forbid,' Marwood said, but he was still nodding at me. 'I say, your new novel sounds splendid.'

My new novel? I said, 'My new book is non-fiction. *A Little Latitude.*'

'Not that,' Marwood said. 'The one you're working on. Sounds smashing.'

Lady Max was smiling at me, hearing everything, seeing everything: the world was naked and hid no secrets from her. But only then, seeing her regal smile, did I remember what I had told her.

'Stick to your own title,' Marwood said. 'Don't let Max put you off. She can be diabolical.'

So she had told them everything.

By then the serving woman had gone round with a tray and I had a drink in my hand.

Heavage stepped over to me. I braced myself to be addressed in French by him—and how would I reply? But in an entirely different and friendly voice he said, 'Super review,'—meaning last week's fiction round-up, in which I had slashed four novels. 'Did you take anything away with you?'

'I thought we agreed to wait until some good ones came along.'

He was unruffled, and did not respond.

'Keen on Henry James?' he said. 'There's a new edition of his letters. Vol. One just out. Supposed to be rather good, some fresh material. Might be fun, you and James, two expats.'

This was a different-sounding Graham Heavage, and he seemed to be offering me a lead piece, the sort of book that V. S. Pritchett usually reviewed. But tonight at Lady Max's, away from his desk at the paper, Heavage looked seedy and powerless. This man, who was naturally and smilingly rude, seemed a little silly and self-conscious trying to be friendly.

'Might give you the chance to talk about that very thing,' he said. 'Expatriation.'

Yes, he was offering me Henry James, a lead piece.

'I could let you have fifteen hundred words,' he said. 'Doesn't come out for ages. You could take your time.'

I said, a little too eagerly, 'I'd love to do it. Do you know that James was apparently hit in the groin by the whiplash of a fire-hose when he was about eighteen?'

'Goodness knows, you might want to animadvert on the implications of this unsolicited kick in the goolies,' Heavage said, without smiling, though Marwood sniggered and Bellamy laughed out loud.

I was certain that it was because he had met me here at Lady Max's that he had offered me the book, and that this laborious comedy from Heavage was a form of friendliness. It was hard for an Englishman of his pitiless sort to attempt generosity without being patronizing, but I did not mind. At least he wasn't speaking French to me in front of all these people.

Lady Max kept her distance, though each time I looked over at her she seemed to be staring at me. Sitting and smoking, she seemed completely in charge, and she was porcelain pretty, her skin so pale in the lovely way it often is with women in this sunless country.

I was disconcerted by her not speaking to me, and by her incongruity—she was so bright, so delicate in this big shadowy house—and I was disturbed by the fact that I could not smell food cooking. I slipped into the hall to look for the toilet. The Filipino woman, correctly guessing what I was looking for, pointed to the door when she saw me hesitating. There were more black shadows, and clammy walls and cold tiles, and again I wished I had stayed home. A satirical print by Rowlandson hung above the basin.

When I returned to the drawing-room, the guests were putting their coats on.

'We're going to dinner,' Lady Max said. 'It's right down the road.'

We trooped out to Brompton Road, to a French restaurant called La Tour Eiffel, and were shown to the sort of secluded wood-panelled private room that I associated with trysting couples or rowdy men. Over the windows hung dusty felt curtains with fat gold tassels. We handed over our coats, and Lady Max seated us. I was confused, and I wondered if the others were too. Mrs Lasch's head was down and she was whispering urgently to her husband. The woman named Pippa was on my right, Marwood on my left.

'Where is Walter Van Bellamy?' Lady Max said.

He had gone—vanished on the way—but Lady Max laughed and said it was just like him. 'He's crackers, you know. The real thing.'

A bored-looking French waiter in a much-too-tight shirt, with damp hair and a hot face, entered the little room and gave us menus and then listed the day's specials and the no-longer-available dishes, speaking in a parody French accent.

Pippa said, 'My menu is sticky. I can't stand that,' and made a face.

'Shall we have some wine?'—Lady Max was addressing the waiter. 'The house wine comes in a filthy carafe and tastes like nail-varnish remover. Two bottles of Meursault, make it three, and you can bring them now.'

She became a brisk attentive hostess from her vantage point at the head of the table. There was a tension of authority in the way she sat, in the angle of her body. She was twitching, alert, full of suggestions.

After the wine was poured, the waiter took up his pad saying, 'And in addition, zere are fresh lobstairs zis ivneen. Zay are not on ze meenue.'

'Not real lobsters,' Lady Max said, shivering as though offended by the word. 'They're just these pathetic little discoloured crayfish from Scotland.'

The waiter simply clicked his ball-point.

'But the potted shrimps are super.'

We all ordered the potted shrimps.

'And the jugged hare,' Lady Max said, and muttered the name in French and sort of licked her lips.

'*Civet de Lievre*,' Heavage said in his pedantic accent.

Lady Max smiled at Heavage—a smile of disapproval—and said, 'They do it with chestnuts here.'

Most of us ordered that too, except Pippa, who was a vegetarian (hearing her announce it, Marwood sighed impatiently). She conferred nervously with the waiter and finally settled on ratatouille.

'And I will bring a selection of vegetables,' the waiter said.

'If you must,' Lady Max said. She lit a cigarette and dismissed him, exhaling and flinging smoke at him with her fingers in a witch-like gesture. 'They do fuss so, and they don't mean a word of it.'

We chatted among ourselves until Pippa called out to Lady Max, 'Do you often have supper here?'

'What is supper? Is it something you eat?' Lady Max said.

Pippa made a terse explanation of the word.

'Surely this is dinner?' Lady Max said.

'Working-class people have supper,' Marwood said.

'Working-class is a euphemism I just adore,' Lady Max said.

The waiter began serving the potted shrimps: a small ceramic dish of pink bubbly paste, with a stack of toast. As we spread it on the toast, Lady Max, still smoking, said, 'I do hate being served promptly. It's like rudeness and I always think it means there's something wrong with the food.'

'I come to that conclusion when the menu's sticky,' Pippa said.

'Tea is a meal for them. Dinner is lunch,' Marwood said. 'I know this through my staff. They have "afters".'

'They are extraordinary,' Lady Max said. 'I always think inventing these ridiculous names for meals is a way of saving money on food.'

'And,' Heavage added in an announcing way, 'they go to the toilet.'

He was at the teasing and silly stage of drunkenness—the teasing that turned cruel and then sadistic. 'That is, working-class people.'

Lady Max smiled disgustedly. She said, 'I cannot stand that word. Does anyone actually say it?'

We laughed, everyone except Pippa, to please the hostess, as though none of us actually used the word.

'Toilets is an anagram of T. S. Eliot,' Mr Lasch said, but no one heard, because Marwood was indignant again.

'And "cheers" is another one I hate,' he said.

Hearing him, or rather mishearing him, Heavage said, 'Cheers,' and emptied his glass.

Looking at me, Lady Max said, 'I love the expression "white trash". Americans are so graphic. Do you suppose we could introduce it here?'

'I'm sorry but I find this whole conversation quite objectionable,' Pippa said.

Marwood leaned in front of me and and put his face against Pippa's and said, 'Miss Lower-Middle-Class-And-She-Knows-It is trying to be the sincere proletarian again.'

'Of course, with the help of your staff, you're an authority on the subtle nuances of class,' Pippa said, blinking but standing her ground.

'Yes, and rather more than I'm given credit for by second-rate book reviewers,' Marwood said, making it obvious that at some point Pippa had given one of his novels an unfavourable review.

'Someone, I think it was a shop-girl, said, "You're welcome" to me the other day,' Lady Max said, ending the stand-off between Marwood and Pippa.

'What a ridiculous American expression,' Heavage said.

'"Have a nice day,"' Mr Lasch said to his wife, who replied, 'Sorry, I have other plans.'

But no one took any notice of them, because Lady Max was saying, '"You're welcome" is not ridiculous at all. It's an effective response. Say "thank you" in England and the other person simply mutters and chews his lips.'

'I suppose it's no worse than *prego*,' Heavage said. 'It's less objectionable than *bitte*. It's rather like *pozhal'st.*'

'You've lost us,' Mr Lasch said.

'One of those useful and happily ambiguous expressions like "I'd like to see more of you,"' Lady Max said, and she smiled at me.

Then the jugged hare was served. It came in an earthenware crock submerged with carrots and chestnuts in a brown stew. The waiter hurried back and forth, sighing, laying out the dishes of vegetables, and when he waited on me his whole body radiated sweaty heat, and I could hear him breathing impatiently.

'Bring more wine,' Lady Max said.

'Thank you,' the waiter said.

'You're welcome,' Lady Max said. 'You see?'

We were still on language. We discussed the correct pronunciation of certain English names, such as Marylebone and Theobalds and Cholmondeley. This, I guessed, was all for my benefit.

Mr Lasch spelled the word Featherstonehaugh and said, 'Fanshaw.'

Marwood smiled and said, 'I've got one. It looks like "Woolfardisworthy".'

'Woolsey,' Pippa said, and turned her cold eyes on him.

'My grandfather pronounced the word "leisure" the American way,' Lady Max said, with another glance at me. 'Leezhah.'

In a solicitous, almost servile way, Marwood asked, 'How is your daughter, Allegra?'

'Flourishing,' Lady Max said. 'That foolish Persian, Mr Pieplate—well, that's what I call him—is still chasing her. He took her to an embassy party and she deliberately wore a transparent lace dress—absolutely in the noddy underneath. It scandalized the Muslims there and it drove him wild. He doesn't even know she's sixteen years old. What an ass he is.'

'She might fall for him,' Marwood said.

'Lucky old Pieplate, if she did. But it won't happen. Allegra's much too heartless. They all are. That's why I don't worry about her. It's her loss. And I know how she feels. At her age I was being squired around by Boothby.'

'Wasn't he a bit fruity?' Heavage asked.

'He was, but not exclusively. Anyway I fended him off.'

She said *orf* as she had said *lorse*.

Her mention of Lord Boothby turned the conversation to the Kray twins and a lot of sixties gossip about the Profumo affair. Again I felt this was for my benefit, as though the dinner were a little seminar on English life that Lady Max had arranged for me.

Seeing a new waiter approach, Lady Max said, 'Another

waiter, another course. And this one has the implacable look of dessert on his face.'

The waiter showed no sign that he had heard this. He said, 'Shall I bring the trolley?'

'It will just be stale gâteau and puddings and sticky buns on wheels.' She was not facing the waiter when she added, 'Why don't you just *flambé* some crêpes for us. There's a good chap.'

For the next twenty minutes the waiter laboured at his portable grill, first making the crêpes—seven of them—and then folding them in a silver dish. He methodically made the sauce, scorching sugar cubes with melted butter in a frying pan and then sousing the crêpes with it. He splashed gouts of Grand Marnier on to them after that, and set them on fire. He then rearranged them on individual plates, still spooning sauce, and served them.

This elaborate procedure killed conversation. We started eating the crêpes and when Pippa made a remark about them ('Delicious. This is only the second time in my life . . . '), Lady Max cut her off, as though it were bad manners to comment on the food.

'Queen Mum's out of hospital today, bless her,' Lady Max said.

'The Royal Barge,' Heavage said, frowning drunkenly.

'I know several of her intimates,' Lady Max said. 'They call her "Cake", you know, behind her back, and I do think it suits her. Her staff are exclusively poofs. One night she got on the phone to them—they were in the kitchen—and she said, "I don't know about the queens down there but this queen wants a drink!"'

It was well after midnight—you knew it from the gloomy resentment on the waiters' faces as they ostentatiously stood around after liqueurs and coffee. They had missed the last tube trains. There was only the chance of an irregular night bus from now on.

The bill, folded in half, had been resting on a saucer at Lady Max's elbow since coffee. She had taken no notice of it.

At last, exhaling smoke on it, she poked it open with her fingers and said, 'I'm terrible at maths. What is ninety-six divided by seven?'

Ninety-six pounds was the amount of my monthly mortgage

payment, and it seemed incredible to me that we had gobbled up a whole mortgage payment. And worse, that I was being asked to pay my share. I remembered Lady Max saying *Bring more wine.*

'Is service included?' Marwood asked.

'Call it fourteen each,' Heavage said.

The Lasches had gone pale, their faces displaying the agony I felt.

'And a quid each for the tip.' Heavage dropped the bill.

'Fifteen even.' Marwood began poking through banknotes in a leather pouch.

Fifteen pounds. It was what I was paid for a book review. Heavage knew that but did not seem to care. I pretended to look through my wallet, but I knew when I heard the figure that I did not have it, nor any sum near it, and neither did Pippa, and this inspired in me a sort of kinship with her. She wrote Lady Max a cheque, and so did Mr Lasch. I fingered a crisp five-pound note. I had some coins but needed them for the bus.

'I'll have to owe you the rest,' I said.

'I'll collect it one way or another,' Lady Max said.

The bus went only as far as the depot at the south end of Battersea Bridge, and so without enough money for another bus fare I walked the rest of the way home in a drizzling mist, kicking the paving stones.

The only certainty in my London life was my writing. I felt this was a way for me to make a place for myself in the city. Although the novel I was writing was a jungle book it was penetrated with London. It was my London work. And I wondered whether the opposite might be true. If I wrote a London story in New Guinea would the book seem jungly and over-bright?

The next day I needed to sit down alone and write. Anne had asked without much interest how the evening had gone and I said fine.

'Rich food, small talk, gossip and indigestion. I didn't even get drunk.'

'I'm glad I stayed at home,' she said.

I somewhat envied her her indifference. It was the reason she could be so serene. I was obnoxiously curious about everything but had to pretend not to be, since it was so unEnglish to be nosy, and to ask probing questions.

I said almost nothing else to her about the strange meal —Lady Max's Dutch treat. I concealed my embarrassment, because I could not tell her the whole truth. How could I tell Anne these misleading details until I knew everything myself? This was a story without an ending, without even a middle. I felt sure there would be more. There would be consequences.

I sat down and continued my novel, as I did every day. I wrote a paragraph that day and a few pages the next. If I wrote nothing in the morning I provoked myself to write something after lunch. And on the days when I wrote well I often turned aside and did a review—I had time for it because I had done my own work first. That week, after I made headway with my book, I read the first volume of *The Letters of Henry James* and wrote notes for what I hoped would be a lead review.

When I was stumped in my writing I wandered around the damp garden behind my house, peering at plants. I tore old birds' nests apart to see how they had been made. I watched spiders feeding, and ants hurrying and snails dragging themselves in their own spittle across the bricks. I put these London creatures into my Central American jungle. I observed a trickle of water and, for my fiction, turned it into a river, with mud-slides and ox-bows.

Sometimes in the black late afternoon, before the pubs opened, I walked—thinking with my feet. *Walking the streets*, I murmured to myself as I was doing it. There were gaps in the day that baffled and intimidated me.

Musprat called, but I put him off. I did not want to be drawn into his life—the disorderly flat, the hasty meals, his intrusive borrowing and bitching, his writer's block and wasted evenings at the Lambourne Club.

I wrote my book. I lived in my house. I loved my family. I had no other life in London, and indeed had not realized there was another life to be had, until Lady Max called again.

'Paul—is that you, dear boy?'

It was affectation, not fooling, and her voice was

unmistakable, dark brown with cigarette smoke. I was alarmed, fearing another of her meals.

But no, she was calling to collect what I owed her. She used those very words. She said I had to go with her to the William Blake exhibition at the Tate Gallery.

'I'll meet you there inside the foyer in about an hour,' she said.

So this was the form my repayment would take. But I had done my work for the day. I did not feel I was being deceitful to Anne, though it was unfair to my sons—I knew that I would not be in the house when they returned home from school. I would miss Marcel making tea and Louis asking, *What page are you on, Dad?* For that I resented Lady Max's sudden presumption and her insistent *Be there.*

She was late. Londoners who regarded themselves as powerful were seldom punctual, though they always expected you to be. She arrived in a taxi and she looked rather small, mounting the wet black steps alone. But this was a passing illusion. I had always seen her in the company of other people, and when I was next to her I felt very plain and out of step, an American again.

Lady Max had hardly greeted me. She said, 'I love being in a museum on a rainy afternoon.'

It was not rain but low cloud, the mist and drizzle of a London winter that made the dark city even blacker.

'There's only one better place to be,' she said. We were passing a sensual Rodin sculpture, all muscles and bumps, a couple entwined, like a big bronze walnut. 'Between the sheets, and preferably not alone.'

She had a knack for uttering statements to which there was no reply. It was like a verbal form of snooker in which I was left holding the cue, unable to use it.

We passed a set of big flat Motherwells, all black shapes like moth-eaten shadows, a slashed and assertively striped Rauschenberg, a Hockney interior that sloped in three directions, a soft sculpture like a big toy, a rusty bike hung on wires, and a triptych the size of three billboards surfaced entirely with broken crockery.

The Blakes were behind this frivolity, in a darkened

exhibition room in low lighted showcases. Walking just behind Lady Max in the darkness I felt her warmth, and her perfume stung my eyes with sweetness. Her white face, her full lips, her large eyes, were reflected in the glass, layered with scenes from *The Marriage of Heaven and Hell.*

'Ruskin called him a primitive,' Lady Max said.

'So unfair. He had great technique, subtle colour, and a kind of visionary quality. Look at that composition of flesh and spirit.'

'Everyone says that about Blake.' She had not even paused or turned.

But this was a standard London put-down, the accusation that you were being hopelessly unoriginal. *Everyone says that.* It sounded cruel, but it was just another move in a chess game. In my earlier years in London I would have hated her for saying it. Now I saw it as glibly defensive—a weak kind of teasing—and she would mock me if I reacted. The London response was not to complain but to do it back and do it better.

'Everyone says it, because it's so obvious and because it's true,' I said. 'Ruskin was the weirdo, if you ask me. Not Blake. Ruskin was shocked by his wife's pubic hair. He thought she was the only woman in the world who had it, like a physical abnormality.'

'There is so much more to Ruskin than that,' Lady Max said.

'But the rest isn't as interesting,' I said.

She liked that. 'I rather like the nympholepsy. He adored little girls.'

'Kiddie porn,' I said.

'You sound so shocked. And yet Ruskin was an incredible romantic.' She was staring down at the Blakes. 'Speaking of pubic hair. Some people shave it into peculiar designs.'

'And some people twine marigolds into it,' I said, 'according to D. H. Lawrence.'

'That's such a silly book,' Lady Max said. 'It's completely unbelievable. It's all Lawrence's lurid fantasies about the English class system—virile gamekeeper, sex-mad aristocrat, emasculated lord. And apart from anything else it gives an utterly inaccurate picture of oral sex technique.'

She was bent over a lighted case of Blake etchings, her face shining at God the Father holding a set of gold compasses among jubilant angels and puffy clouds.

'She could hardly have sucked him off playing with his old job as though it were a cocktail sausage.'

She said *orf* again, slightly dignifying the shocking expression. A shadowy man nearby grunted with unease and disapproval.

Though we were still in the darkened room and I could not see Lady Max's face, I had the impression she was smiling.

'The sexual virtuosity in your novels is much more impressive than Lawrence's.'

This was certainly an advance on *You're much better than Hugh Walpole.*

'Sexual description is the greatest test of literary ability, I always think.'

What was the reply to this?

'The way you handle sodomy,' she said.

My mouth had gone dry.

'You have marvellous penetration,' she said.

Snookered.

'William Blake got married in a church near here,' she said. 'Want to see it?'

She took charge and we were soon outside, in the wet air, walking along the embankment next to the whitish depthless water, which seemed turbulent today.

'There was once a prison here,' she said, at the river's edge. 'Millbank. James described it in *The Princess Casamassima.*'

I had just reviewed a Henry James book and did not know that.

'Notice how the river seems to be flowing upstream?' she said.

It was true—a burst cushion, a broken branch and bits of plastic foam were floating towards Vauxhall Bridge.

'That's because it *is* flowing upstream,' she said. 'It's all tidal as far as Richmond, you know. People in London are for ever staring at the river, but they never see its real character, that its

current changes direction four times a day.'
As she spoke she raised a gloved hand.
'I can't walk any further in these shoes.'
They were the ones Musprat had called her *fuck me* shoes.

Her hailing a cab made me feel useless. And after the privacy, the intimacy of the taxi—the driver isolated, her hand resting on my thigh—there was something unexpected and punitive in the way she stepped out after the short ride and walked on, leaving me to pay the fare. In my confusion I gave the driver an absurdly large tip; he made a mocking noise at me to indicate that he was not impressed.

The church, St Mary's Battersea, was situated directly on the south bank of the river, next to a flour mill and a public house, the Old Swan, the houseboats and brick façades of Chelsea just across the water. The church was in a perfect place, surrounded by light and water, with a Thames sailing barge moored just beside it. Just upriver, above the black railway bridge, the sun was breaking from behind some smoky clouds.

'Ken Tynan showed me this church,' she said. 'It's Georgian. Such a beauty.'

'Tynan the theatre critic?' I asked, unlatching the large church door for her and holding it open.

'And fetishist,' she said, entering the church.

We passed under a low wood-panelled choir loft to an aisle glowing with patches of colour from the light of the stained glass windows. I picked up a leaflet from a side table and saw that Blake had indeed been married here, that Turner had visited, and more.

'Benedict Arnold is buried here, I see.'

'Arnold the brave hero.'

'Arnold the wicked spy.'

'Don't be so predictable.'

I approached the pretty altar and pulpit, thinking how orderly they were. Though somewhat unadorned they were not severe: they had a purity of design, a spareness that had spirit and strength. Lady Max began talking again and looking away.

'The rest of the time, Tynan was gadding about in women's clothes,' she said. 'He had mirrors on the ceiling of his bedroom.

He said to me once, "Have you ever tried soft flage?" I suppose he meant gentle spankings. He had well-thumbed copies of *Rubber News*. This is authentic Georgian, you know.'

She was working her way along the smooth carved pews to the altar rail.

'Is he dead, Tynan?'

'Oh no. He's very ill, but that doesn't stop him,' Lady Max said. 'These days he dabbles in urolagnia with eleven-year-old girls. What do you call it? Golden showers—something like that? I adore these exquisite finials. What's wrong?'

I shook my head, because what was there to say?

'I'm telling you things you need to know.'

'About sex?'

'About London,' she said. 'The love and knowledge of London is in all the great English novels. You're funny. You don't know how good you are, or how great you can be. Now I must go.'

We left the church and walked along Vicarage Crescent to find a taxi.

'Wilson lived there,' she said in front of a two-storey house made of grey brick. 'A vastly underrated painter and great naturalist. He died at the South Pole with Scott.'

Just before she got into the taxi she said, 'I have my accountant tomorrow, so we'll have to meet on Thursday. I'll ring you.'

She did not touch me—the English seldom touched—and that left me feeling even more flustered, in the cloud of her taxi's foul exhaust.

When Thursday came I agreed to meet her in Mortlake that afternoon. As a consequence I had a productive morning writing my novel and, stirred by her talk, I looked forward to seeing her.

The Mortlake excursion was to another church, a Catholic one. In the high-walled churchyard was Sir Richard Burton's tomb, a marble monument in the shape of an Arabian tent.

'This grave has never appeared in any novel of London,' she said. 'I'm giving it to you.'

I read the plaque and began to tell Lady Max how Burton had explored unknown parts of Utah, but she interrupted.

'Because of the polygamy among Mormons there,' she said. 'Burton was sex-mad, but he combined it with scholarship and a love of languages. That's why he translated the *Kama Sutra*, and he was fascinated by fetishes.'

There in the quiet churchyard of St Mary Magdalene, she spoke about some episodes she'd had with men she had known as a girl—older men in every case—and how they had involved some sort of whipping, 'and not soft flage, I can tell you.' The men had been canted over chairs while she had slashed at their buttocks, cutting them with a dog whip.

Then she giggled and pushed a branch aside and said, 'It's all school nonsense. Some Englishmen never get over it.'

'What about English women?'

'We're all sorts, but the most effective kind are matrons —like our new prime minister. Bossy and reliable, with big hospitable bosoms.'

She put her hands on her hips and faced me, but I kept my distance.

That day we finished up at Richmond Park, looking at deer. The following day we met at the London Library, which was a private, hushed, club-like place. Musprat was always mentioning it. Lady Max insisted that I become a member there and then, and I did, writing a cheque for the thirty-pound annual membership fee and making a mental note that I might have to transfer funds so as not to be overdrawn.

After a weekend—Saturday shopping, Sunday outing to Box Hill—I met Lady Max at Blackfriars and she took me across the river to see some rotting Dickensian warehouses at Shad Thames.

'All of these wonderful old buildings will be renovated and made into hideous little flats for awful people one day.'

That week we went to Strawberry Hill, to Hogarth's house in Chiswick, to World's End, to the room Van Gogh had rented in Brixton, to the Sir John Soane Museum. I had crossed Lincolns Inn Fields thirty times and had never been aware of this lovely house that had been converted into a museum of exotic treasures. Often I would be looking at a gable, or some fretwork, or a picture, while she monologued in her off-hand way about something totally unconnected, usually sexual.

'I thought I had seen everything,' I would say.

'Yes, Sir John actually collected these artefacts himself.'

'I mean, about what you just said about—what's the word?'

'Oh that. *Frottage*. It's just French for rubbing. Very subtle. Not very popular. Takes ages. Who has the time, my dear?' And she turned to an inked sheet of petroglyphs. 'I much prefer that rubbing.'

At Turpentine Lane in Victoria she pointed out the fact that the houses had no front doors, and in what perhaps seemed to her a logical progression but was surely a *non-sequitur*, added, 'And I never wear knickers.'

She deconstructed for me (the word was just becoming fashionable among reviewers that year) the Albert Memorial and said, 'You should put this thing into a story some time.' Then she went on to tell me how, after the death of Albert, Queen Victoria developed a passion for her Scottish footman, John Brown.

'But why shouldn't she? Life is short, and passionate people should have what they want. It makes the world go round, and no one is hurt.'

I felt that was true, but she said it with no passion at all.

That day, walking to Kensington Gore from the Albert Memorial, she said, 'I don't live far from here. You could see me home.'

She took me by a circuitous route, to show me where Stephen Crane had lived off Gloucester Road.

'His common-law wife had been a prostitute, but you know that,' she said.

I said yes, but the true answer was no.

'She owned a brothel called the Hotel de Dream in Jacksonville, Florida,' Lady Max said. 'It's perfect, isn't it? But you're much better than Crane.'

She walked briskly—in different shoes—and wore a long black coat and a velvet hat, and she kept slightly ahead of me. Then her great creamy house loomed, looking more weatherbeaten than when I had first seen it—there were patches of yellow water stains near some decayed gutters and broken downspouts.

At the front gate she said, 'Won't you come in?'

129

It was a winter afternoon, blackening into early dusk.

'I should be moving along. I have to be home by six.'

She did not hear my excuses. She batted at some trailing leafless wires of clematis and said, 'This has all got to be cut back.'

I was still hesitating. She lit a cigarette.

'See me to the door,' she said. 'Don't worry. I'm not going to eat you.'

Fixed to the door was a big brass knocker, very tarnished, of a turtle with a tiny head. You banged its shell.

'I'm not worried,' I said. It was impossible not to sound worried when uttering this sentence.

'I have the feeling there is something you want—in your life, in your writing,' she said.

She released the cigarette smoke from her mouth, but with so little force that blue trails of it encircled her head.

'What is it?'

I was restless and a bit fearful standing with her in this vast portico of blistered paint. She had exhausted me with her talk, though she was still bright, as though she had drawn off all my energy. I looked into the little square of the Boltons. I seriously wondered whether there was anything I wanted. My life seemed whole and orderly; there was no emptiness anywhere in it, and so little yearning.

'I've always gotten everything I've wanted.'

'That makes two of us,' Lady Max said.

I smiled. What more was there to say?

'That is what I'm asking you,' she said. 'What is it you want now?'

'Very little,' I said, surprised that I said it.

'Then it must be something crucial,' Lady Max said.

'I wish my writing was more visible. I work hard doing reviews and they're buried in the back of the paper. My book reviews are these round-ups, three or four at a time. I'd like a *solus* review. I'm very happy, really. But I'm indoors all the time. That's why I like these outings of ours, I suppose. I don't have any friends.'

She said, 'That's the proof you're a real writer. How could

you write so much or so well and still maintain your friendships?'

It was what I had often said to rationalize my empty afternoons. I liked Lady Max better for defending me this way.

'But you consider me your friend?'

'Sure.'

'Then you have plenty of well-wishers,' she said, 'and you will have everything you want.'

What could I say to this? I stammered and tried to begin, but she cut me off.

'It's time for you to go home,' she said, as though making the decision for me.

I kissed her cheek.

'I get a kiss,' she said, stating it to the darkness behind me.

But I couldn't tell whether this was gratitude or mockery, and I realized even then that I did not know her.

Sometimes it is only when you turn your back on it that the world gives you what you want.

In a very short time I came to hate Lady Max's promises. I had been content until she made them, but now I disliked myself for hoping. Was it that she had made me want something I felt was unattainable, and that I did not really deserve? No, it was just a matter of *Don't ask*. What you want should be your secret, not spoken aloud. Revealing it had made me feel lonely.

Trying hard not to think about it, I avoided seeing Lady Max. That made life easier. She called three times, and she was sharp and insistent, and I was just dumb and unwilling. It was not only a question of my pride. I had work to do. I turned my back on Lady Max and London. This woman and the world seemed like much the same thing.

I wrote all day at my desk, until the boys returned home. I bought the *Standard* when the Fishmonger's Arms opened. I sat and drank and read, and after a pint or two I went home and made dinner for Anne and the boys. There were whole days when no one spoke to me—days of great serenity and isolation—and I wondered whether this was because I had become a Londoner, or because I was a true alien.

Then one evening the barman in the Fish said, 'Terrible about Jerry,' assuming that I knew.

He had not known me, but I had known Jerry Scully. I went to Jerry's funeral out of curiosity, because I had never seen a cremation in London. And also I wanted to test my anonymity. My going to this service on a weekday morning in London was a form of open espionage.

I did not like him much. He sat under the dartboard that no one used and often grunted at the television. He was a carpenter, a 'chippy', he called himself, a Derry Catholic who could whip himself into a fury in seconds merely at the mention of British troops, or at the sight of a British soldier on the six o'clock news. Watching Jerry, or listening to his talk, I understood the ambushes, the girls who were tarred and feathered for dating British soldiers, the heartless bombings, the fathers shot in front of their children. Jerry approved, Jerry was violent. Now and then I would hear an English person say *What sort of monster puts these bombs in places where they'll kill innocent people?* and I smiled because I knew. It was Jerry.

I happened to be sitting near him once when Prince Charles appeared on the screen. Jerry began to spit. 'Fucking bastard,' he said, with real feeling. I often overheard him, and most of his talk was blaming. In Jerry's eyes, Jerry was Ireland.

But really, Jerry Scully was a Londoner. He lived in a terrace of alms-houses that had been converted to council houses. He was paid in cash for his carpentry and he also drew the dole; he lived alone, his nose dripped, he was nearsighted and wore old wire-rimmed National Health specs, and when he was not drunk he was tremulous and uncertain, his eyes goggling in thick lenses. Thirty years in Clapham.

He shouted when he was drunk, and lately he had complained of a sore throat. He was someone for whom drink was a remedy as well as a sickness. Drink made him ill, and then it made him well. He drank more and his sore throat developed a painful lump that no amount of drinking could ease. He found swallowing difficult, though he could still shout hoarsely at the television set in the Fish. The doctor gave him tablets for his throat, and when these had no effect Jerry saw another doctor, who diagnosed throat cancer, and at last a specialist who told him there was nothing that could be done. He stopped going to the Fish. It seemed a very short time later that the barman said, 'Terrible about Jerry.'

In accordance with his wishes, he was cremated at the cemetery in Earlsfield, on the number 19 bus route, and all the stalwarts from the pub showed up, looking pale and shaky in the thin February light. Some of them looked downright ruined, as though they too were suffering a fatal illness. They had that fearful and unsteady—almost senile—look of dry drunks in the daytime, before the pubs open, and they looked lost here on Trinity Road, so far from the Fish.

There were wreaths on the steps of the red brick crematorium—bouquets wrapped in cellophane, and flower baskets, all with messages to Jerry. One was from Mick, the landlord of the Fish. The strangest flower arrangement was a tankard of beer, two feet high, marigolds representing lager, daisies as froth. The men smiled at it, but not because it was clever. One said, 'Jerry wouldn't touch that.' Jerry drank Guinness.

Filing into the chapel I heard a wheezing man in front of me say, 'These days I get home pissed and want kinky but me missus won't play.'

A small organ was gasping a ponderous hymn. We were handed booklets indicating the details of the crematorium service, and a short sermon was given by a man who, in this glorified furnace, was more a stoker than a priest. He spoke of the immortality of Jerry's soul and the frailty of human flesh, the brevity of our time on earth and our vanity in thinking that earthly successes mattered. Hearing this, I had a sense of Jerry's being precious and indestructible, and that he had carried the secret of his soul around with him all these years. We prayed for Jerry and ourselves, and afterwards Mick opened the Fish early so that we could have a drink. The drinks were free, so opening the pub at ten-thirty was legal.

Lying on the bar of the Fish that day was the early edition of the *Evening Standard*, the one that all the gamblers bought for the horse races, and in the 'Londoner's Diary' column there was a photograph of my face and a short paragraph, with the headline AMERICAN AUTHOR CONTENT TO LIVE IN LONDON, as though it were news.

It was a comment on a quotation from my book review of the Henry James letters—though I had no idea that it had been published. I had said in an aside that I regarded London as 'the most habitable big city in the world,' and that the fact that I lived here was proof that I meant it. The diary item mentioned that I was not one of those Anglophile American professors in stiff matching Burberrys who spent the summer swanking in Belgravia. No, I was a hard-working refugee writing my head off in Clapham. The photograph, printed small and smudgily, flattered me.

I read this three times while the others (who did not know me and would not pay any attention to this section of the *Standard*) reminisced about Jerry. I could not say why but I felt there was a close connection between this gratuitous little paragraph about me, and dead Jerry Scully—perhaps it had been the preacher's speaking about the vanity of earthly success. I was aware of being absurdly pleased.

And there was more. Reading the diary item I was reminded that I had not seen the review I had written. I went next door to Patel's and bought the *New Statesman*. My name was printed large on the cover of the magazine, as large as the prime minister's (the subject of another article), and my piece was the lead for the week, the most prominent book review I had written.

I often had the feeling that only two people cared about any book review, only two people read it—the reviewer and the reviewed. It was public correspondence, a letter from one to the other that no one else read. Sometimes—certainly in London —there was a reply, when the reviewed turned reviewer, answering back, but this was Henry James: did anyone else care?

From time to time Musprat called to say he had seen a piece of mine, but he would use the occasion to tell me he had writer's block. No one else ever commented. But the day after the *New Statesman* appeared Anne said, 'Several people at work today mentioned your review.'

It was a scholarly book. My review had not been brilliant

and I doubted whether people had actually read it. But they had seen my name. The point was that I was now visible. I had been buried in the back pages before.

Heavage called me that same week and offered me a new book by Walter Van Bellamy. Had he remembered that I had met Bellamy at Lady Max's? It was *Alarm and Despondency*, Bellamy's first public mention of being treated for depression. It had to be a favourable review, but a thoughtful one, ruminative, discursive. There was nothing crooked about book reviewing, but often a good book was helped on its way, and the reviewer—in helping—rode along with it.

'I think you'll do it rather well,' Heavage said. 'I can give you fifteen hundred words.'

Space was money—the more column inches, the larger the cheque. This was another lead review, and (because of Bellamy, not me) it was widely read and quoted. It seemed I was now publicly associated with him.

I was asked to be on the radio to discuss Bellamy's book, on *Kaleidoscope*, which was presented by a small yellow-eyed man in a stained cardigan, who had a powerful growly voice and who belittled Bellamy's poems while seeming to praise them. He then asked me leading questions about the book and after a few minutes thanked me out loud, saying my full name. After a burst of music—it was 'I Like New York in June'—he said, 'And now another, curiously different American,' and began discussing the new Woody Allen movie. For this I was paid twenty pounds.

Never mind the fee—'money for jam', as Musprat used to say—the fact was that I had begun to exist in London. In my first years in London my agent had arranged for me to see a producer at *Kaleidoscope*—the idea was that I might become a regular contributor—and I had been rebuffed. It was important for me to have at last appeared on the programme, because I now saw its triviality.

Was triviality the key to success? After the programme, many people mentioned that they had heard me, among them Walter Van Bellamy.

'Dear boy'—he was in a good mood—'I heard you on the wireless.'

He invited me to tea at the Charing Cross Hotel. I wondered whether it might be another of his batty ideas, and I also suspected that he might not come. But there he was, big and wild-haired, standing in the lobby, ten minutes early.

'This was once very grand,' he said, frowning at the worn cushions of the chairs in the lobby, as the Spanish waiter set out the tea things. He was silent a moment. 'More and more I find this city insupportable.'

I was smiling. 'I've just started to like it here.'

'Tell me why.' He fixed his eyes on me like a headmaster and stared until I spoke.

'My work is going well.'

'That I understand.'

'And this city's being good to me. I am making some friends. I have a sense of belonging that I didn't have before.'

'Yes,' he said tentatively. It was not approving. I recognized the tone. He was not happy but he was giving me the benefit of the doubt. He suspected that I was kidding myself. He was exasperated and impatient, but there was too much to say for him to attempt to analyse. My mention of friends made him doubtful—perhaps a little envious and sceptical. All this he put into his *yes*.

'When you first come to London it seems huge—as big as England itself. With each passing year it shrinks around you, until it is a very tight fit—your house, your room, your desk. Your art.'

He poured the tea—milk first, then tea, then sugar. He stirred, and his stirring was like a process of thought.

'I think about people who play with art. Some people in London do it. They are glamoured by it. Don't play with art.'

I wondered whether he meant this personally. Surely he knew better. It was obvious that I worked very hard. I guessed that he was on a medication that was making him serious and single-minded.

He said, 'Who do you see in London?'

It was a sudden question. Yes, he had been provoked by my mention of friends.

'Do you know Ian Musprat, the poet?'

'He doesn't exist,' Bellamy said. 'Not as a poet.'

'His last book won a prize.'

'There are more prizes in this country than there are writers to give them to. Name me an English writer who hasn't won a prize!'

He said this very loudly, curling his lips in triumph, and hooting afterwards. Perhaps his medication was wearing off.

Finally I said, 'And Lady Max. She's a friend.'

'Oh, God,' Bellamy said.

He gave me a twisted smile of disgust, then he sipped some tea and recovered.

'It struck me the other day that the British government ought to sell titles at the post office. They could do it the way they sell television licences. A little booklet with a grid of spaces. You buy stamps, a few at a time, and when you've filled it up you hand it in and get your M.B.E. Two booklets for an O.B.E. Three for a knighthood.'

This little description cheered him up.

'What is a title?' he said. 'What does it mean?'

I said lamely, 'I was only wondering what you thought of her—Lady Max.'

'Years ago, when one first came to London and was being introduced, as it were, when one was impressionable, then one was a bit dazzled. But one was never glamoured by her.'

I saw him to his train and walked home a little shaken by this talk with Bellamy. I had expected him to be crazed and colourful, but this was a sobering talk—a sort of warning. It was clear that he did not approve of Lady Max. And it seemed that he was implying that my new visibility as a writer in London suggested triviality. His warning had been *Don't play with art.*

And he had put me on the defensive. People often did that when they had something to conceal. The more I thought about it, the surer I felt that he had known her in the past. What had she done to him?

But I had turned my back on the world, on Lady Max.

This was in mid-February. I was still working hard on my novel and I had now been writing it for a full year, dating my pages. I wrote two or three pages a day. It was a solemn moment when I realized that a year ago I was sitting here doing exactly the same thing, and still I was not done—not even close. Yet I was not so impatient to finish that I wanted to hurry it and fail to enjoy its surprises, its growth, its improvement—writing, polishing, rereading and moving on.

What had changed? Lady Max had looked into my heart and stirred something and woken it with a word—had made that little animal sit up and beg, then rewarded it with a biscuit. Good dog. Beyond the routine of the day, which I had found satisfying, I had wanted recognition. And I had innocently imagined ways of being recognized—a lead review, my face on an advertisement, mentions in newspaper diaries.

Soon, unexpected rewards came my way—more biscuits—and, surprised and delighted, I began to wag my tail.

The Sunday Times Magazine ran an interview with Sir George Limebaugh, the banker. In the accompanying photograph —a portrait by Lord Snowdon—a copy of one of my novels lay next to a bunch of flowers on Sir George's coffee table, the book title and my name pleasingly visible.

People said, *Now I know who Sir George curls up with.* It was a little miracle, and there were more. A few days later a book of mine was shown on a bookshelf in an ad for Habitat furniture. Another book was mentioned in a celebrity column called *On My Bedside Table.*

These were better, more noticeable, than good reviews and, naturally, people mentioned them. Several of the people were publishers, interested in my next book. Another little miracle: a letter from a movie company in Wardour Street wishing to take out a film option on *The Last Man.*

When had I revealed that title to anyone?

I called the movie producer, Ashley Fleck, and told him that my novel was not finished. He was not dismayed, but sounded enthusiastic—he encouraged me to finish it, and his encouragement gave me hope.

'How did you know about my book?'

'I heard it on the street,' he said. 'There's a lot of talk about it.'

I mumbled that expression to myself. *On the street.* My work had never been spoken about on the street before. In my mind it was a particular street, narrow and interesting, full of pedestrians. A London street.

I had another inquiry from a movie company for a novel I had published a few years before, and a letter from a firm specializing in picture books, asking me to consider writing the text for a volume of London photographs.

'What we want is a sort of excursion,' the picture book publisher wrote. 'Your London.'

My London! Except for what Lady Max had shown me of those churches and monuments and back streets, my London was mainly indoors, as I worked on my book the whole day, confident in the dark.

And all this time there were invitations. Since my lead review and first diary mention I had received more than a dozen invitations. I had received them before—to the sort of it's-a-drink book launches that Musprat always attended. As a reviewer, I was known to the publicity departments of some publishers. But now I began to get invitations to parties at gallery openings, wine-tastings for charity, drinks to publicize new lines of cosmetics, and to film premières. I put them on the mantelpiece, a London affectation—the thick white cards and invitations propped up over the fireplace, looking pompous.

Anne snorted at them, because she never appeared on them, not as 'Mrs', not even as 'and guest'.

She said, 'I wouldn't go even if I were asked.'

I too stayed away. London parties of this kind, always six until eight, were given at the wrong time of day. My work kept me at my desk until five-thirty, and by then it was too late, I was too tired to change my clothes, put on a tie and hurry into the West End. I had the evening meal to prepare, the boys to meet, the *Standard* to read, and rather than standing up in a noisy room drinking wine I preferred a pint of Guinness in the funereal Fish. If I went anywhere these days it was to the topography section in the basement of the London Library to check facts for my novel, which was set in Honduras.

At last I felt obliged to accept an invitation, to a party for the opening of a new exhibition, 'Elizabethan London', at the

Royal Academy. I saw the posters in the underground, and the banners billowing over Piccadilly. We had been near here on one of our London excursions, when Lady Max had shown me the Albany and its courtyard.

Thinking of her in this way, she was fixed in my mind, and so I was startled on entering the foyer of the Royal Academy to see her. Her face was as luminous as ever, her lips as lovely, and she wore a loose shimmering black dress. When she spoke she seemed impatient.

'Where have you been?' she called out, and dropped her cigarette butt, stamping on it with one of her wicked shoes.

If I had been walking down Piccadilly past the Royal Academy that dark winter evening and seen the glowing room and this by-invitation-only preview among the brilliant pictures, I would have hated these party-goers and wanted to throw a brick through the window. What frivolity! What privilege!

But I was inside the Royal Academy, a guest at the private affair, eating smoked salmon and having a wonderful time. It was like a high mass, with all that space and light, and music too—a string quartet sonorously scraping away in a corner. We guests in the foreground were dwarfed by the looming portraits.

Elizabethan London was depicted not only in paintings and period costumes, but in a series of elaborate interiors—a tavern room as it might have looked then, a poor family's kitchen, the bedroom of an aristocrat, an ingeniously conceived view inside the Globe Theatre; each with music, or street sounds, or the speeches of actors declaiming Shakespeare. Some of it was marvellously down-to-earth—whole exhibits given over to objects and pictures describing plumbing or shopping.

'Has this wine corked?' Lady Max was saying. 'They serve bad champagne when a decent Chablis can be had for the same money.'

I was on my second glass. People were chattering with each other, their pink eager faces close together, and no one was looking at the exhibits. Lady Max turned to put her glass down and sniffed.

'You would have thought they'd exhibit something a bit more uplifting than water-closets,' she said. 'Think what an opportunity they lost—what portraits they could have hung. This is all a low-brow cheapie, on the level of a primary school pageant.'

That was not true. It was Elizabethan London from an entirely new angle, and portraits of great Elizabethans were hung everywhere. The pictures in this beautiful room made some guests seem more smug, but most were improved by the setting, and looked more prosperous, hopeful and gentle. There was a sense of eagerness in the place, a vibration running through the room, and I took pleasure in just watching, marvelling at the exhibits. I was glad to be there, delighted to be anonymous—the champagne made me slightly tipsy and gave the party the warmth and blur of a good dream.

'I can't stand another minute of this,' Lady Max said.

She hurried away and, stumbling a bit, I followed her into the foyer, where she handed me her cloakroom tag. I picked up her coat. The lining was still warm—she had not waited long.

'Oh, good. There's a taxi,' she said in the Royal Academy courtyard.

Once again, she was taking charge. She had the capacity to make me feel wonderful, but also stupid and spineless, just a snuffling creature waiting for a dog biscuit.

In the darkness of the taxi, as we tore down Knightsbridge, she said, 'You've been decidedly scarce.'

I agreed, and let myself be bullied, and even paid for the taxi and—fussed by all this abruptness—yet again overtipped the cabbie. Meanwhile, Lady Max had mounted her steps and was in the portico, holding her large black latchkey out for me to take. The turtle knocker caught my eye—it was dark and stained with big damp fingerprints. I made a few feeble pokes with the long latchkey before Lady Max snatched it away from me and expertly rammed it into the keyhole in one thrust, and to the clunking sound of the lock's parts loosening she said, 'That's how it is done.'

She went inside, and I followed, as though by a prior arrangement.

141

She switched on lamps, lighting our way to a side room I had not seen before. It was full of books and framed photographs—clusters of faces staring and smiling from shelves, from tiny tables, from the piano lid. The room was so quiet and so dark at the edges that they were like creatures from another life, another world. As I raised my eyes from all these strangers I saw that she was holding a glass of wine and offering it, much as she had offered me her latchkey.

'Sniff, sniff. You have a novelist's nosiness.'

Her directness embarrassed me. I picked up a bowler hat from the piano seat and put it on—too big. There were the initials T.R.D.A. stamped in gold in the hatband.

'He's out of town,' Lady Max said. 'Please sit down. You're awfully nervy.'

Not nervy, but still tipsy from the Royal Academy champagne.

She sat opposite me on the sofa, then kicked off her sharp-heeled shoes and raised her legs and sank her feet into a blue cushion. She had lovely patterned stockings, and when she swung her legs her dress was hiked up—it was a brief glimpse, but I did see her stocking tops tightened against her white thighs. I remembered, *I never wear knickers.*

'You're frightfully busy these days,' she said.

'No more than usual.'

She pretended not to hear, so as to go on talking—a London habit.

'Absolutely all over the papers,' she said in a tone of approval. 'I can't open one without seeing your name.'

'I'm doing the same amount of work. I'm getting more credit for it, though.'

'No more than you deserve,' Lady Max said, and straightened one stocking with the tips of her fingers. 'You're brilliant, and it's about time people knew it. There will be much more. This is only the beginning. Just watch.'

In the half dark of this shadowy room, speaking from where she sat coiled on the sofa, she sounded less like a well-wisher than one of the witches in *Macbeth.*

'I wasn't doing badly before,' I said, and it seemed to me

that I was whining.

'Of course,' she said—she was amused at my shrill little protest. She patted the sofa with one bloodless hand, and puffed her cigarette with the other. 'Now come here and sit next to me and tell me why you never go to parties.'

Scattering sparks as she poked out her cigarette in the ashtray, she moved her long legs as though to make room, and feeling dog-like I crept across the carpet and sat beside her.

'What parties?' I asked.

'The ones you're invited to.'

'But I just saw you at the Royal Academy party.'

'As though there weren't any others.'

So she knew—and she must have connived at having had me invited. I felt a bit diminished, if not put in my place, by this.

'These parties take place at a very inconvenient time of day.'

'Rubbish. It is a fact of life that there is nothing to do between five and eight most days.'

'I'm pretty busy then,' I said.

She did not hear that. She said, 'As the French say, the hours between the dog and the wolf.'

I wanted to say: In the hours between the dog and the wolf I am usually simmering the spaghetti sauce, or marinating the fish, or chopping vegetables, or reading the *Evening Standard*, or waiting for my wife. But no—while she might have understood the cooking, any mention of my wife seemed out of place or unwelcome at this moment.

'I have been watching for you,' Lady Max said, and slid closer to me. It was a butterfly pattern on her black stockings. 'This is what I had planned. Precisely this.'

She smiled at me and smoothed her hair.

'Thank you for being so co-operative.'

What was I to say to that?

'Do you find me too blunt?' she asked.

'No.'

'I wonder if you could bear to kiss me.'

Her way of speaking threw me and made it impossible for me to refuse. She was deft at throwing me off-balance, and with just the simplest question she could control me, as though tugging at my leash. I thought, *Woof-woof.*

Of course, I was saying, *don't be silly. I want to kiss you.*

And I did, and the kiss was facile, tentative, clumsy, insincere, dutiful, all chilly lips, and made her frown.

'You need practice,' she said. 'Funny. One of my favourite scenes in literature is when you have that man in your book fuck the woman in front of the fire.'

In a single motion, flicking her fingers, she pushed her dress off her shoulder—there was no strap beneath—and slipped her hand down and inside and moved it over her breasts. I could see her knuckles move against the silk as she traced her nipples.

'I know I'm no great beauty,' she said. 'I have small boobs and a biggish bum.' She smiled teasingly because what she said defied me to glance at her body. 'But honestly I think I could show you a thing or two.'

She was still sipping her wine and moving her hand inside her dress, caressing herself, still fluttering her fingers over her nipples.

'Do I surprise you?' she said. She moistened her lips. 'I think I could surprise you in lots of other ways.'

I was aware that I was leaning close to her. She removed her wandering hand, and shrugged, straightening her dress. Then she was looking past me as though at the window, listening hard—I could see it in the concentration of the eyes. She was hearing something clearly that I heard only faintly.

'Wouldn't you know,' she said with utter disgust, but not to me.

The front door creaked open—I heard the chink of the turtle knocker before the door slammed—there was a stamping in the hall, a sigh, and our door was flung open. A tall girl stood smiling in the doorway, wearing a dark cape and boots. She had tumbling blonde hair, and from the pinkish glow highlighting her pale skin you knew she had walked home this frosty evening. Her standing there breathless and apologetic made her seem even more attractive. It was the daughter, Allegra.

'Hello, Mummy—sorry to burst in.'

'Shut that fucking door this instant, you silly girl, and go to your room!'

The girl reacted as though she had been slapped, her face contorted, her pinkness contracted to points of colour on each cheek. And she was off—the door was shut even before Lady Max stopped shrieking.

The spell was broken and all my ardour died. It was a tone I had never heard—harsh, angry, pitiless, ignorant, more an animal's snarl than a human noise. It startled me and made a little welt on my memory. And I knew that after this I would never be able to look at Lady Max without also thinking of this ugly person inside her.

But she had gone quiet. She had slipped her dress off her shoulder again, farther than before, and was holding one breast like a Madonna in a Renaissance painting, proferring the nipple in her fingers for me to suck.

'Take it.'

The bluish veins in her breast made it look as cool as marble. A suggestion of pale hair surrounded the russet brown of the areola and the nipple. Against the delicious softness of her breast, the nipple looked thick, like the stem of a fruit.

Seeing me hesitate, she said, 'It's Allegra, isn't it?'

She held her breast, but casually, like an apple she was holding for me in case I might be hungry.

'She had arranged to meet a friend—that's what she told me. She never makes a plan and sticks to it. She's so selfish, the way she comes and goes.'

A shudder of gratitude passed through me. I was thankful to the daughter for showing up—for provoking the mother and revealing her. And I was touched by the daughter's humiliation.

'God, I hate the young,' Lady Max said, and stroked her breast sourly before tucking it into her dress.

She looked older and unreasonable, though I could only think of the daughter's sweet startled face in the doorway, her uncertain posture, her sudden fear.

Lady Max glanced at me. I said nothing and felt I was a coward for not defending the daughter. But there was a deeper reason: I had been so touched by the daughter's hurt I felt I might betray myself, because in a sense I fell for the girl then, for her wounded innocence.

145

'I hate them for being young,' Lady Max said. 'I hate their talk.'

Now, for my own self-respect, I felt I had to speak up for the girl. I began to say how the young seemed connected to the world—they lived close to the ground, they travelled light, and they were most alive in old safe cities like London.

But Lady Max was shaking her head.

'I hate the way they tell you things you already know, as though it's news,' she said. 'They are for ever discovering things —that Soho is charming, that the Kings Road is stylish, that Oxford Street's a bore. And in their little papers and magazines they write about it all in sickening detail. I hate the things they buy, I hate their music.'

She lit a cigarette but without any flourish, simply snatched one from a silver box at her elbow and set it on fire and gasped on it.

Speaking through rags of smoke—and the smoke itself made the words visible—she said, 'And as if that's not bad enough, they tell you things you know are wrong. You want to say "Balls!" but you can't talk them out of it, so you listen, and in a month or so you have to sit through them contradicting themselves.'

She tapped the ash off the cigarette and sulked as she exhaled more smoke, blowing it as though spraying poison, blighting the air with her breath.

'That's the worst of it, listening to them change their minds —watching the young grow up.'

'It happens so fast, though,' I said, thinking of my own children.

'Not true. It takes too bloody long. I have been listening to this nonsense for years,' she said. 'And I hate the way they think out loud. I hate their ignorant opinions. I can't stand the way they change their mind.'

Saying these things with such conviction she seemed old and cranky, and I felt at a greater distance from her—young, or at least younger than she.

'Isn't it all part of growing up?'

'Why can't they do it more quietly?' she said. And with

menace in her eyes she glanced up at where Allegra's room probably was. 'She was supposed to be with her friend.'

It was the most passionate she had ever been with me face to face, and though she could be a tease and an insincere mocker I knew she meant every word of this.

And her words were tainted by the dark whiff in her breath. She was a heavy smoker and I was sitting near. It was the odour of her lungs—not a rancid thing in her mouth, but deeper. It seemed especially odd and offensive because she was so lovely. She had stubbed out her cigarette, but she smelled strongly of smoke, of black clammy London, of sooty air.

First her shriek, then her rant and finally her breath. She stank. And yet from a little distance she seemed so pale and fragile. In her rant she had lost interest in me, and she had emptied her glass. She looked peevish and distracted, though for a long while afterwards she sat there saying nothing. Then she saw me sneaking a look at my watch.

'You're going to be late.'

'It's all right.'

'Your wife is going to wonder where you are.'

I hated that, and said nothing. Seeing me squirm made her smile.

'Will I keep seeing your name everywhere?'

'Who knows?'

'I think I will,' she said, and paused, then added, 'If I want to.'

A nother London walk, homeward from Lady Max's, through winter streets. I needed the ritual to calm me. Each time I saw her I had to sort out where I was, and what did she mean, and who was I, and who was she? Part of her witchery came from her power to spread confusion, and the rest of her witchery was her beauty. But I was still confused.

I had gained a measure of visibility. She knew that and from what she said might even have pulled a string or two. But the writing was mine—I had done the work. And she had revealed herself as rather a pest—it seemed she had been to those other parties I had stayed away from, and apparently had lain in wait for me.

I was still walking, still remembering. There are certain awful sounds that enter your ears and penetrate your whole body. Her howl at her daughter was one of those. It startled me and made me fearful. Now I was nearing the river, walking south towards Battersea Bridge and home. The odour of soot and burning coal fires on these narrow streets reminded me of her breath—the chimney smell of her lungs.

Though I was flattered by her interest and her praise, her sudden sexuality threw me. She made me feel like an idiot for not responding, but—really—did she expect me to kneel and suck on her breast and then go home and kiss my wife?

By the time I reached Clapham I had worked myself into a state of grievance against her—feeling she was presumptuous and unsubtle. I hated her greed. And she was niggardly too—I had not forgotten the dinner at La Tour Eiffel.

The phone was ringing as I climbed the steps to my house. The ringing stopped when I opened the front door. Anne was holding the receiver towards me.

'It's for you,' she said. She covered the mouthpiece. 'A woman. Frightfully posh.'

It was Lady Max.

'I was wondering whether you had any plans for tomorrow,' she said.

'Just work.' Writing at home gave me no convincing excuses.

'Good. Then you can take the day off and have lunch with me.'

But my walk home had filled me with resentment.

'Sorry,' I said.

She hung on, she made me struggle, but I stood firm and at last I got her off the line.

A week passed. More invitations. My book was going so well that I accepted an assignment to write a piece the following week about Brighton, for a British travel magazine. Lady Max called on Monday.

'You weren't at the Heinemann party,' she said.

'I'm pretty busy. I have to go to Brighton tomorrow.'

'I know. It's for *Travel World*, isn't it? I'll go with you.'

She was not only blunt, she was quick. I couldn't think. I

said, 'I'm staying overnight.'

'Even better.'

Now she made me work.

'It's not a good idea.'

'I think it's an excellent idea. Brighton's a marvellously scruffy place, and in The Lanes there are some splendid restaurants.'

Feeling spineless and desperate I said, 'My wife might be going with me.'

Lady Max did not hesitate. 'I thought your wife worked.'

'Yes. She does. But she's taking the day off.'

She had made me squirm, she had frightened me, and now she was making me lie. I hated her for that most of all. We had entered a new phase of the relationship, deeper and more treacherous, like some of the streets she had shown me in London, the strange alleys and cul-de-sacs off wide and well-known thoroughfares. She was insistent, I was desperate. And she had a meddling interest. How did she know, and what business was it of hers, who I was writing this Brighton piece for?

That night, after putting the boys to bed, Anne was chatty.

'Everyone's talking about you these days. "Are you any relation to the writer?" That sort of question.' She smiled. 'I'm not sure I like it.'

I was opening my mail in front of the fire.

'What's wrong?'

'Nothing. Look at this—two publishers have written to ask about my new novel. It's not even finished and they're competing for it. And here's something from the *Observer*. They want to know if I can go to China.'

Anne was looking puzzled. 'Aren't you glad?'

'Of course.'

'Then why do you look so haunted?'

Again I thought: Most writers are balder and smaller than you expect. I was entering the Members' Reading Room of the London Library. Men were scribbling, some seated at tables, others hunched in leather chairs. There were women writing, too, but they seemed altogether more efficient, tidier, less conspicuous. It was a warm room, with an odour of leather and old bindings, and quiet except for the rustle of pages being turned and the hiss and ping of radiators.

With his back to the room, Ian Musprat was writing. He was facing a window pane that was so black, so stippled with raindrops, it looked liquefied, like a tall trembling sheet of water which diffused the yellow street lamps of St James's Square. He clutched his head with his bitten fingers. Peering over his shoulder, I could see his open notebook page—crossed-out lines and doodles and *A distant toilet flushing is like the sound of the human voice, a sigh becoming water and collapsing into a pipe—a little sad* and the scattered words and phrases, *Humptulips* and *distemper* and *How terribly reassuring.*

They were the makings of a poem—I could tell from the way the lines were set out, not reaching the right-hand margin of the page.

Seeing this small untidy man writing made me respect him, even like him again. Writing made him seem admirable and civilized. This was what he was for, and I was impressed by his bravery. His posture gave him a look of concentration and struggle, and in his very plainness was an aura of strength. There was also something in his silence, and the way he wrote with the notebook on his lap, that gave him the appearance of a conspirator. He was so engrossed he did not notice me.

At his elbow was a plump volume with *Mythologiques—Vol 3: The Origin of Table Manners* printed on the spine.

Only when I stood in his light did he look up at me, with the scowling face of a hamster waking from a nap in its nest. He said, 'God, I'm sick of doing this.'

'How about a cup of tea?'

'There's a poxy tea-shop in Duke Street.'

He tripped leaving the Reading Room and shouted loudly, 'Knickers!' No one stopped writing, though one man looked over the top of his newspaper.

'How long have you been a member of the library?' he asked on the stairs.

'Since Lady Max insisted I join.'

He said nothing.

'What are you writing?'

'A desperate piece of crap about hermeneutics,' he said.

'Could you elaborate?'

'It's really about Lévi-Strauss.'

'The American blue jeans?'

'The French structuralist,' he said. And he smiled. 'That's nice.'

In the tea-shop I said, 'I want to ask you about Lady Max.'

Musprat did not reply. He stared at the floor and then blew his nose with a stiff and wrinkled handkerchief that he held balled-up in his hand. He then frowned at the thing and said, 'I'm disgusting,' and stuffed it into his pocket.

Stirring his styrofoam cup of tea with a wooden stick, he said, 'I sort of hate her. Sometimes I'd like to punch her in the face.' He sucked the tea from the wooden stirrer and said, 'Sorry. I know you're a big fan.'

'I'm not a fan at all.'

He sipped his tea, then faced me with a little more confidence.

'You write short stories. Want an idea for one?'

He began to gnaw his wooden stirrer.

'You meet someone early in your career, when you are weak and they are strong. They are bloody rude to you. Time passes. You get a little recognition, and you meet this person again. This time they are very pleasant. They don't remember that they were rude. They actually believe they were part of your success. Yet their rudeness is all you remember—the only thing.'

He had reduced his wooden stirrer to a mass of wet splinters. He lifted the paper cup in his thin anxious fingers.

'The first time Lady Max met me she more or less mocked me. I knew she didn't fancy me at all. Anyway, why should she? I'm a pig. After I won the Hawthornden she remembered my name and tried to be nice to me.'

'And that's why you want to punch her in the face?'

'No. I think I envy her, actually. I'd like to have her money. I'd like to have a house in the Boltons. I'd like to go around saying, "I never wear knickers." That's her war-cry, you know.'

Having finished the tea he began chewing the top edge of the styrofoam cup.

'Her mother's a marchioness. Only a marquis or a marchioness can be addressed as "the most honourable,"' he said. 'I'm surprised you don't know that. That's the sort of thing Americans tend to know.'

'What if Lady Max had fancied you?'

Now he smiled, he was strengthened, as though I had played the wrong card. He looked timidly triumphant.

He said, 'I should have thought you could tell me a thing or two about that.'

The English could be so pompous and wordy when they thought they were in the right.

'I haven't touched her, Ian.'

'I don't want to know about it,' Musprat said, and made it sound like a teasing accusation. 'But it's easy to talk about her, because she makes no secret of her life.'

'Meaning?'

'She's been to bed with everyone,' he said. 'Didn't you know that?'

'I guessed,' I said. Yet I had not wanted to think about it.

'Heavage?' I said.

'She had a fairly public thing with him,' Musprat said. 'Most editors have had a leg over her. Most writers in the news. Writing's a sort of aphrodisiac to her. She's very old-fashioned that way.'

'She mentioned Kenneth Tynan.'

'They used to show up at parties wearing each other's clothes.'

'Do you know a movie producer called Ashley Fleck?'

'No, but Lady Max does.'

I named the other men at the dinner party—Marwood the novelist, the South African named Lasch.

'I suppose so. She's fairly rapacious. I know you're shocked and all that, but looking in from the outside I find it boring.' In his off-hand way, blowing his nose, chewing shreds from his plastic cup, he named others, as though listing people involved in a conspiracy. They included journalists who must have put my name in 'Londoner's Diary', publishers who sent me invitations to book launches, museum directors and the editor of the travel magazine who had asked me to write a piece about Brighton. And Walter Van Bellamy. I had thought she had pulled a few strings, but it was more than that—she had manipulated all the attention I had been receiving lately. She had tipped a wink to these old lovers, perhaps collecting on a debt from them.

'I'm not shocked,' I said.

But I was.

I decided to avoid the germ-laden commuters and walked home. It was only when I took a London bus or train in the rush hour that I caught a cold. It was an easy one-hour walk through St James's Park, past the palace, through Victoria and Chelsea, and across the river and uphill to Clapham.

Walking along, I thought again about Musprat. He seemed almost virtuous in his detachment and his mockery. His detachment had given him a perspective. He looked on, he was touched by forgivable envy, but he had not been lured into Lady Max's orbit. And that was his strength.

Putting these questions to him about Lady Max, I understood Musprat better—and that had been the case in my talk with Bellamy too. She was the key. She had shown me London, but seeing London through her eyes had distorted the city for me—and there was another price to pay. Yet seeing Lady Max through the eyes of others helped me to understand London better. And of course she had helped me. The more visible I became, the clearer I could see London, because she had given me access.

But I was left with a sense of woe and a feeling of obligation. What to do about her?

She phoned me again several more times. She did not give her name or say hello. She said, 'Well?' and waited impatiently until I thought of something to say, and when I did my evasiveness seemed to rouse her.

'I'm afraid I'm not very gregarious.'

Even then I did not say her name—I didn't know what to call her.

'We'll see.'

She regarded me as an interesting problem. But, as before,

she worked obliquely. From other quarters came more invitations to parties, more offers of writing assignments. A television producer asked me whether I was interested in writing a play for television. Another literary editor inquired about the possibility of my reviewing for him. These were substantial offers, involving contracts and terms, with the promise of serious money.

As with Musprat, knowing these people helped me to know Lady Max better. I could place her now, I understood her society and what she needed, and that was a London knack, being able to put a person in context. It was a sprawling, complex city, and Londoners fitted in, but each one was a tight fit.

She phoned once more, was off-hand again, and asked whether I were free for dinner that very night.

'No, I have another dinner,' I replied—and I did, with Anne and one of her friends from work.

'Where will you be going?'

I named the restaurant.

She said, 'I'd love to join you.'

She could not have been more blunt.

'And my wife?'

'I don't cope very well with wives ordinarily, but we do have something in common, she and I.'

I could not imagine what that might be, and I said so.

'You, dear boy,' Lady Max said, a contemptuous edge in her voice.

But I resisted, feeling foolish, and out of cowardice cancelled the dinner, fearful that Lady Max would show up and make a scene.

After that, I seemed to see her everywhere in London. It was a city of shadows, of memories and suggestions. It was a city of lowered voices. And at this dark and rainy time of year, with all its shining lights and the mirrors of its winter streets, a city of reflections.

It was also a city of look-alikes—people dressed similarly, a familiar hat, that identical coat, the same umbrella. There were London clothes, there was even a London walk. Londoners didn't saunter, they walked with purpose, rarely looking at one another, their faces fixed, or else averted. I often saw Lady Max's drawn-back hair, her white face, her cloaks and capes, and I believed she was watching me. Anonymity was a valuable asset here, but now I was afraid I had lost mine. Lady Max had shown me the city, its secret places, but now that I had begun to inhabit her London it seemed that I was exposed. I felt she might turn up anywhere, at any time.

It was easy enough to stay home. Life in London had given me a taste for privacy: Londoners valued their isolation—they liked to be, as Musprat said of himself in one of his own invented words, 'ungetatable'. Unlike in New York, you could never get lost here, but you could hide.

I loved the seclusion of my house, and my absorption in my novel made me happy. Except for the ring of the telephone—but it was never her these days, she had stopped calling—I worked without anxiety. What other cold northern city was so protective that it allowed you to be able to write, undisturbed, of the jungle? It was the effect of all that winter darkness. Yet even at the end of February there was a suggestion of spring, the first flowers of the year—snowdrops, some early crocuses. Even in London gardens there was a sense of rural England, the residue of the old fertile land—old roots and shrubs, old bulbs and tubers blooming in the mud.

And then the worst, most dreaded event in London, a sudden knock at the door.

London taxis with their engines idling make an unmistakable rattle and clack, an impatient shivering of metal that accompanies the paying of the fare; the door slams and, still shaking, the cab drives off. All this I was dimly aware of as I sat upstairs at the back of the house, writing *The Last Man*. It was an afternoon of white winter light, the flowers in the back gardens showing some small tongues of colour.

The front doorbell rang, and only then did I connect this visitor to the sound of the taxi.

'Aren't you going to ask me in?'

Only in bad dreams did you meet someone you knew in the oddest place—your mother in a locker-room; or it might be a total stranger, or someone you feared, in the seclusion of your

155

home. I wanted her to go away, but she had a slender claim on me, so how could I be rude?

Inside the house, looking at pictures, touching furniture, she said, 'This is not at all what I expected.'

Already she was sneering, as though anticipating rejection.

Passing me on her way into the sitting-room—she had not waited to be asked—I had a sense of other men on her, and I recalled how the bronze shell of the turtle door-knocker at her house was stained and black with fingerprints. But this was more an odour than anything visible, and it enclosed her body like an atmosphere she carried with her.

'How very interesting,' she was saying.

Her manner was a little chilly. Every encounter I had had with Lady Max was like a job interview, but it was she who was turned down. Today was slightly different. She was responding to me in a defensive and remote way, treating me as a male—not a friend, or someone with a name, but a man. There had been so many other men. And men were so predictable. This was her weakness, her poor judgement, her bad timing; and this was the reason she would fail in the end: she believed that all men were the same.

It made me dislike and even fear her, because a woman with that belief would blame me for the harm another man had done her. Seeing her prowling in my house, looking two storeys down at the garden below, gave me pause. Impulsive and greedy, loving to shock—these traits made her seem destructive.

'Don't worry. I'm not going to throw myself out of the window.'

It was precisely what I feared.

'But if I did you'd be in a jolly awkward position explaining it.'

'If you jumped out this window,' I said, 'it seems to me that you'd be the one in the awkward position.'

'Yes. Maybe I should push you out instead.'

'Why would you do a silly thing like that?'

I tried to appear calm, but what she said terrified me, and I was watching her, so that she couldn't lunge and catch me off-balance.

'Because you've been avoiding me, and I don't like it.'

It was simple, really. What made her passionate was that I was unwilling. And she was also stubborn. My refusal made me different from the others, and it made her more insistent.

She had paused near a stack of magazines and papers on a side table, each of which contained something I had written.

'I put those people on to you.'

'But I did the writing.'

She raised her face to me and pursed her lips, to jeer.

'There are so many writers in London,' she said. 'Many of them are just as clever as you, but much more polite. They would have thanked me.'

She lit a cigarette, and again I had the impression, when she exhaled, of someone blowing poison into the room.

'I don't think you realize what I've done for you.'

'Do I seem ungrateful?'

'Very,' she said, and looked around. 'Your little house. Your little life. Your little wife.'

She peered across the back garden to the row of houses beyond. The sun was casting its last redness over the roofs and through the black branches of the trees.

'Places like this make my heart sink.'

'I can't do what you want me to do.'

'I don't know why I came here,' she said.

In that moment she looked abandoned and truly lost. Some women could seem so pathetic in rejection, almost tragic, as though they were about to lose their lives. For most men rejection was not a tragedy, but simply bad luck—the breaks.

'I don't think I want you any more,' she said, turning away, looking sad. I had never seen her in this mood, and it shocked me, her mute face, her small shoulders, her slightly hunched, defeated-looking posture.

I almost said, *Tell me what to do to please you, and I'll do it.* But I couldn't say it. I seemed prissy. It was not a fear of sex—on the contrary, I liked her, I was attracted to her. But sex with her was not a meal—it was only the first course. She would not have been satisfied until she had all of me. She wanted more than passionate afternoons and the occasional party—I had the powerful fear that she wanted to suck my soul out of my body.

Without speaking, she wandered out of the room and found the telephone in the hall. She simply picked up the receiver and dialled, and I felt sorry for her again, as I watched her struggle—calling for help. I assumed she was calling a taxi.

'Julian!' she said.

What was this new voice? It was gleeful, it was hearty, it was false. There was something diabolical in the way this utterly different voice rang out of her body, as though she were a lump of ectoplasm that could be sorrowful one moment and coquettish the next. Like London itself—Dickensian in one street, dreary in another, renovated, crass, cosy, dangerous—not one city, but many.

'It's me. What about our drink, then?' she was saying. She stopped and listened, then said, 'Perfect.'

In this new voice she rattled on, mentioning a publisher, a magazine, an editor, a café, and she settled on a day and a time, tomorrow, in fact. The voice quacking at the other end of the line sounded surprised and grateful—a young man's eager voice, thankful for the sudden interruption on an otherwise empty afternoon. I knew the feeling.

She kept me waiting a while longer while she chattered, and then she hung up and said over her shoulder, 'Must be off. Thanks for the use of the phone.'

I touched her arm, so that she would turn and listen to me.

'A prostitute did that to me once in a hotel,' I said. 'She had finished with me. She was calling her next customer.'

'You are a shit,' Lady Max said.

I opened the front door. In our passing from one room to the other, from the back of the house to the front, night had fallen. The word 'shit' was still on her lips as she stepped on to the landing. I had always regarded her as lovely, even in her pestering and greed, but now I felt I knew her well, and she seemed ugly, bony, bloodless, witch-like.

'Don't be surprised if you find life in London rather different after this.'

It was a threat, and she left believing that I was doomed, that I would be lost and forgotten. She went into the street and disappeared, swallowed by the London darkness. I was not afraid. At once my house again seemed large and safe. I did not mind being left behind if it meant I would never have to see this woman again.

The children came home from school a few minutes later. It was Friday—two free days ahead of them—and they purified the house with their laughter. From that day the weather in London improved.

Spring came. Anne knew nothing except that for a period I was very happy and productive. My book was still unfinished. But a book was not a job or a project, it was part of my life—and I liked my life.

Still, when I wrote a review or took a trip, I remembered Lady Max's threat, which sounded more and more like a witch's curse. Defying it strengthened me, and I became even bolder when I realized that she could not destroy me. It meant that my writing mattered, and that she had not created me or connived at granting me my success.

Once, I saw her at a publisher's party. She seemed ugly, almost monstrous to me, with her huge white forehead and popping eyes and her greedy mouth and red claws. I intended to say hello, but I had ceased to exist for her. There was a London way of dealing with people you had written off. She cut me—did not see me, although she certainly had noticed I was there. She radiated a poisonous awareness of me as she made a bee-line for a young writer at the far side of the room, the same Julian she had called from my house that last day.

I went home happy and did not see her again. Lady Max had taken Julian as her lover. He was a northerner, new to London, and he lived in Hampstead and wrote of misery in provincial coal towns. Was Lady Max the reason he was all over the papers, being helpfully mentioned and reviewed and offered work and short-listed for the spring book prizes? Time would tell. In the meantime, Julian became known—as perhaps I had been—as one of Lady Max's young men.

'I think Julian is a fearful little tick,' Musprat said.

We had resumed our snooker games, but not at the

Lambourne Club. Musprat was avoiding the Lambourne because he owed so much money, both in club dues and bar bills. We played these days at the Regency Snooker Hall in Clapham Junction, two pounds an hour, tea and pork pies extra, and a cockney with ear-rings and tattoos at the cash register saying, *Is that the lot then, guv?*

'But she's worse,' he said. 'You know that.'

I said I didn't. I wanted to encourage him, to hear his version.

'I think about her every time I do my taxes,' he said. 'She doesn't pay them, since she's not English.'

'Of course she is.'

'She's American. For tax reasons. Carries an American passport. How else do you suppose she manages to go on living in London?'

Yet I was grateful to Lady Max. She had shown me that I would never be a Londoner. That was a valuable lesson. And because I had not been her lover I could see her clearly, and London too. So I knew the simple fate of being an alien here, and I felt certain of a time when I would leave for good and write about her and her city.

Every issue of Granta features fiction, politics, travel writing, photography and more. So don't miss out — subscribe today and save up to 40% from the £6.99 cover price.

Don't miss out on major issues. Subscribe now to Granta and save up to 40%.

Don't let your friends miss out either. One year gifts (4 issues) are only £19.95.

GRANTA

FREEPOST
2-3 Hanover Yard
Noel Road
London
N1 8BR

NO
STAMP
REQUIRED

FREEPOST
2-3 Hanover Yard
Noel Road
London
N1 8BR

WILLIAM T. VOLLMANN
AN AFGHANISTAN
PICTURE SHOW

Alaska: While an increasingly desperate Hafizullah Amin was conducting pacification operations in every province, while his superior, Mr Nur Mohammad Taraki, began the last six weeks of his presidency (and, incidentally, his life), while Babrak Karmal waited in Moscow, while the Soviet Union was bland (for this was still five months before the invasion of Afghanistan stunned and horrified us); in the month of July I first visited Alaska. At that time I had no suspicion that I ever might go to Afghanistan. We were on the ferry from Seattle to Haines, my friend Erica and I. She was older. The inland passage narrowed, and on either side of us evergreen forests ascended mountain shoulders until they met snow, white fogs lying in all the hollows, and we passed rocky grassy beaches and the wind smelled of salt. When the two shores began to draw away from each other again, the sky to open, we stood on the cabin deck, our hair beating against our faces. We could see for a long way. The windbreakers of the passengers standing at the rail fluttered violently.

Erica pointed down. 'If your child fell overboard, would you jump down and save it?'

'If it were a wanted child,' I said flippantly.

'If it wasn't, you'd just let it drown?'

'Sure,' I said, straight-faced.

When I was growing up, my little sister drowned because I hadn't paid attention.

My Leader: 'This is the life!' laughed Erica, who had taught at Outward Bound. Her hair was a wild cloud of curls. She had a ruddy, happy face; her skin was so thick, she said, that no mosquitoes could bite it. She was as strong as a bear. How many weaklings had she saved?

Above the River: Tenting in the rain with Erica was always the best part. We were all set up, which was a relief, because I was bad at that and other things; we were resting, going nowhere, and I could feel as though I were in the *Arabian Nights*, the tent covered with tapestries and furs, perhaps, with a brazier of incense between our sleeping-bags, and a silver bowl of dates (actually, we ate them from one of Erica's zip-lock plastic bags), and when she

163

slept she kept on smiling, which made me happy too—the Land of Counterpane was not dangerous at all—we had hours left before I'd have to prove myself again, a good respite to tell each other fantastic stories (the rain being reliable that way); so Erica told me about being married and climbing the mountain in South America that later got named after her, Pico Erica; and being in the Peace Corps and snorting heroin and breaking into people's houses solely to steal ice-cream and living with the Navajos and all the other things she had done that left me wide-eyed and determined to do things like that (and at the very end of that year, when I was reading the Christmas newspapers in Switzerland, and there it was in black and white and French. *Afghanistan had been invaded!* I suddenly thought: 'Someday I would like to go there,' and it was not because Afghanistan was Afghanistan, but because Afghanistan was invaded); and my tent mate snuggled her sleeping-bag up against me and asked me to rub her back and I said that I would and she laid her head on my knee and said, 'Go ahead, scratch! Long, hard strokes, all the way down my back! Harder!'—for she was from a military family.

'You really want me to *scratch* your back?' I said.

'You got it!'

'All right,' I said dubiously.

'What do you mean, "all right"? My body is different from yours.'

'It must be.'

'It's getting monotonous now.'

'Sorry.'

'Oh, that feels good.'

'Thank you.'

'That's nice. Could you go just a little lower? And make your strokes harder. Oh, that's wonderful. Oh, keep doing that.'

The rain thundered and thundered.

'Isn't this exciting?' said Erica sleepily.

It was. The tent shuddered and flapped. Water was leaking in. We had no idea whether or not the evening wind would rip it apart—a dessert of uncertainty which pleased Erica; Erica loved to climb mountains because they brought her so close to death. She'd seen another climber fall a thousand feet; she'd seen a frozen

German couple in the Swiss Alps. Because danger fulfilled Erica so much, it also fulfilled me—or at least the thought of it did. Or at least I thought that the thought of it did. I had a crush on Erica.

We were up at McGonagall Pass. To the east were the stony cones of Ostler Mountain and the trail that we had come up from the river. To the west below us was a plain crawling with the black rivers of glaciers, peaks dolloped with snow and ice everywhere we looked (or at least our maps told us that they were peaks; *we* could see only massive pillars, some blue, some white, some gravel-brown, that disappeared into the clouds). That plain was mainly gravel piles and raw earth so soggy with glacial melt that it swallowed our boots to the ankle. There were heaps of loose stones: white granite flecked with black, or rusty shale, or yellow-tinted crystals that Erica thought were sulphur. We had both become very quiet; I was almost frightened by everything. Stones trickled into pools of a strange pale green. The water tasted sweet and silty. Between the gravel country ('No Man's Land,' Erica called it) and the titanic black-earth mounds of the glaciers was a river with the same green pallor, too wide to cross, eating deeper and deeper into a sculpted channel of ice. Not even Erica dared to go very close to it. What I most remember now is the still steady trickling of water everywhere, a sound which seemed uncanny to me because in that vast nature-riddled place everything should have been roaring and booming and I kept waiting for something to happen, for the black mountains to explode, for the ice to break, for thunder and lightning to come . . .

Happiness: It was a dark, stifling tent. Flies buzzed outside and inside. The Young Man felt as if he could barely breathe. The refugees sat in the hot darkness. The whites of their eyes gleamed.

'Are you happy here?' he asked the head of the family.

'Oh, you see,' explained the Pakistani administrator of the camp, 'We are trying to make them happy, but they have left their own country, so it is *difficult* for them to be happy! But we want to make their stay here as comfortable as we can. They are satisfied with the help that we are giving them and the United Nations is giving them, and they are appreciating that.'

'Do you think they'll stay here for the rest of their lives?'

165

The Young Man apparently had a knack for surprising the administrator.

'Why should they?'

'Because the Russians will not give Afghanistan up.'

'No, that is impossible!' cried the administrator. 'The whole world is against them, you see!'

'I hope you're right.' The Young Man turned to the refugees. 'Why did you leave Afghanistan?' he asked.

'Russian . . . attack us,' the man said slowly. 'Their . . . airplanes and tanks. Russian came, and they . . . tease our womans, they hurt them . . . and we are very in trouble. Their . . . airplanes come, and . . . bombs *destroy* our places . . . '

'Are you happy living here?'

'No, sir. We are not happy. We are satisfied here, but in summer season, we . . . are in troubles.'

'Do you have enough food to eat?'

'Yes, sir. Enough food.'

'And enough water?'

'It is hard. We don't have enough drinking water. And the food is not of such good quality, sir. Afterwards we feel ill. And there is giant insects that scare us . . . '

Happiness: 'Don't be apprehensive,' Erica had said.

'I'll do my best.'

'It's really a very trivial crossing.'

'Good,' I said politely.

We sat down on the moss for a while and gathered blueberries into my wool hat. I could not stop thinking about what had happened in the river. Erica picked about four times more blueberries than I did. The sun was very hot and sweet in our faces.

'Let's go,' Erica said at last. We put our packs back on, and I tightened my sweaty straps and hip belt as we went down the incline. The closer I got to the edge of the river, the less I liked it. There were two channels. The first was easy enough: I could see the rocks on the bottom. The second, however, was of the treacherous kind, a wide, deep, smooth stretch of water that might be thigh-deep and slow, or maybe chest-deep and very very fast underneath, and the bottom might be slippery, and that second channel might drown me on this sunny afternoon.

Erica looked at me, scanned the river and looked at me again. She waded the first channel, stepped on to the sand bar in the middle, peered into the water again and came back to me. 'Good news,' she said. 'We're crossing tomorrow.'

I felt horribly depressed and ashamed.

'Today's your birthday,' Erica said. 'You set up the tent and I'll make you a special birthday dinner. I don't want you to help. Just get in your sleeping-bag and relax.'

'You're so nice to me, Erica,' I said.

Erica sat by the stove, singing songs in Navajo and French. The evening was very beautiful. 'You know,' she said, 'one Christmas all my brothers and sisters and I were fighting. My father used to be a brigadier general. All of a sudden he lost control and barked out, "*I command you to be happy!*" We kids just burst out laughing.'

I smiled.

'So,' said Erica, 'I command you to be happy!'

Erica Bright and Erica Green-Eyes: By this time I had separated Erica into two personalities: Erica Bright, who was sweet, playful and girlish (and who liked me), and Erica Green-Eyes, who could best be described as *prowling* and *competent*. Green-Eyes was the one whom I continually offended; and it was Green-Eyes who made my first thoughts so filled with dread as I lay beside her in the small hours of a sunny morning, knowing that in minutes she'd awake and hustle me along to another river crossing, snapping at me, glaring at me, shoving me because I was slow and we had to cross before the glaciers began their morning melt. It maddened Green-Eyes that I continued to lose tent stakes, that I had no sense of balance, that I was a poor map reader. 'Come on!' Erica said as we canoed up Moose River. '*Hard*, deep strokes! Dig into that water! Come on; there's a tribe of hostile Indians behind us and we have to *stroke* for our lives! They're going to catch us at this rate! *Stroke! Stroke! Stroke! Hard*, deep strokes! They're coming closer; they're cocking their bows; let's see you put yourself into your *stroke*! Dig in! *Bend* at the waist, *move* your shoulders; STROKE!' As we went farther upriver, my stroke actually began to get smoother and better. Erica was happy, believing that maybe I'd actually learned something. I paddled us around for a little while as she lay back and watched the clouds. Presently we felt an impulse to piracy, so we tied up at a private dock, tiptoed into somebody's garden, and stole a handful of strawberries. 'Now stroke . . . ' said Erica very sleepily, laughing and yawning in the sun, and the sunbeams danced on the water and a faint breeze stirred her hair. Going back downriver, I also stroked creditably. We had a good time until we reached the landing. I jumped out to pull the canoe up on to the shore. Still inside, Erica giggled as it wobbled, thinking that I was playing, and as I summoned my energies for a return smile I stumbled, tipping it and her into the water . . . 'God *damn* it,' she said . . . In general, no matter whether I did or did not learn things from Green-Eyes (and I do remember a few occasions where she nodded at me in a satisfied way, and once because I had located our position so accurately she gave me the McGonagall Pass topo map for my own), the lessons were neither easy nor pleasant. I would look down at the ground, apologizing for my latest stupidity and feeling a strange tightness in my chest which I thought then was pure self-loathing (but which I now suspect was anger, too); and Erica threw her head back despairingly, reached to me and cried, '*Think!*' Then she would feel a pitying impulse to rally me, would make herself smile and say, 'Your river crossings are a hundred times better than at the start.'

'Thank you,' I said.

The Knot, the Robot and the Knife: Once when we were hitch-hiking, Erica Bright stood on the empty road, ready to play the pretty part (even when it was cold she kept her sweater off so that the drivers would see that she had breasts). She was singing a song by Jacques Brel. Her face was young and clear. She combed her hair, sang a song in Spanish (she knew eight languages); got impatient and sprang upside down, walking on her hands in the middle of the highway, smiling and singing. Then Green-Eyes decided to make me exercise, and she was yelling because I couldn't twist my neck and arms in the way she wanted. 'You move like a robot!' she cried after half an hour. 'There's no use trying to get you to do anything, is there? You might as well sit down.' She cheered up, though, a moment later, when I tied a perfect knot (Erica was always making me practise things). 'Good,' she said to me. 'Very good.'

'Thank you,' I said.

'You're being sarcastic,' said Bright. Her feelings were hurt.

'No, I'm not.'

'Yes, you are,' said Green-Eyes. 'That really bothers me about you, that you'll never admit it when you're being sarcastic.'

'What are you doing with your knife?' said Erica.

'Not much.'

I got up and started walking. It was my plan at that moment to walk into the woods until I died. Erica called my name, tentatively. I kept walking.

'Come back!' cried Bright.

I stopped.

'Let's just try to enjoy each other,' she said. 'OK?'

I didn't say anything.

'What are you thinking?'

'I'm not thinking anything.'

Carrying my Sweater: Ten days later we were climbing the side of a steep ravine in the mountains, with a frozen stream below and the dusk-blue wall of a glacier above, and it was snowing but we both felt hot.

'Let me carry your sweater,' Erica said.

'No, that's all right.'

'Come on, we'll go faster if I have it. Just give it to me.'

'All right. Thank you.'

'You're welcome,' said Erica, smiling at me.

A Thought (1989): Erica carried my sweater. What did I do for anyone in Afghanistan? Well, once I brought a few armloads of wood for a fire. Somehow this should be worth as much as Erica carrying my sweater, in terms of mass carried over a distance for a utilitarian purpose; and somehow it seems to me that in Afghanistan I never did a goddamned thing.

Raspberries (1979): One night we camped in a boggy, grassy place by the highway near Anchorage. It was finally starting to get dark late at night, because we had achieved the month of August, and the tent, which hung loosely on its poles in the soft grass, took on a primeval quality, the walls seeming like shaggy, wrinkled skins in the dusk and the thick grass beneath our bodies feeling like them; and reeds whispered all around us, reddened through the back window of the tent by the alpenglow. Erica's features, hard and shadowy and strong, were in relief as she lay beside me. Her sweater looked like mail. She lay still with her eyes closed. We slept late; there were no more river crossings to make. The next morning was a happy one, a relapse in the progress of Green-Eyes's contempt for me. She talked to me a little and even smiled at me. She said she'd make breakfast beside the railroad tracks across the highway. When she'd gone I got up and struck camp, shaking the tent-fly clean of slugs, pulled my pack on and hiked over. Erica was just fixing my breakfast: a big dish of granola, heaped with brown sugar and beautiful raspberries that she had picked for me.

The River: It was four-thirty in the morning when we struck the tent and left the wooded sand bar. Green-Eyes hustled me along. It was very warm and sunny; the water level was rising fast. Our boots filled up with cold water and gravel in the first channel. Within a few minutes my feet were completely numb. 'Listen,' Green-Eyes told me as we ran through toe-deep streams and gravel beds. 'No, don't slow up, just listen. You hear that noise like thunder coming from the east? That's the ice beginning to break up for the day. Look, the water's getting higher! Can you hear how it sounds different?'

We had reached the first of the difficult channels. Green-Eyes tied a bowline around my waist and showed me how to step *into* the rope to pay it out across my hip. '*Watch* for me as I go across!' she said. 'Be ready to pull me in if I fall. If you can't do it, you'll have to throw off your pack and run for me. Give me slack when I call for it.'

'Right.'

'Now, remember, you have to pay attention!'

170

'I will.'

She undid her hip belt and started across. The grey water was rising very quickly now. The stump on the sand bar behind us, which had been dry a quarter-hour before, was now almost entirely underwater.

'*Tension!*' Erica screamed from the middle of the river channel. I could barely hear her. The water roared.

'All right,' I said, pulling in rope.

Erica stumbled in the current. 'No! Slack, goddamnit; give me slack! I tell you to *pay attention* and you pull in rope!'

'Sorry,' I said. She couldn't hear me.

I paid out rope, and Erica crossed the channel. 'Come on!' she called, 'Hurry!' I started into the water, remembered to unbuckle my hip belt, and crossed slowly, carefully, thinking only *left foot, right foot, left foot, right foot* so that I would not be thinking about where I was, and I did not look around me more than I had to. Green-Eyes pulled in the rope from her side of the channel. The water was waist deep. It pushed at me, trying to knock me down. I missed my footing for a moment, aborted the step, and reached with the other toe until I found a rock. Carefully, my arms outstretched in proper Outward Bound fashion, I made the crossing and pulled myself up on to Erica's gravel bank. I was numb from the waist down.

'You're going to have to go faster than that,' Erica said.

'That's true,' I said. 'I can see that.' We went to the next channel at a run. I was terrified. The water was somewhat deeper here, and Erica crossed with difficulty. I could see the look of complete concentration on her far-away face.

'OK—come on!' she called faintly.

I stepped into the water, my open hip belt swinging loose against my thighs. My pack did not feel properly balanced. The current was very strong. I took another step, and another. The bottom dropped away suddenly, and the water was above my belly. The pack twisted on my shoulders as the river shoved me back and forth. 'Erica!' I screamed from the middle of the channel. I was falling; I fell; the current was pulling me down, and my heavy pack held me underwater, trapping the back of my head against the hard frame so that I could not reach air. The

171

world sang in my ears. I could not get up, and the cold, cold water was paralysing me. I thrashed stupidly. Then Erica was pulling the rope tight and calling something to me in a firm voice. I couldn't understand her, but I knew that I had to get up. The water was very cold. My arms and legs still responded somewhat, and I floundered forward, clawing at the rope, until at last the channel was only knee-deep again and I got to my feet.

'Good recovery!' Erica called encouragingly.

'Thank you,' I said.

I waded up on to the sand bar, shivering, and stood beside her, looking at the next channel. The water was grey and swollen; it was quick and calm and deep. As soon as I saw it, I knew that I was going to fall.

'Let's go,' said Erica. 'We've got to get across soon. The water's rising faster.'

'All right.'

'Watch me! Be ready to run for me! Pay attention!'

'All right.'

The water was already up to her hips. As I watched, she staggered and righted herself. Carefully I paid out rope. Then she was across and looking anxiously at me. 'OK!' she called. 'Come on!'

'This doesn't look too bad,' I said across the channel to her, knowing that she couldn't hear. I stepped into the water. For the first time that day I allowed myself to look ahead, and saw that the other side of the river was a long distance away. We were less than halfway to it. The bank became a green ridge of tundra that met the horizon, topped by the squat white shape of Mount McKinley thrusting into the blue sky.

'Come on!' Erica called through cupped hands.

I wasn't frightened any more. I felt doomed. I started stumbling when the water was only calf-deep. Arms spread wide, I kept on. The current pushed at me rhythmically with each step. The cold water was up to my knees. The only noise I could hear was the gravel churning in the water. My legs were numb. I decided to hurry to get it over with. Paying no attention to my footing, I bolted towards Erica. I looked up at her on that distant sand bar ahead of me; she was pulling in rope complacently. She was pleased, no doubt, that I had finally gotten the knack of river crossings and could perform them with all deliberate speed—when actually, of course, I was rushing through the water in a panic. My pack slammed into my back; I felt relief when I finally fell. The river slugged me, chilly, strong and hateful, and ground me into the rocks. I was shooting downstream, scraping across the rocks as I went. I was breathing in water. I didn't even try to raise my head. I considered myself dead.

Then I stopped moving with a jerk. Erica had thrown herself down to the ground and began to haul me in. I felt myself being hauled but I could not help her. Slowly, slowly she dragged me out of the river. I could hear her grunting with the effort. At last I was lying in only three or four inches of icy water. I tried to get up, but I couldn't. My body was without feeling, and my pack was heavy with water. I undid one shoulder strap, pulled myself slowly out of the other, and dragged myself and my pack very slowly along through the wet stones, as if I were a snail.

'Come on!' Erica was calling. 'Get up!'

I tried to keep moving.

'You can do it! You've got to do it! Get up!'

Erica called my name again, breathlessly.

We were on another big sand bar. Erica Bright was pulling off my shoes and my torn, bloody jeans; she was unrolling my sleeping-bag, which had stayed dry in its double stuff sack; she was holding me tight. My legs and face were bloody. 'Hurry up and get into your bag,' Erica Green-Eyes said. 'You have hypothermia.'

'Erica,' I said. It took all my effort to say her name.

'My heart really went out to you, too,' she said. 'Now get in.'

For a long time I shivered in the sun. Erica sat beside me all afternoon. 'You know,' she said finally, 'I'm starting to get fond of you.'

I smiled up at her.

The next day we crossed McKinley all the way. In the last channel, Erica fell. We were side by side in the water, holding on to each other by my belt. There was a heavy clank as Erica hit the rocks with her pack and then a grinding. I was pulled down.

173

'Get up!' I shouted in my best Green-Eyes manner. I pulled her up; she slipped off her pack. We were in calm shallow water. I helped her to her feet, and the two of us dragged her pack on to the final sandbank. She looked at me, wet and smiling, and threw her arms around me and kissed my cheek.

Of course, she hadn't needed my help at all.

The Other Side: I will never forget that morning, which was so sunny and joyous, with the river behind us and ahead of us a rolling tundra ridge sparkling with wet blueberries, beyond which (although we could not see that yet) was a valley of beautiful little lakes in which we could bathe, and then ankle-deep moss, some red, some green; and then more ecstatic days and terrible days until one morning we woke up in someone's bedroom, she in the double bed, I in my sleeping-bag on the floor (for we never slept together), and the shades were down so that the room was so dim that we could hardly see each other; we had woken up at the same time; she reached down from the bed, I reached up, and we gripped each other's wrists in that solid way that gives support on river crossings, and I have not seen Erica again, but I went back and back to the Arctic and crossed rivers by myself because dear Erica showed me how; and as Erica and I came out of the river on that morning in late July I somehow knew all this and was so happy as we ate blueberries out of Erica's enamel cup; and of course within hours came the edge of that mossy plateau, and below waited our next river and I could hear the heavy sound of the water, and the river was just as dreadful as ever; but while we were eating blueberries it was a long way away yet; and the place where we found ourselves was so beautiful, so beautiful, and I was stunned by the sunlight and the sound of the river behind me and the unknown vastness ahead of me; I was stunned by it all.

I think now that if my purpose in going to Afghanistan was at all good, then it must have been to learn if there was a way to help people get across rivers—as I said, I didn't help them, but they helped me. When I went into Afghanistan, my friend Suleiman carried me across the rivers on his back.

ALAN LIGHTMAN
EINSTEIN IN BERN

instein and Besso walk slowly down Speichergasse in the late afternoon. It is a quiet time of day. Shopkeepers are dropping their awnings; others are getting out their bicycles. From a second-floor window, a mother calls to her daughter to come home for dinner.

Einstein has been explaining to his friend Besso why he wants to know time. He says nothing of his dreams.

They will soon be at Besso's house. Sometimes Einstein stays there through dinner, and Mileva has to come and get him, toting their infant. That happens when Einstein is possessed by a new project, as he is now, and all through dinner his leg will twitch under the table. Einstein isn't good dinner company.

Einstein leans over to Besso, who is also short, and says, 'I want to understand time because I want to get close to the Old One.'

Besso nods, but points out the problems. For one, perhaps the Old One isn't interested in getting close to his creations. For another, it is not obvious that knowledge is closeness. And then again, this time project could be too big for a twenty-six-year-old.

On the other hand, Besso believes that his friend might be

Albert Einstein moved to Bern in 1902, having been hired on a trial basis as 'technical expert third class' at the Swiss patent office. The position was made permanent two years later, although the twenty-five-year-old Einstein was unable to advance further until he had 'fully mastered machine technology.' The following year, 1905, is known as the 'miracle year'. On 17 March, Einstein, writing after office hours, completed an article on photoelectric effects that would later earn him the Nobel Prize. On 30 April, he submitted a new version of his doctoral thesis (his first thesis had been rejected in 1902). On 10 May, he published a paper on Brownian motion. And on 30 June, he completed his special theory of relativity (a theory of time), dedicated to his 'loyal friend M. Besso'—Michele Angelo Besso, his old school friend and patent-office colleague.

The following year, on 1 April 1906, Einstein was promoted to 'technical expert second class' at the patent office.

capable of anything. The current project actually began as an investigation of electricity and magnetism, which, Einstein suddenly announced one day, would require a reconception of time. Besso is dazzled by Einstein's ambition.

For a while, Besso leaves Einstein alone with his thoughts and wonders what Anna will have cooked for dinner. He looks down a side-street, where a silver boat on the Aare glints in the low sun. As the two men walk, their footsteps softly click on the cobbled stones. They have known each other since their student days in Zürich.

'I got a letter from my brother in Rome,' says Besso. 'He's coming to visit for a month. Anna likes him because he always compliments her figure.'

Einstein smiles absently.

'I won't be able to see you after work while my brother is here. Will you be all right?'

'What?' asks Einstein.

'I won't be able to see you much while my brother is here,' repeats Besso. 'Will you be all right by yourself?'

'Sure,' says Einstein. 'Don't worry about me.'

Ever since Besso has known him, Einstein has been self-sufficient. Like Besso he is married, but he hardly goes anywhere with his wife. Even at home, he sneaks away in the middle of the night and goes to the kitchen to calculate long pages of equations, which he shows Besso the next day at the office.

Besso eyes his friend curiously. For such a recluse and an introvert, Einstein's passion for closeness seems odd.

Einstein's dream, 19 April 1905. It is a cold morning in November and the first snow has fallen. A man in a long leather coat stands on his fourth-floor balcony on Kramgasse, overlooking the Zahringer Fountain and the white street below. To the east, he can see the fragile steeple of Saint Vincent's Cathedral; to the west, the curved roof of the Zytgloggeturm. But the man is not looking east or west. He is staring down at a tiny red hat left in the snow below, and he is thinking. Should he go to the woman's house in Fribourg? His hands grip the metal balustrade, release it, grip it again.

Photo: Hulton Picture Company

Should he visit her?
Should he visit her?

He decides not to see her again. She is manipulative and judgemental, and she could make his life miserable. Perhaps she is not interested in him anyway. So: he will not see her again. He will, instead, keep the company of men.

He works hard at the pharmacy, goes to the brasserie on Kochergasse in the evenings with his friends and drinks beer, learns to make fondue. Then, in three years, he meets another woman in a clothing shop in Neuchatel. She is nice. Over a period of months, she makes love to him very, very slowly. After a year, she comes to live with him in Bern. They live quietly, take walks together beside the Aare, become companions, grow old and contented.

In the second world, the man in the long leather coat decides that he must see the Fribourg woman again. He hardly knows her, she could be manipulative and her movements hint at volatility, but there is that way her face softens when she smiles, that laugh, her cleverness. Yes, he must see her. He goes to her house in Fribourg, sits with her on the couch, feels his heart pounding, grows weak at the sight of her white arms. They make love, loudly and with passion. She persuades him to move to Fribourg. He leaves his job in Bern and begins work at the Fribourg Post Bureau. He burns with his love for her. Every day he comes home at noon. They eat, make love, argue; she complains that she needs more money; he pleads with her; she throws pots at him; they make love again; he returns to the Post Bureau. She threatens to leave him, but does not leave him. He lives for her and is happy in his anguish.

In the third world, he also decides that he must see her again. He hardly knows her, she could be manipulative and her movements hint at volatility, but there is that smile, that laugh, her cleverness. Yes, he must see her. He goes to her house in Fribourg, meets her at the door, has tea at her kitchen table. They talk of her work at the library, his job at the pharmacy. After an hour, she says that she must leave to help a friend; she says goodbye to him; they shake hands. He returns to Bern, feels empty during the thirty-kilometre train ride, goes to his fourth-floor apartment on Kramgasse, stands on the balcony and stares down at the tiny red hat left in the snow.

These three events all happen simultaneously. For in this world, time has three dimensions, like space. Just as an object may move in three perpendicular directions, corresponding to horizontal, vertical and longitudinal, so an object may participate in three perpendicular futures. Each future moves in a different direction of time. Each future is real. At every point of decision—whether to visit a woman in Fribourg or to buy a new coat—the world splits into three worlds, each one filled by the same people but each having a different fate. In time, there are an infinity of worlds.

Some make light of decisions, arguing that all possible decisions will occur. In such a world, how could one be responsible for his actions? Others hold that each decision must be considered and committed to, that without commitment there is chaos. Such people are content to live in contradictory worlds, as long as they know the reason for each.

Einstein's dream, 24 April 1905. In this world there are two times: mechanical time and body time. The first is rigid and as metallic as a pendulum of iron that swings back and forth, back and forth, back and forth. The second squirms and wriggles like a bluefish. The first is unyielding, predetermined. The second makes up its mind as it goes along.

Many are convinced that mechanical time does not exist. When they pass the giant clock on the Kramgasse they do not see it; nor do they hear its chimes while mailing packages at the Postgasse or strolling among the flowers in the Rosengarten. They might wear watches on their wrists, but only as an ornament or a courtesy to those who gave them as gifts. They do not keep clocks in their houses. Instead, they listen to their heartbeats. They feel the rhythms of their moods and desires. Such people eat when they are hungry, go to their jobs at the millinery or the chemist's whenever they wake from their sleep, make love all hours of the day. Such people laugh at the thought of mechanical time. They know that time moves in fits and starts: that it struggles forward with a weight on its back when they are rushing an injured child to the hospital; and that it darts away when they are lying in the arms of a secret lover.

Then there are those who live by mechanical time. They rise at seven o'clock in the morning. They eat their lunch at noon and their supper at six. They arrive at their appointments on time, precisely by the clock. They make love between eight and ten at night. They work forty hours a week, read the Sunday paper on Sunday, play chess on Tuesday nights. When their stomach growls, they look at their watch to see if it is time to eat. When they begin to lose themselves in a concert, they look at the clock above the stage to see when it is time to go home. They know that the body is not a thing of wild magic, but a collection of chemicals, tissues and nerve impulses. Thoughts are electrical surges in the brain; sexual arousal, a flow of chemicals to certain nerve endings; sadness, a bit of acid transfixed in the cerebellum. In short, the body is a machine, subject to the same laws of electricity and mechanics as an electron or clock. As such, the body must be spoken to in the words of physics. The body is a thing to be ordered, not obeyed.

Taking the night air along the River Aare, one sees evidence for two worlds in one. A boatman gauges his position in the dark by counting the seconds as he is carried by the water's current. 'One, three metres. Two, six metres. Three, nine metres.' His voice cuts through the black in clean and certain syllables. Beneath a lamp-post on the Nydegg Bridge, two brothers stand and drink and laugh. They have not seen each other for a year. The bell in the Cathedral of Saint Vincent sings ten times. In seconds, lights in the apartments lining Schifflaube wink out, as though in a perfectly mechanized response. On the river bank, two lovers, wakened by the distant bells, look up lazily, surprised to find that night has come.

Where the two times meet, desperation. Where the two times go their separate ways, contentment. For, miraculously, a barrister, a nurse, a baker can make a world in either time, but not both times. Each time is true, but the truths are not the same.

Einstein's dream, 28 April 1905. One cannot walk down an avenue, converse with a friend, enter a building, browse beneath the sandstone arches of an old arcade without meeting an instrument of time. Time is visible in all places. Clock towers, wrist-watches, church bells divide years into months, months into days, days into hours, hours into seconds, each increment of time following the other in perfect succession. And beyond any particular clock, a vast scaffold of time, stretching across the universe, lays down the law of time equally for all. In this world, a second is a second is a second. Time paces forward with exquisite regularity, at precisely the same velocity in every corner of space. Time is an infinite ruler. Time is absolute.

Every afternoon, the townspeople of Bern convene at the west end of Kramgasse. There, at four minutes to three, the Zytgloggeturm pays tribute to time. High on the turret of the tower, clowns dance, roosters crow, bears play fife and drum, their mechanical movements and sounds synchronized exactly by the turning of gears, which in turn are inspired by the perfection of time. At three o'clock precisely, a massive bell chimes three times, people verify their watches and then return to their offices on Speichergasse, their shops on Marktgasse, their farms beyond the bridges of the Aare.

Those of religious faith see time as evidence of God. For surely nothing could be created perfect without a Creator. Nothing could be universal and not be divine. All absolutes are part of the One Absolute. And wherever absolutes, so too time. Thus the philosophers of ethics have placed time at the centre of their belief. Time is the reference against which all actions are judged. Time is the clarity for seeing right and wrong.

In a linen shop on Amthausgasse, a woman talks with her friend. The woman has suddenly lost her job. For twenty years, she worked as a clerk in the Bundeshaus, recording debates. She has supported her family. Now, with a daughter still in school and a husband who spends two hours each morning on the toilet, she has been fired. Her administrator, a heavily oiled and grotesque lady, came in one morning and told her to clear out her desk by the following day. The friend in the shop listens quietly, neatly folds the table-cloth she has purchased, picks lint off the sweater of the woman who has just lost her job. The two friends agree to meet for tea at ten o'clock the next morning. Ten o'clock. Seventeen hours and fifty-three minutes from this moment. The woman who has just lost her job smiles for the first time in days. In her mind, she imagines the clock on the wall in her kitchen, ticking off each second between now and tomorrow at ten, without interruption. And a similar clock in the home of her friend, synchronized. Tomorrow morning, twenty minutes before ten, the woman will put on her scarf and gloves and coat and walk down the Schifflaube, past the Nydegg Bridge and on to the tea shop on Postgasse. Across town, at fifteen minutes before ten, her friend will leave her own house on Zeughausgasse and make her way to the same place. At ten o'clock they will meet. They will meet at ten o'clock.

A world in which time is absolute is a world of consolation. For while the movements of people are unpredictable, the movement of time is predictable. While people can be doubted, time cannot be doubted. While people brood, time skips ahead without looking back. In the coffee houses, in the government buildings, in boats on Lake Geneva, people look at their watches and take refuge in time. Each person knows that somewhere is recorded the moment she was born, the moment she took her first step, the moment of her first passion, the moment she said goodbye to her parents.

Einstein's dream, 28 June 1905. 'Stop eating so much,' says the grandmother, tapping her son on the shoulder. 'You'll die before me and who will take care of my silver?' The family is having a picnic on the banks of the Aare, ten kilometres south of Bern. The girls have finished their lunch and chase each other around a spruce tree. Finally dizzy, they collapse in the thick grass, lie still for a moment, then roll on the ground and get dizzy again. The son and his very fat wife and the grandmother sit on a blanket, eating smoked beef, cheese, sour dough bread with mustard, grapes, chocolate cake. As they eat and drink, a gentle breeze comes over the river, and they breathe in the sweet summer air. The son takes off his shoes and wiggles his toes in the grass.

Suddenly a flock of birds darts overhead. The young man leaps from the blanket and runs after them, without taking time to put on his shoes. He disappears over the hill. Soon he is joined by others, who have spotted the birds from the city.

One bird has alighted in a tree. A woman climbs the trunk, reaches out to catch the bird, but the bird jumps quickly to a higher branch. She climbs further up, cautiously straddles a branch and slowly moves outward. The bird hops back to the lower branch. As the woman hangs helplessly up in the tree, another bird has touched down to eat seeds. Two men creep up behind it, carrying a giant bell jar. But the bird is too fast for them and takes to the air, merging again with the flock.

Now the birds fly through the town. The vicar at Saint Vincent's Cathedral, standing in the belfry, tries to coax the birds into the arched window. An old woman in the Kleine Schanze gardens sees the birds momentarily roost in a bush. She walks slowly towards them with a bell jar, knows she has no chance of entrapping a bird, drops her jar to the ground and begins weeping.

And she is not alone in her frustration. Indeed, each man and each woman desires a bird. Because this flock of nightingales is time. Time flutters and fidgets and hops with these birds. Trap one of these nightingales beneath a bell jar, and time stops. The moment is frozen for all people and trees and soil caught within.

In truth, these birds are rarely caught. The children, who alone have the speed to catch birds, have no desire to stop time. For the children, time moves too slowly already. They rush from moment to moment, anxious for birthdays and new years, barely able to wait for the rest of their lives. The elderly desperately wish to halt time, but are much too slow and fatigued to entrap any bird. For the elderly, time darts by much too quickly. They yearn to capture a single minute at the breakfast table drinking tea, or a moment when a grandchild is stuck getting out of her costume, or an afternoon when the winter sun reflects off the snow and floods the music room with light. But they are too slow. They must watch time jump and fly beyond reach.

On those occasions that a nightingale is caught, the catchers delight in the moment now frozen. They savour the precise placement of family and friends, the facial expressions, the trapped happiness over a prize or a birth or romance, the captured smell of cinnamon or white double violets. The catchers delight in the moment so frozen but soon discover that the nightingale expires, its clear, flute-like song diminishes to silence, the trapped moment grows withered and without life.

Einstein on 30 June 1905. In some distant arcade, a clock tower calls out six times and then stops. The young man slumps at his desk. He has come to the office at dawn, after another upheaval. His hair is uncombed and his trousers are too big. In his hand he holds his new theory of time, written on twenty crumpled pages, which he will mail out today to a German journal of physics.

Tiny sounds from the city drift through the room. A milk bottle clinks on a stone. An awning is cranked in a shop on Marktgasse. A vegetable cart slowly moves through a street. A man and woman talk in hushed tones from an apartment nearby.

In the dim light the desks in the room appear shadowy and soft, like large sleeping animals. Except for the young man's desk, which is cluttered with half-opened books, the twelve oak desks are all neatly covered with documents left from the previous day. In two hours, when the clerks arrive, each will know precisely where to begin. But at this moment, in this dim light, the documents on the desks are no more visible than the clock in the corner or the secretary's stool by the door.

Ten minutes past six, by the invisible clock on the wall. Minute by minute, new objects gain form. Here, a brass wastebasket appears. There, a calendar on a wall. Here, a family photograph, a box of paper-clips, an inkwell, a pen. There, a typewriter, a jacket folded on a chair. In time, the bookshelves emerge from the night mist that clings to the walls. The bookshelves hold notebooks of patents. One patent concerns a new drilling gear with teeth curved in a pattern to minimize friction. Another proposes an electrical transformer that holds constant voltage when the power supply varies. Another describes a typewriter with a low velocity typebar to eliminate noise. It is a room full of practical ideas.

Outside, the tops of the Alps start to glow from the sun. A boatman on the Aare unties his small skiff and pushes off, letting the current take him beside Aarstrasse to Gerberngasse, where he will deliver his summer walnuts and figs. The baker arrives at his store on Marktgasse, fires his coal oven, begins mixing flour and yeast. Two lovers embrace on the Nydegg bridge, gaze wistfully into the river below. A man stands on his balcony on Schifflaube, studies the pink sky. A woman who cannot sleep walks slowly down Kramgasse, peering into each dark arcade, reading the posters in half light.

In the long, narrow office on Speichergasse, the room full of practical ideas, the young patent clerk still sprawls in his chair, head down on his desk. For the past several months, since the middle of April, he has dreamed many dreams about time. His dreams have taken hold of his research. His dreams have worn him out, exhausted him so that he sometimes could not tell whether he was awake or asleep. But the dreaming is finished. Out of many possible natures of time, imagined in as many nights, one seems compelling. Not that the others are impossible. The others might exist in other worlds.

The young man shifts in his chair, waiting for the typist to come, and softly hums from Beethoven's *Moonlight Sonata*.

THE
WOMAN'S
DAUGHTER

'Dermot Bolger distills a
dark brew... laced with
a poet's fevered
imagination and horrors
temporal and spectral
from two centuries...
powerful with a strong
aftertaste'
- The Guardian

DERMOT
BOLGER

£5.99
Out now
in Penguin

ANDRÉ BRINK
AFRIKANERS AND THE
FUTURE

André Brink

What is the future of Afrikaners in South Africa? Speculation ranges from the over-optimistic and rather naïve conviction of President de Klerk that Afrikaners will in some way continue to control, or at the very least check, power in the future South Africa, to the equally firm conviction, curiously shared by both the extreme left and the extreme right, that Afrikaners as a distinct tribe will be swept from the scene, leaving no trace of their history, political systems, language or culture.

The nature of Afrikaner political power and the way in which it has been established in South Africa make it significant for the future. In other ex-colonies, independence has brought a straightforward confrontation, peaceful or otherwise, between the colonizer and the colonized. But in South Africa at the time of the British occupation (temporarily from 1795–1803 and permanently after 1806), the Boers saw themselves, at least regarding the new colonizers, as part of the indigenous population. This does not diminish the fact that vis-à-vis the 'real' indigenous peoples, the Boers continued to fulfil in many respects the role of oppressors, but certainly their identification with other Africans was such that on several occasions during the nineteenth century Boers and Blacks joined forces against what to them was the common enemy, the foreign invader: the British. And after the British imposed their permanent presence, Afrikaners fought several wars of liberation against the colonizers—winning at least once, in 1881, before being temporarily crushed in 1902. For well over a century they regarded themselves as part of the oppressed; and by the time they finally won political power it was interpreted largely as the vindication of their right to rule the country in which they had been 'stepchildren' for three centuries.

The Afrikaner political establishment has for so long cultivated the image of a monolith that it has become difficult to acknowledge, even within Afrikanerdom, that this white tribe has never really been a homogeneous group in terms of politics, culture, socio-economics or even religion. What unity has been perceived from outside, or imposed from inside, has largely been brought about by the pressure of circumstances and a gut-felt need to survive against the odds.

Certainly, the grim face of apartheid has led most outsiders, and gradually even many insiders, to believe that dour Calvinism, power politics vested in violence and racism based on an Old Testament-like faith in being God's chosen people are the defining characteristics—the only characteristics—of the Afrikaner people. And crude popular representations by writers like Wilbur Smith or James Michener have done much to confirm the stereotypes. The results of the recent white referendum in the country, which has seen a remarkable majority of Afrikaners effectively and consciously voting themselves out of power, will perhaps dispel some of the false perceptions of the past (although a touch of cynicism in one's evaluation of that vote may not be out of place: the prospect of international competition in rugby, cricket and athletics may well have weighed more heavily with white voters than considerations of political realism).

Part of the historical heritage of Afrikaners is a deep-rooted pragmatism, without which survival would not have been conceivable. It was only late in the nineteenth century that burghers of the Transvaal Republic—the immediate ancestors of today's Treurnichts and Terreblanches—consciously began to devise a mythology of racial supremacy which soon hardened into ideology. Behind the face of ideology still hides the pragmatist who wishes not only to survive, but to survive in Africa, and who has now acknowledged that if the choice is between death and life, or between clinging to principles (which means exile) and pragmatism (which means negotiating the terms of remaining in Africa with a black majority), most of them will be practical.

Afrikaners have survived in Africa for over three hundred years not only because they have been better than everybody else at oppressing others, but also because from a very early stage of Dutch settlement they have defined themselves, not in terms of a foreign 'patria' (as Holland was called for a long time) but in terms of Africa. Through the need to survive the physical ordeals presented by the interior of a strange country, these Boers (and within fifty years of the arrival of the Dutch at the Cape those born in Africa were already calling themselves 'Afrikaners') had

191

to attune themselves to the rhythms of the continent. In the worst circumstances, their interaction with indigenous peoples was violent and destructive; in the best circumstances they acknowledged a mutual dependence: protection and a new kind of know-how in exchange for the kind of 'natural' knowledge that made survival possible.

In terms of a common history and a collective memory of a peasant, tribal, nomadic existence in Africa, Afrikaners share a great deal with black Africans, as acknowledged in numerous contacts between Afrikaners and ANC representatives during the dark and dangerous years when the ANC was still a banned organization. And both sides are prepared to negotiate a common future. Some may do so grudgingly, others cynically; but ultimately Africa is the deciding factor. And that ferocious attachment to the continent—which most foreigners often mistake for romanticism or sentimentality, but which Russians understand when they speak about 'Mother Russia'—will ultimately promote the kind of interdependence and co-operation which is essential to a secure future in South Africa.

This is precisely what is happening in Namibia at the moment, in spite of convulsive problems of racism, economic straits (created largely by the West characteristically reneging on pre-independence promises), and a legacy of mistrust: in Namibia, too, a hard core of nationalist Afrikaners threatened to shoot their way to survival. But once independence was achieved and these chauvinists discovered that it was not the end of the world, they began to accept the inevitable. And already there are indications in South Africa after the referendum that, except for perhaps a very small minority, most Afrikaners on the extreme right will accept survival through a negotiated settlement with the majority, rather than exile or death or irrelevance.

What is to become of the Afrikaans language in the process? One should bear in mind that this language came into existence in the mouths of slaves and indigenous African peoples through their attempts to speak Dutch: for a long time Afrikaans was the language of the oppressed, a kitchen patois banished as much from English-speaking courts of law as from Dutch religious and official institutions. Only at the end of the nineteenth century, when a handful of white men consciously wrested the language from its original humble speakers and turned it into an instrument of war against Dutch and English alike in order to foster political aspirations, did Afrikaans gradually become the language of apartheid, and of white males.

But in the last few decades more and more Afrikaans writers have been using the language as their weapon against the establishment and against apartheid: just as German was not only the language of Hitler, but also of Goethe and Thomas Mann, so Afrikaans has gradually become larger than the ideology which originally tried to entrap it. More importantly, in recent years so-called 'Coloured' speakers have begun to reclaim 'their' language, turning it into an instrument of liberation and cultural affirmation. Almost half the mother tongue speakers of Afrikaans are not white. Once Afrikaans sheds the burden of being an official language, and once its ordinary usage confirms that it is no longer the language of oppression, it has every chance of a worthy survival as one of the many indigenous languages of a new South Africa.

With the indigenous peoples, Afrikaners are becoming the children of Adamastor, that great dark brooding guardian spirit of the Cape who has for so long stood watch over the southern tip of the continent to keep out those who come only for gain or war. In this respect they have a very real contribution to make to the future: provided they acknowledge that, by the same token, they have an increasing—but inspiring—burden of responsibility.

DAVID GOLDBLATT
DIE HEL

Die Hel is a remote valley in the Swartburg Mountains of the south-western Cape. White people first settled there in the latter part of the last century. They left the valley only twice a year when they took a caravan of donkeys over the mountains to the nearest town, Prince Albert, to trade the fruit they grew.

I took these pictures when I visited Die Hel in 1967 and 1968. On both occasions it was Christmastime. In many ways the people—three or four families—seemed to embody an unattainable Afrikaner ideal; I was struck by their industry and self-sufficiency, and by their innocence. They expressed no prejudice; they did not know the word 'kaffir'.

But even then their society was changing. In the 1950s the provincial government had driven a road through the mountains; some of the young men had bought small trucks—'bakkies'—and looked for work outside the valley. The children had begun to attend schools in Prince Albert.

When I returned to Die Hel last year, the houses were in ruins and the orchards were barren. Only one of the families remains.

Caught in a Story

CONTEMPORARY FAIRYTALES
and FABLES
edited by
CHRISTINE PARK *and* CAROLINE HEATON

From twenty of our finest contemporary
writers, a rich and subversive collection of
modern fairytales

£5.99
A VINTAGE PAPERBACK

V

NADINE GORDIMER
LOOK-ALIKES

Nadine Gordimer

It was scarcely worth noticing at first; an out-of-work lying under one of the rare indigenous shrubs cultivated by the Botany Department on the campus. Some of us remembered, afterwards, having passed him. And he—or another like him— was seen rummaging in the refuse bins behind the Student Union; one of us (a girl, of course) thrust out awkwardly to him a pitta she'd just bought for herself at the canteen, and she flushed with humiliation as he turned away mumbling. When there were more of them, the woman in charge of catering came out with a kitchen hand in a blood-streaked apron to chase them off like a band of marauding monkeys.

We were accustomed to seeing them panhandling in the streets of the city near the university and gathered in this vacant lot or that, clandestine with only one secret mission, to beg enough to buy another bottle; moving on as the Druids' circle of their boxes and bits of board spread on the ground round the ashes of their trash fires was cleared for the erection of post-modern office blocks. We all knew the one who waved cars into empty parking bays. We'd all been confronted, as we crossed the road or waited at the traffic lights, idling in our minds as the engine of the jalopy idles, by the one who held up a piece of cardboard with a message running out of space at the edges: NO JOB IM HUNGRY EVEYONE HELP PLeas.

At first; yes, there were already a few of them about. They must have drifted in by the old, unfrequented entrance down near the tennis-courts, where the security fence was not yet completed. And if they were not come upon, there were the signs: trampled spaces in the bushes, empty bottles, a single split shoe with a sole like a lolling tongue. No doubt they had been chased out by a patrolling security guard. No student, at that stage, would have bothered to report the harmless presence; those of us who had cars might have been more careful than usual to leave no sweaters or radios visible through the locked windows. We followed our familiar rabbit-runs from the lecture rooms and laboratories back, forth and around campus, between residences, libraries, Student Union and swimming-pool, through avenues of posters making announcements of debates and sports events, discos and rap sessions, the meetings of Muslim, Christian or

Jewish brotherhoods, gay or feminist sisterhoods, with the same lack of attention to all but the ones we'd put up ourselves.

It was summer when it all started. We spend a lot of time on the lawns around the pool, in summer. We swot down there, we get a good preview of each other more or less nude, boys and girls, there's plenty of what you might call foreplay—happy necking. And the water to cool off in. The serious competitive swimmers come early in the morning when nobody else is up, and it was they who discovered these people washing clothes in the pool. When the swimmers warned them off they laughed and jeered. One left a dirt-stiff pair of pants that a swimmer balled and threw after him. There was argument among the swimmers; one felt the incident ought to be reported to Security, two were uncomfortable with the idea in view of the university's commitment to being available to the city community. They must have persuaded him that he would be exposed for élitism, because although the pool was referred to as the Wishee-Washee, among us, after that, there seemed to be no action taken.

Now you began to see them all over. Some greeted you smarmily (*my baas*, sir, according to their colour and culture), retreating humbly into the undergrowth; others, bold on wine or stoned on meths, sentimental on pot, or transformed in the wild hubris of all three, called out a claim (Hey man, *Ja boetie*) and even beckoned to you to join them where they had formed one of their circles, or huddled, just two, with the instinct for seclusion that only couples looking for a place to make love have, among us. The security fence down at the tennis-courts was completed, reinforced with spikes and manned guardhouse, but somehow they got in. The guards with their Alsatian dogs patrolled the campus at night but every day there were more shambling figures disappearing into the trees, more of those thick and battered faces looking up from the wells between buildings, more supine bodies contoured like sacks of grass cuttings against the earth beneath the struts of the sports grandstands.

And they were no longer a silent presence. Their laughter and their quarrels broadcast over our student discussions, our tête-à-tête conversations and love-making, even our raucous fooling about. They had made a kind of encampment for

207

themselves, there behind the sports fields where there was a stretch of ground whose use the university had not yet determined: it was for future expansion of some kind, and in the meantime equipment for maintenance of the campus was kept there—objects that might or might not be useful, an old tractor, barrels for indoor plants when the Vice-Chancellor requested a bower to decorate some hall for the reception of distinguished guests, and—of course—the compost heaps. The compost heaps were now being used as a repository for more than garden waste. If they had not been there with their odours of rot sharpened by the chemical agents for decay with which they were treated, the conclave living down there might have been sniffed out sooner. Perhaps they had calculated this in the secrets of living rough: perhaps they decided that the Alsatians' noses would be bamboozled.

So we knew about them—everybody knew about them, students, faculty, administrative staff, Vice-Chancellor—and yet nobody knew about them. Not officially. Security was supposed to deal with trespassers as a routine duty; but although Security was able to find and escort beyond the gates one or two individuals too befuddled or not wily enough to keep out of the way, they came back or were replaced by others. There was some kind of accommodation they had worked out within the order of the campus, some plan of interstices they had that the university didn't have; like the hours at which security patrols could be expected, there must have been other certainties we students and our learned teachers had relied on so long we did not realize that they had become useless as those red bomb-shaped fire extinguishers which, when a fire leaps out in a room, are found to have evaporated their contents while hanging on the wall.

We came to recognize some of the bolder characters; or rather it was that they got to recognize us—with their street-wise judgement they knew who could be approached. For a cigarette. Not money—you obviously don't ask students for what they themselves are always short of. They would point to a wrist and ask the time, as an opener. And they must have recognized something else, too: those among us who come to a university because it's the cover where you think you can be safe from surveillance and the expectations others have of you—back to play-school days, only the sand-pit and the finger-painting are substituted by other games. The drop-outs, just cruising along until the end of the academic year, sometimes joined the group down behind the grandstands, taking a turn with the zoll and maybe helping out with the donation of a bottle of wine now and then. Of course only we, their siblings, identified them; with their jeans bought ready-torn at the knees, and hair shaved up to a topknot, they would not have been distinguished from the younger men in the group by a passing professor dismayed at the sight of the intrusion of the campus by hoboes and loafers. (An interesting point, for the English Department, that in popular terminology the whites are known as hoboes and the blacks as loafers.) If student solidarity with the underdog was expressed in the wearing of ragged clothes, then the invaders' claim to be within society was made through adoption of acceptable fashionable unconventions. (I thought of putting that in my next essay for Sociology II.) There were topknots and single ear-rings among the younger invaders, dreadlocks, and one had long tangled blond hair snaking about his dark-stubbled face. He could even have passed for a certain junior lecturer in the Department of Political Science.

So nobody said a word about these recruits from among the students, down there. Not even the Society of Christian Students, who campaigned for moral regeneration on the campus. In the meantime, 'the general situation had been brought to the notice' of Administration. The implication was that the trespassers were to be requested to leave, with semantic evasion of the terms 'squatter' or 'eviction'. SUJUS (Students for Justice) held a meeting in protest against forced removal under any euphemism. ASOCS (Association of Conservative Students) sent a delegation to the Vice-Chancellor to demand that the campus be cleared of degenerates.

Then it was discovered that there were several women living among the men down there. The white woman was the familiar one who worked along the cars parked in the streets, trudging in thonged rubber sandals on swollen feet. The faces of the two

209

black women were darkened by drink as white faces are reddened by it. The three women were seen swaying together, keeping upright on the principle of a tripod. The Feminist Forum took them food, tampons, and condoms for their protection against pregnancy and AIDS, although it was difficult to judge which was still young enough to be a sex object in need of protection; they might be merely prematurely aged by the engorged tissues puffing up their faces and the exposure of their skin to all weathers, just as, in a reverse process, pampered females look younger than they are through the effect of potions and plastic surgery.

From ASOCS came the rumour that one of the group had made obscene advances to a girl student—although she denied this in tears, *she* had offered *him* her pitta, which he had refused, mumbling 'I don't eat rubbish.' The Vice-Chancellor was importuned by parents who objected to their sons' and daughters' exposure to undesirables, and by Hope for the Homeless who wanted to put up tents on this territory of the over-privileged. The city health authorities were driven off the campus by SUJUS and the Feminist Forum while the Jewish Student Congress discussed getting the Medical School to open a clinic down at the grandstands, the Islamic Student Association took a collection for the group while declaring that the area of their occupation was out of bounds to female students wearing the *chador*, and the Students' Buddhist Society distributed tracts on meditation among men and women quietly sleeping in the sun with their half-jacks, discreet in brown paper packets up to the screw-top, snug beside them as hot-water bottles.

These people could have been removed by the police, of course, on a charge of vagrancy or some such, but the Vice-Chancellor, the University Council and the Faculty Association had had too much experience of violence resulting from the presence of the police on campus to invite this again. The matter was referred back and forth. When we students returned after the Easter vacation, the blond man known by his head of hair, the toothless ones, the black woman who always called out *Hullo lovey how'you* and the neat queen who would buttonhole anyone to tell of his student days in Dublin, *You kids don't know what a real university is*, were still there. Like the stray cats students (girls again) stooped to scratch behind the ears.

And then something really happened. One afternoon I thought I saw Professor Jepson in a little huddle of four or five comfortably under a tree on their fruit-box seats. Someone who looked the image of him; one of the older men, having been around the campus some months, now, was taking on some form of mimesis better suited to him than the kid-stuff garb the younger ones and the students aped from each other. Then I saw him again, and there was Dr Heimrath from Philosophy just in the act of taking a draw, next to him—if any social reject wanted a model for a look-alike it would be from that department. And I was not alone, either; the friend I was with that day saw what I did. We were the only ones who believed a student who said he had almost stepped on Bell, Senior Lecturer from Math, in the bushes with one of the three women; Bell's bald head shone a warning signal just in time. Others said they'd seen Kort wrangling with one of the men, there were always fights when the gatherings ran out of wine and went on to meths. Of course Kort had every kind of pure alcohol available to him in his domain, the science laboratories; everybody saw him, again and again, down there, it was Kort, all right, no chance of simple resemblance, and the euphoria followed by aggression that a meths concoction produces markedly increased in the open-air coterie during the following weeks. The papers Math students handed in were not returned when they were due; Bell's secretary did not connect calls to his office, day after day, telling callers he had stepped out for a moment. Jepson, Professor Jepson who not only had an international reputation as a nuclear physicist but also was revered by the student body as the one member of faculty who was always to be trusted to defend students' rights against authoritarianism, our old prof, everybody's enlightened grandfather—he walked down a corridor unbuttoned, stained, with dilated pupils that were unaware of the students who shrank back, silent, to make way.

There had been sniggers and jokes about the other faculty

members, but nobody found anything to say over Professor Jepson; nothing, nothing at all. As if to smother any comment about him, rumours about others got wilder; or facts did. It was said that the Vice-Chancellor himself was seen down there, sitting round one of their trash fires; but it could have been that he was there to reason with the trespassers, to flatter them with the respect of placing himself in their company so that he could deal with the situation. Heimrath was supposed to have been with him, and Bester from Religious Studies with Franklin-Turner from English—but Franklin-Turner was hanging around there a lot, anyway, that snobbish closet drinker come out into the cold, no more fastidious ideas about race keeping him out of that mixed company, eh?

And it was no rumour that Professor Russo was going down there, now. Minerva Russo, of Classics, young, untouchable as one of those lovely creatures who can't be possessed by men, can be carried off only by a bull or penetrated only by the snowy penis-neck of a swan. We males all had understood, through her, what it means to feast with your eyes, but we never speculated about what we'd find under her clothes; further sexual awe, perhaps, a mother-of-pearl scaled tail. Russo was attracted. She sat down there and put their dirty bottle to her mouth and the black-rimmed finger-nails of one of them fondled her neck. Russo heard their wheedling, brawling, booze-snagged voices calling and became a female along with the other unwashed three. We saw her scratching herself when she did still turn up —irregularly—to teach us Greek poetry. Did she share their body-lice too?

It was through her, perhaps, that real awareness of the people down there came. The revulsion and the pity; the old white woman with the suffering feet ganging up with the black ones when the men turned on the women in the paranoia of betrayal—by some mother, some string of wives or lovers half-drowned in the bottles of the past—and cursing her sisters when one of them took a last cigarette butt or hung on a man the white sister favoured; tended by the sisterhood or tending one of them when the horrors shook or a blow was received. The stink of the compost heaps they used drifted through the libraries with the reminder that higher functions might belong to us but we had to perform the lower ones just like the wretches who made us stop our noses. Shit wasn't a meaningless expletive, it was part of the hazards of the human condition. They were ugly, down there at the grandstands and under the bushes, barnacled and scaled with disease and rejection, no one knows how you may pick it up, how it is transmitted, turning blacks grey and firing whites' faces in a furnace of exposure, taking away shame so that you beg, but leaving painful pride so that you can still rebuff, *I don't eat rubbish*, relying on violence because peace has to have shelter, but sticking together with those who threaten you because that is the only bond that's left. The shudder at it, and the freedom of it—to let go of assignments, assessments, tests of knowledge, hopes of tenure, the joy and misery of responsibility for lovers and children, money, debts. No goals and no failures. It was enviable and frightening to see them down there—Bester, Franklin-Turner, Heimrath and the others, Russo pulling herself to rights to play the goddess when she caught sight of us but too bedraggled to bring it off. Jepson, our Jepson, all that we had to believe in of the Old Guard's world, passing and not recognizing us.

And then one day, they had simply disappeared. Gone. The groundsmen had swept away the broken bottles and discarded rags. The compost was doused with chemicals and spread on the campus's floral display. The Vice-Chancellor had never joined the bent backs round the zoll and the bottle down there and was in his panelled office. The lines caging Heimrath's mouth in silence did not release him to ask why students gazed at him. Minerva sat before us in her special way with matched pale narrow hands placed as if one were the reflection of the other, its fingertips raised against a mirror. Jepson's old bristly sow's ear sagged patiently towards the discourse of the seminar's show-off.

From under the bushes and behind the grandstands they had gone, or someone had found a way to get rid of them overnight; somewhere else.

213

KEN LIGHT
THE MISSISSIPPI DELTA

I n the last three years I have driven along some of the smaller, less-travelled roads of the Mississippi Delta.

I had in my mind the famous photographs taken by Dorothea Lange and Marion Post Wolcott during the Depression, and pictures from *Life* magazine of the civil rights era. I had also done some research. I knew that there were parts of the Delta where more than half the population lived below the official poverty line (a rate higher than that for the inner cities); that the incidence of children born outside marriage was sixty per cent; and that thirty-four per cent of the houses lacked adequate plumbing or heating.

But I was not prepared for what I saw: in a landscape dotted with wooden churches, cotton gins and shacks made from planks of cypress wood at the edges of plantations were scenes from an America I believed had disappeared long ago.

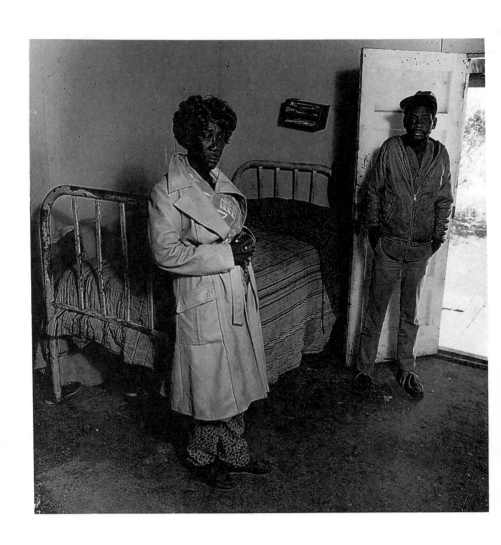

R̲ICHARD R̲AYNER

L̲OS A̲NGELES

I live in a Spanish-style villa in Los Angeles, at the corner of Franklin and Grace, two blocks from Hollywood Boulevard and only one block from Yucca and Wilcox, known as 'crack alley'. One morning my girl-friend walked down into the garage beneath the building and found human excrement on the windscreen of our car. The excrement had not been thrown or carelessly daubed, but somehow painted in a perfect rectangle, thick, four feet by two. Someone had gone to a lot of trouble; from a distance the excrement looked like a nasty modern painting; it also smelled powerfully and took over an hour to wash and scrape off. 'Why didn't they just steal the fucking car?' she said. I did my best to be urbane about another unpleasant reminder of the nature of our neighbourhood. The homeless, I told her, couldn't afford the gas, and the homeboys wouldn't be seen dead in a Volvo; they preferred old Cadillacs and new BMWs, white, loaded with extras.

Several times during the past year I'd watched from my study window as officers of the Los Angeles Police Department staged elaborate busts on the streets. The officers, always white, wore sun-glasses and had Zapata moustaches and carried shotguns or had handguns strapped to their thighs. A car was surrounded and stopped. The suspects, always black, usually young, often well-dressed, were dragged out and made to lie on the ground. They were cuffed with plastic thongs that, from a distance, looked like the tags with which I closed up bags of rubbish. Then they were searched and made to kneel, one on this side of the street, one on the other, while the officers talked among themselves or, swaggering to and fro, conducted an ad hoc interrogation: 'Shut the fuck up and don't move,' I heard on one occasion. 'Feel clever now, black boy?' 'Be careful now, I'm in the mood to hit me a homer.' Every now and then a helicopter would appear, a roaring accompaniment to the scene's edgy surrealism. Sometimes my neighbours came out: an old lady who used to sit in her car, although she never drove it (that was what she did most mornings: she sat there, in her car, not driving it); a long-haired heavy metal musician; a blonde from Texas, pretty, but probably not pretty enough to make it in the movies; a black one-time boxer whose presence was always a comfort. They

Photo: Lester Sloan

watched without any sign of animation—it was all fairly routine —and after fifteen minutes or so the suspects were driven away in the back of a black and white police car, known to the officers as 'a black and normal' ever since police chief Daryl Gates said that the reason why so many blacks died from the carotid chokehold —the controversial technique once used to detain suspects—was that 'their veins and arteries do not open up as fast as they do on normal people.'

I was surprised, not by the fact that this was happening in my neighbourhood, but by the fact that the people of my neighbourhood accepted it all with such indifference. There was, it was apparent, nothing remarkable about the behaviour of the LAPD, which was seen less as a police force than an army at war, a perception encouraged by the department's chief. Gates referred to black drug dealers as 'Viet Cong'. He told a Senate Committee that even casual drug users 'ought to be taken out and shot.' And part of his strategy, Gates said on another occasion, 'is to put a lot of police officers on the street and harass people and make arrests for inconsequential kinds of things.' Gates was known to model his police department on the US Marines; its stated aims were to be fast, mobile and extremely aggressive.

'You're *supposed* to be frightened of the LAPD,' a friend told me. 'The question is why you live in the neighbourhood you do.'

My apartment, I explained, was a particularly beautiful piece of history, designed and built in the 1920s by the movie director Cecil B. De Mille.

'Are you insane?' my friend said. 'Move somewhere else, move away from that shit, move to the Westside,' by which he meant a small rectangle within the new 310 area telephone code: west of La Cienega Boulevard and north of the Santa Monica freeway. My friend stressed the borders: these weren't just streets; they were magical divides. By entering this area, I would be safe, secure and white. Hispanics would be the people who didn't speak English; they would clean the house and clip the lawn, then get on the RTD and disappear back to the nether worlds of East and South Los Angeles. And blacks wouldn't exist at all, unless they wore Armani and worked at CAA.

Seeing a black in Los Angeles, I had come to realize, wasn't the same experience as seeing a black in New York. I found myself making categories. There were the smart professional blacks—lawyers, entertainers, film-industry schmoozers. These I greeted with a smiling 'Ciao!' There were middle-class blacks, who ran businesses and owned property in more or less exclusively black and Hispanic areas—Inglewood, Compton, Crenshaw. These I knew about but never met: our worlds didn't intersect. There were the bums on Hollywood Boulevard, asking for a quarter or shouting their rage among the tourists, the runaways, the hustlers and hookers, the followers of L. Ron Hubbard and his Scientology Church. These it was safe to ignore. And then there were the homeboys, the gang-bangers, who pulled up alongside at a stop-light, or ran whooping through the aisles of smart movie theatres in Westwood and Century City, or strutted along that same stretch of Hollywood Boulevard in Nike Air Jordans, baggy shorts, Gucci T-shirts and baseball caps with an X on the front. Perhaps they really were in a gang, perhaps not, but they behaved with an anger, an arrogance, an aura of fearlessness that suggested they might be. With them, I was the one who became non-existent. Staring straight ahead, I would quicken my step, but not enough to attract attention, and was most comfortable if I happened to be wearing sun-glasses, so that no eye contact was possible. I would hold my breath. I would be invisible.

I knew that my fear was out of all proportion to the true nature of the threat, but, like the earthquake that must happen eventually, the black street gangs of South Los Angeles were a part of the city's apocalyptic demonology. They were armed with Uzis and AK-47s and even rocket launchers, killing each other, and sometimes innocent bystanders, not just for money or 'turf', but for wearing the wrong colour of shoelace or baseball cap. There were said to be as many as 100,000 hard core gang members. Their tags were sprayed on the wall of our building and on the sidewalk outside, an indecipherable crossword, a labyrinth of black paint on white concrete that our Mexican

231

gardener washed away with Chlorox and whitewash. A few days later the crossword was always back.

So it was: don't go here, don't go there, lock the car doors, never spend more time than you have to in parking lots, avoid eye contact on the freeway. This wasn't *just* paranoia. One Friday night I happened to glance at an old Cadillac Coupe de Ville cruising alongside us on the Hollywood freeway. I saw a black kid hand a gun to a friend in the back, not even looking, passing the gun over his shoulder as casually as if it were a pack of cigarettes. So it was: don't go south of Wilshire, here's a homeboy, here's a cop car, a black and white, a black and *normal.* Good. The police spoke about perimeters and containment and points of control. They spoke about South-Central as if it were a township.

Los Angeles was a lot like South Africa. The apartheid wasn't enshrined by law, but by economics and geography, and it was just as powerful. In Los Angeles I was afraid of blacks in a way I had never been. I behaved in a way that would have disgusted me in New York or London. I was a racist.

The Taser stun gun was introduced by the LAPD in 1980, and it was used against Rodney King, the black motorist whom LAPD officers Lawrence Powell, Ted Briseno, Timothy Wind and Sergeant Stacey Koon were accused of unlawfully beating shortly after midnight on 3 March 1991. Despite all that had been written about the incident, I had read very little about the operation of the Taser. It was, I discovered, a weird-looking device, a crude, chunky grey pistol which fired darts into people. The darts were attached to wires, which on pushing a button administered a shock of 50,000 volts. 'Seems to cool off most people pretty good,' said a representative of Ray's Guns of Hollywood. It had been used more and more to restrain suspects following the banning of the carotid chokehold in 1984.

Rodney King was stopped after a high speed pursuit, first on the Foothill freeway, and then on the streets of Pacoima, during which he drove at speeds in excess of 100 miles per hour and ignored a number of red lights. The initial pursuit was made by Melanie and Timothy Singer, a husband and wife team of the

California Highway Patrol, but when LAPD cars arrived on the scene it was Sergeant Stacey Koon who took charge. As Koon notes in an as yet unpublished autobiography, he looked at the petite Melanie Singer and then at the six foot three inch, 225-pound Rodney King (who, according to Koon, had dropped his trousers and was waving his buttocks in the air), and decided that this was about to develop into 'a Mandingo type sex encounter,' a reference to a Hollywood movie which involves black slaves raping white women.

Koon used his Taser stun gun, firing two darts into Rodney King and giving him two shocks. One was enough to subdue most suspects and even the Mandingo Rodney King himself was on the ground by now, showing little sign of resistance. Koon and the three other officers then kicked him and hit him fifty-six times with their batons, breaking his ankle, his cheek-bone and causing eleven fractures at the base of his skull, as well as concussion and nerve damage to the face. The force of the blows knocked fillings from his teeth.

The last of the not-guilty verdicts was announced in Simi Valley at three forty-five p.m. on Wednesday, 29 April 1992. As Stacey Koon left the court-house, it was declared that he had hired an entertainment attorney to sell the movie and book rights to his story, which would be titled *The Ides of March*, since he had been indicted on 15 March of the previous year.

After the verdict, I went to the Mayfair Market, to a bookstore, to a bar on Franklin. People were nervous, excited. Something was going to happen in South-Central; the question was how bad it would be. When I got home, the phone was ringing. Crowds had gathered downtown at the Parker Center, LAPD headquarters. A police car had been turned over. Looting was said to have started in other places, though the moment when the riots began in earnest was easy to spot: it was broadcast live on TV.

At six-thirty p.m., Reginald Denny stopped at a traffic-light at the intersection of Florence and Normandie. He was on his way to deliver twenty-seven tons of sand to a cement-mixing plant in Inglewood. Denny, thirty-six, would have been driving through South-Central to avoid the rush-hour traffic on the freeways. It was the territory of the Eight-Trey Gangster Crips, one of the city's most famous gangs. While waiting for the light to change, he was pulled from his rig by five or six black youths. Two news helicopters were overhead, watching the crowd which had been gathering since the verdict was announced, and the incident turned into an uncanny mirror-image of the Rodney King beating, though where the King video had been dim and murky, captured by an onlooker from his balcony with a newly acquired Sony camcorder (a few days earlier, on the same tape, he'd bagged Arnold Schwarzenegger, filming a scene from *Terminator 2* in a nearby bar), what I saw now was shot by professionals—the camera zooming in and out, the images well-defined and horribly colourful.

Denny was kneeling in the middle of the street, now empty. Two blacks entered the frame and beat Denny's head with their fists and then kicked him. Another black raised his arms and hurled the truck's fire-extinguisher, hitting Denny on the side of his head, which lurched from the impact. Denny tried to move and rolled on to his side. The helicopter circled for a better angle. You could now see how Denny's white T-shirt, which had slid up his belly, was saturated with blood. A black appeared briefly, smashing what appeared to be a lamp-base over Denny's head. He collapsed again. Another black appeared: this one was holding a shotgun at arm's length, very casual, and shot Denny in the leg. A black was wheeling a bicycle in the background. A black ran up, leaped athletically in the air and kicked him in the head. Denny tried to stand up. The right side of his face was a mess of red, as if it were melting. A black hit him with a tyre-iron; Denny went down. A black hit him with a beer bottle and then raised his arms in triumph. Another black appeared, went through Denny's left pocket, right pocket, back pocket and then ran away with his wallet. A black in baggy shorts stepped up and kicked Denny in the head and danced away on one leg very slowly.

It happened in silence since the scene was filmed from a helicopter, but later I watched a video shot by an eyewitness —again the uncanny mirror image. In this one there was sound;

you could hear the voices: 'No mercy for the white man, no mercy for the white man.' It seemed to be choreographed and went on for a very long time—thirty minutes. Watching the Rodney King video, I had thought it reasonable for American blacks to hate the police and be suspicious of all whites. This didn't make me suspicious of these particular blacks; it made me want to kill them. If any of them had been in my power in that moment, as Reginald Denny was in theirs, I would have done it gladly. I actually saw myself with a gun in my hand. Pow. Pow. Pow.

A few feet from Reginald Denny's truck was Tom's Liquor and Deli; it was the first store looted. The first fire-call was received thirty minutes later at seven-thirty p.m. Forty-five minutes later was the first fatality, Louis Watson, thirty-two blocks and three miles (a distance which in Manhattan takes you from Greenwich Village to Central Park) from where Denny's truck had been, yet still in the heart of South-Central. Watson, an eighteen-year-old black who had wanted to be an artist, was shot to death at Vernon and Vermont, hit by a stray bullet while waiting for a bus.

The TV showed a fire, then another and still more. Soon there were so many that fires normally requiring ten trucks were dealt with by one. A fire captain was threatened with an AK-47 to the head by a gang-banger called 'Psycho'. Another fireman was shot in the throat, and more people began to die, a lot more people. Dwight Taylor, forty-two, was shot to death at 446 Martin Luther King Boulevard. He had been on his way to buy milk. Arturo Miranda, twenty, was shot to death in his car on the way back from soccer practice. Edward Travens, a fifteen-year-old white youth, was shot to death in a drive-by attack in the San Fernando Valley. Patrick Bettan, a white security guard, was shot to death in a Korean supermarket at 2740 W. Olympic. But the dead were mostly black. Two unnamed blacks were shot to death in a gun battle with the LAPD at the Nickerson Gardens Housing Project. A robber shot to death at Century and Van Ness. *Shot to death*: the phrase itself had a velocity, a connectedness to the violence it described, that even constant repetition couldn't reduce to TV babble. At ten-forty: Anthony Netherly, twenty-one, was shot to death at 78th and San Pedro. At eleven-fifteen: Elbert Wilkins, thirty-three, was shot to death in a drive-by attack at 92nd and Western. Ernest Neal, twenty-seven, was shot to death in the same incident. Time unknown: an unknown black male shot to death at 10720 Buren Street. A man *of unknown race and age* was dead of 'riot-related injuries' at Daniel Freeman Memorial Hospital: what possible state was he found in?

Thirteen dead by the end of the night, 1,600 fire-calls, and in the moments when TV stations had nothing new to show, they always went back to Reginald Denny, a white man, for ever on his knees, being beaten. Outside, the choking, fried-plastic smell of the fires wafted across the city.

On Thursday morning people were wanting the riots to be over, hoping they were, believing that they had been a one-day affair. At nine-thirty the radio weatherman was still trying to be wacky. 'Our weather today calls for hazy sunshine. Let's change that,' he chortled, 'smoky sunshine.' If the riots were going to start again, I wanted to see them for myself, and I wanted to see them with a black, not, I'm afraid, because I thought I'd get a special insight (although that was the way it turned out), but because I knew I'd be safer. I called Jake, a black screenwriter. He had grown up in Los Angeles, in South-Central in fact, where his father had been a preacher, and he had gone to college in New York. He had only recently moved back. 'I've been talking to people, not just the gang-bangers, and they're saying they just ain't gonna take it. They've been resting a couple of hours, but it's all going to start up again.' Today, he predicted, the rioters and looters would march across the city. He said he'd pick me up soon.

Jake arrived by eleven and we drove down Normandie, a helicopter overhead, following us south.

Hispanic families stood in doorways, waiting. A street was taped off where a building had burned the previous night, and twice we were passed by LAPD cars, not moving singly, or even in pairs, but in groups of four and five. 'For safety,' said Jake.

236

'Those guys are nervous. The LAPD got burned last night.' He exchanged a fisted salute with the black driver of a Chevrolet. 'The way they left that guy there, at the intersection? The *po-lice*,' he said, as if it were the rock group he were talking about. 'The homies think they've got something on them *for ever*.'

A palm tree was on fire. Flames ran up from the base to the leaves above and seconds later the entire tree was ablaze. Five or six young black kids were running. For a moment I thought they were frightened, running away, and then I realized, of course, they'd set it alight. There was the sound of a gunshot, though it wasn't clear who had fired it; it seemed some way off.

But it was my first experience of the riot close at hand. I was afraid and began to babble. I explained to Jake that I hated gunfire. Americans were obsessed with guns. Before New Year the city authorities had found it necessary to place billboards all over Los Angeles, in English and Spanish, warning people not to fire their guns into the air at midnight. So lots of people fired their guns *into the ground*. Sometimes, lying in bed, or finishing dinner in our Cecil B. De Mille dining-room, with its wood beam ceiling and baronial stone fireplace, I heard shots outside the building. 'Car backfiring again,' I'd say, and my girl-friend would roll her eyes.

'I'm the sort of person,' I told Jake, 'who lies awake in bed thinking someone's about to break in and slit my throat.' No doubt I'd be like that if I lived in the Cotswolds or on the Isle of Skye. Unfortunately I lived in a neighbourhood where corpses were found stuffed into our garbage bins or decomposing in closets in nearby apartments. These stories never made it into the *Los Angeles Times*.

'Move to the Westside,' said Jake, and I presumed he was joking, though I remembered the first time he'd visited our apartment when he walked around checking the locks; then he'd gone around the block and advised us not to walk on Yucca.

Jake wasn't joking. 'You can afford to move away. Move the fuck away,' he said. 'What's your problem?' He'd been living down at the ocean in Santa Monica since returning from New York. He said, 'You live in a marginal neighbourhood, so it's real for you, because you know it's there, but at the same time

237

it's not real, it's just this big bad boogie thing you glimpse from time to time.' The 'it' he was talking about was violence. 'But it's never reached out and really hurt you.'

I agreed; I was lucky.

'I was lucky too. I grew up in a bad neighbourhood. Guys I went to school with are in jail now, or long dead, or crippled in wheelchairs, or have had twelve feet of intestine ripped out by a gunshot.'

On Vermont we passed a furniture store, burnt out and still smoking, and then a mini-mall from which people were running with armloads of loot, or calmly wheeling laden checkout trolleys. It seemed extraordinary that traffic was moving about quite normally at these places, and that these events were visible as we cruised about, snug inside Jake's Honda with the radio and air-conditioning on. We drove past a Blockbuster video store—its window already smashed—as two police officers struggled to cuff a black who was kicking out at them from the ground. Three black kids were getting out of a white Toyota that had just driven up. They walked past the black on the ground and the two officers trying to hold him there, entered the shop and started filling up their arms with videos.

I wanted to say, this is it, we're really in the riot now, it's starting up again, but Jake was so casual about it all. He said that these kids had no hope of getting out as he had. Everything about society told them they were worthless, non-people. They had nothing, so they had nothing to lose, something I'd hear a lot of blacks say over the next days.

We drove east on Pico, past blocks that were quiet, then past blocks where crowds had gathered in anticipation of something happening, and then, once again, past blocks where something *was* happening already. There was a mob inside a Payless shoe store and a black kid, very young, emerged running with two boxes, stopped for a moment, then sat down in the parking lot to try the shoes on. There was a Vons supermarket that Jake had passed some hours before, while it was being looted, which was now on fire, flames leaping through the roof, a fire-truck yet to arrive.

Jake said, 'Sometimes they do it at the same time, other

times they clean it out and come back hours later and burn it then. Keeps the cops on their toes.'

I nodded, as if to say, yes, I could see the logic of that. Two Hispanic youths appeared, casually wheeling a piano around a corner. I was beginning to get a sense of the sheer scale of what was going on. It was huge. The radio was announcing a curfew. After sundown tonight people on the streets anywhere in Los Angeles would be stopped and questioned. The National Guard was on its way, and 2,400 federal troops, veterans of the Gulf war, were set to follow.

'Hubba, hubba,' said Jake.

By one o'clock we were looping back to the east. We came up to 3rd and Vermont. There was a big crowd and a fire in the distance, and now another one, closer, but just starting, and to my left, a column of thick black smoke which made my eyes water and got into my throat almost at once. I began to cough. Twenty or so young men of various races, not running and not walking either, but hurrying as if towards a very serious appointment, crossed the street and kicked down the door of a toy shop. The Korean owner stood by, offering no resistance, shaking his head. On the other side of the intersection three black looters were running, away from the Unocal station, lugging cans of oil in either hand. I didn't need a diagram to figure out what they were going to do with the cans. A hydrant was shooting a plume of water high into the air. At the Thrifty Drug Store, there was a line of people waiting to enter through a door, its glass smashed out, while others made their way out with plastic bags or trolleys filled with stolen goods. A man kicked some glass aside and emerged leaning backwards like in a Monty Python silly walk, his cradled arms piled so high with white and brown boxes that I couldn't see his face.

The traffic lights were out at the intersection. Making a left turn, not a simple exercise at the best of times in Los Angeles, was now a game of chicken, with fire trucks speeding up the hill and drivers nosing forward anxiously, or stopping and then making perilous surges across the intersection, windows open. A mouth and a yellow baseball cap in a Ford truck was yelling: 'MOTHERFUCKER.' The TV hadn't prepared me for the deafening noise of the riot—breaking glass, engines, sirens, smashing, shouting. Everyone was shouting. The noise of the riot was a shape, and it approached and receded like a wave, surging this way and that.

There was another thing: a lot of people had guns, in the waistbands of their trousers or even in their hands. They weren't firing the guns, they merely had them, but that was frightening enough. In England people don't carry guns.

Patrol cars must have pulled up, because there was now an LAPD sergeant shouting commands, and a line of officers— perhaps fifteen in all—was forming at the far end of the Thrifty Drug Store parking lot. The sudden phalanx of officers had no effect on the looters, and, as it advanced, they tended merely to drift into the next store. One sprinted straight at the police line, yelling, and then swerved off at the last moment, jumping over the low wall of the parking lot. A looter stopped to say cheese for a cameraman wearing a flak jacket. Another, a bearded black in a long white T-shirt, and with a cigarette in his mouth, was pointing to his penis, inviting the officers to suck it. The phalanx of police advanced a few steps further; they began beating on their riot shields with their batons.

A kid stepped up and hurled a rock into the street. I didn't see if anyone was hit. The kid threw another rock, launching it from low behind his back as if it were a javelin. Suddenly there were lots of kids, all of them throwing rocks, and then more police cars, coming up behind the phalanx. Jake said in his view the situation was about to get nasty.

In my view the situation had gone some way beyond that. This wasn't at all like the quite pleasurable thrill of fear I'd felt at first. I was terrified. A young black, a teenager, stopped in the middle of the street with a bottle of Budweiser which he was getting ready to throw at a car, ours. The bottle was nearly full. He stared at me, saw I was white, glanced at Jake, saw he was black, and made an obvious calculation. He ran on.

It was about two o'clock when Jake dropped me home. I didn't go out again until the early evening. I made a Waldorf salad, thinking: Now I'm making a Waldorf salad. It seemed

241

a startling way to be carrying on. I had to force myself to eat it. The radio said that a fire was being set every three minutes. That night's performance of *The Phantom of the Opera* at the Amundsen Theatre was cancelled; for some reason this piece of information was repeated over and over again. An interview with an analyst from Harvard was cut abruptly short for another repeat of the crucial *Phantom* announcement, and then it was back to the Harvard man, who was interrupted again, but this time for news of yet another fire and looting.

On TV, Tom Bradley, LA's black mayor, appeared, calling for calm. As he spoke, the screen was split, one half showing a respectable black man urging restraint, the other showing the looting of a clothing store. Mayor Bradley urged everyone to stay at home and watch the final episode of *The Cosby Show* that night; perhaps that would help us solve our problems, he suggested. Then Pete Wilson, the Governor of California, quoted Martin Luther King. His face wasn't shown, but King's words, spoken by Wilson in a slow and sanctimonious tone, were used as the soundtrack as hundreds of black youths rampaged through a mini-mall.

A friend called, a little hysterical, having been trapped in a gridlock for over an hour at Century City. It was like a scene from a Godzilla movie, she said, with Westsiders heading for hotels in Santa Barbara and San Diego, leaving the city in droves. She often had trouble because of her very blonde hair; it gave her the appearance of a Nazi, she said, and homeboys sometimes took exception. She explained all this as if it were no more remarkable a fact of her life than having a mole on her cheek. She was from Sweden and nothing about America surprised her. She'd been on Olympic when someone threw a rock through the passenger window of her car with such velocity that it passed directly in front of her face and then shattered the window on the driver's side. She'd held the steering-wheel so tight on the way home that her arms were still trembling.

A t six o'clock on the Thursday night, my girl-friend and I drove to the hills above Silver Lake. I wanted the view. A smart Korean gentleman in his early forties was watching as well. He had on a blue silk shirt and blue linen trousers, baggily cut, and his sun-glasses were by Oliver Peoples. He was a *very* smart Korean gentleman and he remarked with a world-weary air that he had a business in the mid-Wilshire district, right next door to the Sears building, which now appeared to be ablaze. He wasn't going to defend it, though he knew some of his countrymen had armed themselves with shotguns and machine-guns in Koreatown. But they were shopkeeeepers and he—he shrugged, a little apologetically—was not a shopkeeper. 'Nor am I Clint Eastwood,' he said. 'I pay America lots and lots of taxes so I don't have to be.'

I asked what line of business he was in.

'I have a gallery,' he said. 'You're English?'

'That's right.'

'Two foreigners together,' he said. 'And here we are, watching Los Angeles burn.' He smiled, revealing his teeth, very white and even. Ah me, he seemed to be saying, the wicked, wicked way of the world.

On a clear day I'd seen the ocean from here, but not this evening; the entire Los Angeles basin was covered in a thick grey haze. The twin towers of Century City, a little more than halfway to the sea, were invisible, and looking south and east, the sky was darker still. Black smoke indicated fires that were out of control; white smoke, those that were now contained. The sound of sirens came from all over, and there was a convoy of army vehicles on the Hollywood freeway.

I said, 'Do you think they'll ever feel the same about the city again?'

He asked, 'Who?'

'The rich.'

'The rich?' he said and laughed, a sudden explosion. 'The *rich*?' He found this very amusing. 'Oh my dear, you're so naïve. They might feel guilty for a day or two. Some of them might even be panicked into leaving, for good I mean, for Paris or London or Seattle, not just getting the children into the buggy and high-tailing it for the Sierras. The rest will pull the wagons in even tighter than before. Watch those security bills soar!'

We were on the way back from Silver Lake, driving down Sunset towards a sun that was in fact setting, when I realized that the looting had got very close to my home. I'd been expecting it all day, and I felt a thrill as I saw a pair of homeboys, shouting and jumping, dodging among the cars on Sunset, their arms full of bandannas and Ray-Bans and studded leather jackets, looted, I presumed, from L. A. Roxx, a store which pulled in tourists from the Midwest, relieved them of a couple of hundred dollars and sent them away looking like clones of the whitebread rockers Guns 'n' Roses. I wondered how the homeboys would manage to dispose of all *that* in South-Central.

I didn't know why, but I felt a little proud. The riot had reached my neighbourhood.

This time I was determined not to be such a wuss. I got out of the car at Highland and walked east along Hollywood. There were people running towards me. There was a small boy, he couldn't have been more than seven years old, with two cartons of Marlboro tucked under his arm; a middle-aged white woman was clutching a beat-box still in its box, saying as if she couldn't quite believe it, 'For free.'

A photographer stood beneath the awning of the Ritz Cinema, shooting down the street. 'It's a party now,' he said. 'It's carnival time.'

There was a big crowd between Cherokee and Whitley. They were the type of people I usually saw in the neighbourhood, which is to say tourists, teenagers from the Midwest who still dressed like punks, some kids, a few homeboys, even a few young middle-class types in suits. There was a balding fellow who worked in the Hollywood Book City bookstore. They had all gathered round to watch a very bewildered police officer.

The back of a car was hooked to the steel protective shutter in front of an electronic appliance store. The driver was black, about twenty, with a scrubby beard and a woollen hat. The oblong badge on the officer's chest said: *Barraja*. Officer Barraja wore a helmet with the visor down and sun-glasses behind it. In any other circumstances, we would all have been very frightened of Officer Barraja. But the moment he walked forward and aimed his shotgun at the head of the driver, I knew, and the crowd knew and the bearded man certainly knew that Officer Barraja had put himself in an absurd situation; I knew, the crowd knew and the bearded man certainly knew that Officer Barraja would not shoot. Officer Barraja did not know this yet; he learned it a few moments later when the bearded driver turned and grinned and, gunning his engine, then accelerated until the protective shutter gave way with a groan. Officer Barraja stepped back and shouldered his weapon and then: did nothing. People were hooting and clapping. Someone paused to take his picture. Outside the electronics store a queue was forming, as the people in front ducked through the wrecked fence and stepped inside.

The swap-meet was on fire at the corner of Wilcox, making my eyes smart again, sirens in the distance. I had an exhilarating sense of chaos. I wondered what was going to happen next, when up ahead I spotted a black teenager smashing the door of Frederick's of Hollywood with a hammer. Another pitched a chair and then climbed through the shattered window into the display. Alarm bells sounded, and the crowd, my neighbourhood crowd, responded as though to an invitation, and so I went along as well, not trying to resist as I was almost lifted off my feet in the dense mass of bodies that suddenly crushed forward. I had somehow become part of a mob about to loot and trash what passed in Hollywood for a landmark: a lingerie store.

Someone found a switch and turned on the lights. Frederick's was classier than I'd imagined. The floor was slippery marble tile. The lingerie was red and pink and emerald green, as well as black and white, and each piece had its own hanger, its own place in the spacious arrangement of spinners and wall racks.

No one but me appeared to be admiring it. A girl ran to the far corner of the store, ahead of the pack, earning herself just enough time to be a little selective, as she lifted down hangers one by one. A fat lady in white appeared at the back, pushing, shouting at a man, 'Let's go, let's go.' She, along with the others crushing in behind her, were panicking at the prospect of having arrived too late. The members of this new lot had a strangely fixed expression, concerned perhaps that everything had gone, and were determined to make up for lost time. Broken glass crunched under my feet. Someone had found a ladder and was carefully prising loose an imitation art-deco light fixture. There was no anger or fear; just bedlam. A black teenager in a T-shirt with a big cross around his neck made for the door with a mannequin under his arm. Pieces of other mannequins, stripped and smashed, were lying in the window display. The fat lady in white was on her hands and knees, her broad butt swinging in the air, as she rushed to fill up a suitcase. The suitcase had price-tags; she'd just taken it from somewhere else. She looked at me, a round, chubby face, and smiled, nodding, a gesture that I'm sure was supposed to say to me: *Go on.* I wasn't sure how to behave. I must have looked a little odd, standing there. I fingered some silky stuff.

'Hi!' someone shouted. Not at me, I assumed, but then it came again: 'Hi, Richard.' It was the not-quite-pretty-enough Texan from the building next to mine, on her way from something called the Lingerie Museum at the back of the store. She picked up an intricate lace bra. 'What do you think?' she said, and, without waiting for my reply, folded the bra carefully inside her black leather duffel bag. 'I'm having a ball,' she said, though she was disappointed that the Madonna bustier—the prize exhibit of the Lingerie Museum—had gone before she got to it; there'd been quite a race. She could have got a leather bra belonging to the pop star Belinda Carlisle, but she didn't care for that sort of music and, in any case, 'Definitely a D-cup.' She had the same pouty expression I'd seen on her face once before, when a producer of violent action films had brought her home one morning and ridden off on his Harley-Davidson, leaving her without so much as a kiss.

Frederick's, five minutes after being broken into, was picked bare.

A block and a half away, back up on Grace Avenue, a man was wetting the roof of our building with a hose in case somebody set fire to it. Some of our other neighbours were out on the street. They'd formed a vigilante committee, they said.

But of course, I replied, a little dazed, why not? I felt like

Bertie Wooster. A fat man I'd never seen before wore a baseball cap that said FUCK EVERYBODY.

The black ex-boxer said, 'This town is lost, man. This town is so *lost*.'

The heavy metal musician, standing nearby, opened his jacket to reveal an Ozzie Osbourne T-shirt and, stuffed inside the waistband of his jeans, a gun. 'Browning automatic,' he said proudly. It turned out he was English too.

'Oh, my God,' said my girl-friend. This fellow didn't look like he should be let loose with a water-pistol. Was I the only person in Los Angeles who *didn't* have a gun?

'I was in the Falklands, man,' said the heavy metal musician. 'I've seen this kind of stuff before. Let 'em come.'

'Let them not,' said the ex-boxer. 'I can't afford to move again. I've been moved too many times.'

I wondered what he meant by 'been moved', but then it was the heavy metal musician again, saying, 'The curfew's in force already so you folks had better go home now, OK?' It struck me that he was a strange authority figure. Had he really been in the Falklands? Everything was so extraordinary now I could almost believe he was for real. He walked towards the corner, not without a certain John Wayne swagger. 'You all take care now. OK?'

Nine-thirty, Thursday night, and the death toll was up to thirty. Howard Epstein shot to death at 7th and Slauson. Jose L. Garcia shot to death at Fresno and Atlantic. Matthew Haines pulled off his motorcycle and shot to death in Long Beach. Eduardo Vela shot to death at 5142 W. Slauson. Some of the dead were very young. Fourteen, fifteen. Keven Evanahen died while trying to put out a fire in a cheque-cashing store at Braddock and Inglewood. At least that made for variety. I blinked and shook my head as soon as that thought popped out. I'd been amazed by the riot, thrilled by it, swept along by it, terrified by it. It wasn't just that events had moved at such speed; the actual nature of what had occurred seemed to be shifting all the time. The riot had started with a particular angry focus: race. It had turned quickly into a poverty riot and then, diffused, became interracial anarchy. I wasn't sure what I'd seen, but I felt changed. Los Angeles itself seemed more tangible, now that everyone, even the players themselves, would have to acknowledge that there was more to the city than the make-believe Medici court of the movie business.

The Gap was being looted on Melrose.

The TV news was replaying a bulletin from earlier in the day. At 3rd and Vermont an unknown Latino had been shot with his own gun and was lying dead in the back of his car. No ambulance had been able to get there. This was the very intersection where I'd been with Jake. The reporter, talking to camera, was trying to describe the situation, while black teenagers milled around behind him, clowning it up. At last the reporter gave up. 'There's a dead person here and it's a big joke. Back to you at the studio.'

At midnight we went for a drive. Hollywood Boulevard was blocked off by National Guardsmen in combat fatigues—they were on every corner—so we got on to the Hollywood freeway. Even at his hour, the freeway was normally crowded; now it was deserted. Los Angeles had become another city. We headed south and just as we were passing L. Ron Hubbard's Church of Scientology Celebrity Center, a police car came up alongside. A voice came through the patrol car's loudspeaker. '*A curfew is in force. You are breaking the law. Go home. Get off the streets. You are breaking the law.*'

In the middle of the afternoon on Friday, it became clear that it was probably over, and, curiously, there was a sense not of relief but of disappointed expectation: people wanted more. The rioting had become an entertainment. Announcers at KWIB —news twenty-four hours a day, all day, give us twenty minutes and we give you the world—actually apologized for the fact that the station was now returning to its true obsession, sport, and it occurred to me that during the time of the riot the city had gathered round a spectacle, as it might during the Super Bowl.

I wanted to see the damage where it had been worst, in South-Central, so I went to see Beverley, a black school-teacher I had recently been introduced to. I was cadging a ride with blacks again, this time so that I wouldn't feel threatened while I looked at their burnt-out neighbourhoods.

We started off on Vermont, heading towards South-Central. Straight away Beverley's eleven-year-old daughter Maya declared that she was thirsty, so I said I'd keep my eyes peeled for a store still standing to buy her a soda. The task turned out not to be so easy.

'Burned,' said Beverley, pointing to one store, and then to another. 'Razed . . . Looted and burned. See that cheque store over there? Korean-owned, looted and burned.' Above it was a bright green sign, still intact: INSTANT CASH. On top of the sign stood a National Guardsman with his assault rifle.

'Burned,' she said, as we continued on our quest. 'Levelled to the ground.' Delicatessens, liquor stores, furniture stores, a Fedco warehouse where six hundred workers had turned up and found, literally, no job to go to—building after building was burned. Before the riots, there was one store for every 415 residents, less than half the Los Angeles average. That ratio looked pretty good now. On some stores metal cutters had been used. Solid steel shutters had perfect triangles cut into them, like cans popped with an opener. At the intersection of Vernon and Central all four corners had been wiped out.

'Burned, burned, burned, burned. That's the deli where Latasha Harlins was killed,' Beverley said, pointing to the store whose Korean owner Soon Ja Du had been fined $500 for shooting dead a fifteen-year-old black girl in a dispute over a $1.79 bottle of orange juice. It was one of the first stores attacked (nearly 1,000 Korean businesses were destroyed, I would learn later). 'Homies,' Beverley continued, 'tried to burn that deli three times, but they were ready. Not open now, of course.' In the Watts riots of 1965 many Jewish businesses had been burned in South Los Angeles, and the Jews had left the neighbourhood for good; this time the Koreans had been a target. Yet here, ironically, a BLACK OWNED sign had been a less effective guarantee of safety than in other areas of the city, because the destruction had been so general. 'See that furniture store over there? A black family ran that for twenty-five years. Razed. Look at the job they did there, that was a liquor store, burned to the ground, Korean owned.'

Beverley had been ten in 1965. 'This was much worse,' she said. 'Spread further and faster. More people died. The abuses that people reacted to in 'sixty-five were just the same—police abuse, economic discrimination, lack of jobs, but those riots were about hope. We had hope then. Gone now.' It had taken twenty years to get a shopping centre built in Watts after 1965. How long would it take to recover from this?

There was graffiti everywhere, on the remains of the buildings that had been burned, on the walls of every one that was still standing:

FUCK THE POLICE

FUCK WHITE PEOPLE

FUCK LAPD

FUCK GATES

FUCK THE LAW

POLICE KILLA

FUCK WHITIES

FUCK THE LAW

FUCK WHITEBOYS

NO JUSTICE, NO PEACE

GATES KILLA

BLOODS 'N' CRIPS TOGETHER FOR EVER

POLICE 187

And then: THIS IS SOUTH-CENTRAL.

When I'd first spent time in Los Angeles in the mid-1980s, I'd had no more thought of coming here than to the moon, though I did go with friends to the Los Angeles Coliseum or the Forum, sports arenas close enough to make us very careful about planning the way back to the freeway. Turn a corner, I'd thought, and there I'd be, with bad street lighting and people dreaming of doing me damage. For me South-Central hadn't been just a small, bad neighbourhood of the sort that existed in any city; it had been a very big bad neighbourhood the size of a small city, and it had existed in my mind not as a real place—with stop-lights and movie theatres and stores on the corner—but as a black hole stretching from downtown to Long Beach. I was ashamed of that. It seemed quite possible, now that South-Central had had the effrontery to impose itself on the rest

of the city, that the rest of the city would respond by turning it into an even grimmer ghetto.

'Security Pacific Bank, burned, razed to the ground,' said Beverley. 'Burning a corner store, that's one thing. But to get into a bank and leave nothing except the empty safe still standing at the back. That takes dedication.'

Beverley's daughter Maya reminded me that she was still thirsty, and Beverley said there was a 7-Eleven over on the edge of Inglewood. The rioting hadn't been so bad there, and we drove for another ten minutes only to find another destroyed building. 'Looted,' said Beverley. 'Burned *to the ground.*' She began to laugh, and it did seem funny all of a sudden; we'd spent forty-five minutes driving through the geographical centre of America's second largest city, and we'd been unable to buy a Coca-Cola.

I had never seen Simi Valley, the town where the four officers had been found not guilty of beating Rodney King and from where, every morning, more than 2,000 LAPD officers, county sheriffs and other law-enforcement personnel commuted to their jobs in distant Los Angeles. I wanted to make the journey myself. My girl-friend and I drove there from South-Central.

The journey took us about an hour; in traffic, it could take two hours: the Harbour freeway to the Hollywood freeway, short stretches of the Ventura and San Diego freeways and the bland sprawl of the San Fernando Valley. It was on our last freeway, the Simi Valley, that the landscape changed. This had all been part of Southern California's ranch country; its nineteenth-century history concerned trails and horses and men who did what men had to do. But now housing estates could be seen on most hillsides, and freeway exit ramps were marked CONSTRUCTION VEHICLES ONLY, where new dormitory suburbs were being built. It was like a passage between continents.

At the far end of Los Angeles Avenue, there was a sale of 'recreational vehicles', where a short man called Ted said that, while he had been shocked by the verdicts, and horrified by the riots, this was all good news for him. He was a real estate agent. He predicted a boom in Simi Valley, and indeed throughout the whole of Ventura County, as more and more fled black street crime and the Dickensian hell of Los Angeles. 'You know the worst thing about the looting all those niggers did down there?' he asked. *'They couldn't afford it.'* Ted paused. 'Just kidding,' he said.

We drove through the city. Los Angeles Avenue itself consisted of shopping malls: Simi Valley Plaza, Mountain Gate Plaza, Madre Plaza, the Westgate Center. In these plazas huge parking lots were surrounded by stores of all kinds. A cavernous home improvement centre issued the smell of wood. Everything else issued the smell of air-conditioning. You could buy things here: a new Ford, a taco, a garden hose, and ice-cream, an airline ticket to Lake Tahoe, a pair of jeans, a carton of frozen yoghurt, a CD player, a hair-cut, a chilli burger, a spade, a doughnut, a bag of enriched soil fertilizer, a vegetarian health sandwich, the *Simi Valley Advertiser*, a novel by Stephen King, a new tie, a bathing suit that dries in minutes, spark plugs, a suit for $250, a non-stick frying pan, a small plastic container of Anacin, the *New York Times*, a set of plastic poker chips. You could collect interest on your savings, wash your car or go bowling. You could buy beer, Gatorade and many different kinds of California Chardonnay. You could buy a Coca-Cola. I bought a Coca-Cola.

You could tell who lived in Simi Valley (they were white) and who worked there but lived elsewhere (they were Hispanic). We didn't see any blacks but we may not have stayed long enough. I'm sure there were blacks in Simi Valley.

At the East County court-house, where the King verdicts had been reached, I was confronted by a local resident, a middle-aged woman in a beige suit made of an indeterminate fabric. She smiled at me coldly.

'You're not from here, are you?'

'No,' I replied, a little surprised. Was I really so obvious? Perhaps I looked a little thin. Simi Valley seemed to be a place where fat people got fatter.

'I thought so,' she said. 'And you've come because of that Rodney King thing.'

I said yes.

'I don't feel guilty,' she said, answering a question I hadn't asked. 'I refuse to feel guilty. I did everything I could back in the sixties for those people. They just refused to make the most of their opportunities.'

'Why was that?'

'Oh, they're lazy,' she said. 'Those people are just plain lazy.

'Go back to Los Angeles,' she said, 'and take your issue with you. It has nothing to do with Simi Valley. Those people on the jury did the best job they could, and for you to assume that twelve white people can't hand down a fair verdict in a case like that, well, that's racist in itself, isn't it?'

She was right: if thinking that twelve people like her couldn't be relied upon to hand down a fair verdict was racist, then I was a racist. I hated her. I wanted to hurt her. I didn't want to argue or protest. I wanted her injured. I saw myself doing it. Pow. Pow. Pow.

We returned to Los Angeles.

The riots began on Wednesday, 29 April 1992. Monday, 4 May, was the first day—the first of many—that gun sales topped 2,000 in Southern California, twice the normal figure, a gun sale every forty seconds. By that Monday, this was the riot toll: 228 people had suffered critical injuries (second and third degree skin burns; blindness; gunshot wounds to the lung, stomach, neck, shoulder and limbs; knife wounds; life-threatening injuries from broken glass), and 2,383 people had suffered non-critical injuries (requiring hospital treatment); there were more than 7,000 fire emergency calls; 3,100 businesses were affected by burning or looting; 12,111 arrests. As this goes to press there are reports of 18,000 arrests. Fifty-eight people are dead.

VOX

NICHOLSON BAKER

'A brief, hilarious, insistently sensual, ferociously
inventive paean to phone sex.'
James Kaplan, Vanity Fair

'Tender, funny and supremely honest.'
Harry Ritchie, The Sunday Times Magazine

'Let us all admire Nicholson Baker's act of aplomb, let the prudish
grit their teeth and let us all read his book.' *Fay Weldon, Guardian*

'What is rare is the laughter Baker provokes us to at his own
expense: he's so willing, so generous with his neuroses and his outré
metaphors! ... The sexiest thing about Baker may be, finally, that
he's a funny guy.' *Deborah Garrison, New Yorker*

£7.99

GRANTA BOOKS

Notes on Contributors

Richard Ford was born in Jackson, Mississippi, and is the author of four novels and a volume of short stories, *Rock Springs*. He is also the editor of *The Granta Book of the American Short Story*, which will be published in the United States in August. He is currently living in Rhode Island and is at work on a new novel. **Paul Theroux** arrived in London on 4 November 1971 and lived there for the next eighteen years. 'Lady Max' was written shortly after he left England, while travelling through the Pacific islands. His account of these travels is included in his new book *The Happy Isles of Oceania: Paddling the Pacific*. It is published in Britain in September. **William T. Vollmann** lives in Sacramento, California. He travelled to Afghanistan in 1982; 'An Afghanistan Picture Show' is drawn from a memoir of that journey and will be published by Farrar, Straus and Giroux later this summer. **Alan Lightman** is Professor of Science and Writing and a senior lecturer in physics at MIT. He has published a range of different kinds of writing—poems, essays, a science column, an interdisciplinary textbook—and a number of books. 'Einstein in Bern' is drawn from *Einstein's Dreams*, his first novel, which will be published next spring by Pantheon in the United States and by Bloomsbury in Britain. **Nadine Gordimer** was awarded the Nobel Prize for Literature last year. She lives in Johannesburg and her fiction has regularly appeared in *Granta*. **Ken Light** teaches photography at the Graduate School of Journalism at the University of California, Berkeley, and has published two books of social documentary, *With These Hands* and *To the Promised Land*. **André Brink** is the author of several books in both Afrikaans and English, including *A Dry White Season*, *States of Emergency* and *Looking on Darkness*, the first novel in Afrikaans to be banned. 'Afrikaners and the Future' was originally broadcast on Radio 4. For the past nine years **David Goldblatt** has been working on a personal project photographing buildings, selections from which appeared in *Granta* 28. **Richard Rayner**, brought up in Bradford, is now living in Los Angeles. His memoir of the city, *Los Angeles without a Map*, is being made into a film. *The Elephant*, his first novel, was published in the United States last spring. He is completing a new novel.